"This is a truly remarkable book. Dyron [...] numerous expressions of the Christian [...] humour. For those unacquainted with Christian traditions, it is an outstanding introduction; and committed Christians will discover much about their own roots as well as those of other traditions."

—**George D. Chryssides,** York St John University, UK

"When you first open *Roots*, you might think you are getting a simple primer to Christian life and practice. Only when you delve a little further do you realize just how smartly the author identifies and confronts the key questions facing all denominations, and how deep and wide-ranging are the scholarly resources with which he tackles them. This is a truly deceptive book, and admirably so. And an enjoyable read throughout."

—**Philip Jenkins,** Distinguished Professor of History, Institute for Studies of Religion, Baylor University

"Evangelical Christians care deeply about the Bible and Christian faith, but they sometimes treat the two thousand years since Jesus walked on earth as if they are thoroughly inconsequential. That is unfortunate. The thoughts and actions of Christians today are rooted in holy habits that have been nurtured, refined, criticized, and reformed over centuries. In this winsomely written volume, evangelical scholar Dyron Daughrity shows how much can be gained when the historic roots of today's Christian faith and practice are unearthed and examined."

—**Douglas Jacobsen,** Distinguished Professor of Church History and Theology, Messiah College

"Dyron Daughrity has written a well-documented book providing the theological and historical roots of common Christian traditions. Dr. Daughrity skillfully weaves biblical truth, arguments from early church fathers, reformation practices, and contemporary developments to demonstrate Christian liturgy and customs through the ages. *Roots* is an important read for all interested in the traditions of Christianity."

—**Terry G. Carter,** Associate Dean of the Pruet School of Christian Studies, Professor of Christian History and Ministry, Ouachita Baptist University

"Digging deep into the Bible, the *roots* of the Christian faith, Dyron Daughrity explains in a clear and accessible style why churches adopt certain practices. While deeply rooted in his evangelical tradition, Daughrity brings to his discussion a rare ecumenical sensitivity and theological open-mindedness. *Roots* is an admirable example of practical ecclesiology which will prove helpful to pastors as well as the laity."

—**Peter Phan,** The Ignacio Ellacuria, S. J. Chair of Catholic Social Thought, Department of Theology, Georgetown University

"Reading church history can be a dry and boring experience unless it is written by an author who loves it passionately and understands it intimately. Dyron Daughrity is just such an author. *Roots* is a dramatic and revealing flight through centuries of religious history that is both illuminating and, dare I say, entertaining!"

—**Jeff Walling,** Director, Youth Leadership Initiative, Pepperdine University; Teaching Pastor, Shepherd of the Hills Christian Church, Porter Ranch, CA

"Dr. Daughrity has provided the church with a real gift in this book. Perhaps most helpful is how he locates each of these church practices within a developing history. This book would serve as a good resource for generating lively conversation among church study groups."

—**Jeff Cary,** Associate Professor of Theology, Lubbock Christian University, author of *Free Churches and the Body of Christ*

"*Roots* answers the most frequently asked questions on Christian practice. A renowned scholar and a former minister, Dyron Daughrity has a gift for presenting potentially complex topics in a way that is theologically impeccable, amiably concise, and pastorally wise. His book is a wonderful bridge between the real world of practice and the rigor of academic scholarship. A great book for students, practitioners, clergy, and educators."

—**Enrico Beltramini,** PhD, Professor of Theology, Santa Clara University

"This book sheds much light on the fascinating and often unpredictable twists and turns in the development of church practices and traditions. Understanding the traditions that have shaped us and appreciating what we have inherited will go a long way to helping us practice our faith with greater wisdom and humility."

—**Andy Wall,** Minister, Conejo Valley Church of Christ

"Christians have often felt called to change the way they live out faith, reforming the ancient church to better serve the needs of the age. Too often, we have undertaken these changes without understanding how things have come to be the way they are. We need guidance from someone who loves the church and its mission and who understands the church's story. With his expertise in church history and a discernment honed by his years of ministry, Dyron Daughrity provides that guidance to help us live out our faith more intentionally."

—**Ron Cox,** Blanche E. Seaver Professor of Religion, Pepperdine University

"Dyron Daughrity, a recognized scholar of global Christianity, turns his attention to the sweep of Christian history, deftly surveying basic features of church: the role of the Bible, baptism, the Lord's supper, pastors and bishops, church buildings, preaching, and music. Solidly rooted in the best scholarship. Wonderfully clear and readable. Generous in spirit yet firm in conviction. Dive into this fascinating book and be enlightened, humbled, and more deeply rooted in the rich, diverse stream of Christian faith across the ages."

—**Leonard Allen,** Lipscomb University; author of *Distant Voices*

Roots

Roots

UNCOVERING *WHY WE DO*

WHAT WE DO

IN CHURCH

DYRON DAUGHRITY

LEAFWOOD
PUBLISHERS
an imprint of Abilene Christian University Press

ROOTS
Uncovering Why We Do What We Do in Church

an imprint of *Abilene Christian University Press*

Cover design by Kent Jensen
Interior text design by Sandy Armstrong, Strong Design

Leafwood Publishers is an imprint of Abilene Christian University Press
ACU Box 29138
Abilene, Texas 79699

1-877-816-4455
www.leafwoodpublishers.com

16 17 18 19 20 21 22 / 7 6 5 4 3 2 1

This book is dedicated to the faith communities that have nurtured and sustained the author throughout the years:

Southside Church of Christ (Portales, New Mexico)

Edmonson Church of Christ (Edmonson, Texas)

Woodlawn Church of Christ (Abilene, Texas)

Calgary Church of Christ (Calgary, Alberta, Canada)

Campbell-Stone United Church (Calgary, Alberta, Canada)

University Church of Christ (Malibu, California)

Pasadena Church of Christ (Pasadena, California)

Conejo Valley Church of Christ (Thousand Oaks, California)

With gratitude and deep respect, the author of this volume would like to pay tribute to the life and work of Dr. Everett Ferguson, the author's church history professor at Abilene Christian University. Dr. Ferguson is without equal in the field of early Christianity, and it was a privilege to sit at his feet and listen. His work will impact the academy and the church for many generations to come.

Contents

Acknowledgments

First off, I would like to acknowledge the good work of Abilene Christian University Press & Leafwood Publishers, especially the excellent leadership of Jason Fikes. I am grateful to have been given the opportunity to write for them.

I extend a sincere thanks to my colleagues at Pepperdine. It is a joy to go to work each morning. The Religion Division accepted me with open arms in 2007, and they are still (yes, even still!) so gracious and kind. I make special mention of my divisional dean, Dr. Tim Willis, for encouraging me at every turn. I also want to mention my provost, Dr. Rick Marrs, for taking a personal interest in my work and providing opportunities for my continued development. I am indebted to my friend and colleague Dr. Ron Cox for reading this book carefully in its earlier stages and offering many valuable insights that have made it better.

With great thanks, I want to acknowledge the support of my pastor, Dr. Andy Wall. I appreciate his support of this book; yes, even after reading it.

I acknowledge my wonderful students at Pepperdine, especially those with whom I have worked personally. I must single out my graduate assistant Mike Gaston and my undergraduate-research-student Brianna Hill for assisting me during the time I was writing this book.

I gratefully acknowledge the loving support of my wife Sunde, and our four children: Clare Soleil, Ross Dyron, Mande Mae, and Holly Joy. You give to me such happiness.

"Now unto him that is able to do exceeding abundantly above all that we ask or think, according to the power that worketh in us, Unto him be glory in the church by Christ Jesus throughout all ages, world without end. Amen" (Eph. 3:20–21 KJV).

Dyron B. Daughrity
Jerusalem, Israel
May 30, 2016

Introduction

Why Read This Book?

This book explains why we do what we do in church. It is a short history in plain language. I want people to enjoy reading about how we got to this point in Christianity. I want Christians to say to themselves, "I have always wondered why we did it that way." Hopefully this book will provide some answers.

I will focus on some of the noteworthy practices we have in our churches today. First, let's look at where each particular teaching may have its roots in the Bible. Then, let's see if we can track chapter by chapter how these practices evolved through the medieval era, the Reformation, and into modern times. The chapter on priests and pastors, for example, focuses heavily on the biblical and patristic eras, since these periods are vital to understanding how the leadership of the church became so hierarchical. In other chapters, I will emphasize a global perspective on the issue. Christianity no longer is the possession of the Western world. Today, it is stronger in the Global South than in Western Europe or North America. Along the way we will look at how churches in the Global South are reinventing the teachings and practices they inherited from Western missionaries.

Any of us can look at some practice in a church and say, "What they're doing is not biblical!" Each of us, however, takes a unique angle in interpreting scriptural topics. Before we rush to judgment about somebody else's perspective, we at least need to understand how we arrived at our own. This book provides some instruction here. Perhaps it can raise our awareness of why Christians disagree. My goal is not necessarily to cause Christians to agree on everything. That would be an unrealistic and unattainable goal. But all of us do at least need to know the background of our faith debates, as well as the history of our own practices. Thus equipped, we will be able to carry on a much more fruitful dialogue with each other.

Being Biblical

As I write this book, I assume that my readers will be familiar with the Bible and will have high respect for it. My target audience is Christian readers who believe that the followers of Christ in every age ought to be faithful to the biblical witness. A person who rejects the authority of the Bible or sees the Bible as no more important than other religious texts probably will not understand the assumptions made in this book. Nor will they understand its rationale or goals.

Put succinctly, my aim in these pages is to help Christians understand the roots of their beliefs and practices, so that they can be more gracious toward each other, more informed about the history of their faith, and more faithful to the earliest ideals recorded and preserved in the biblical text. Truth-in-packaging requires me to identify myself from the start as a Protestant who strongly believes that Christians should do their best to be faithful to the biblical text. I realize that all Christians do not ascribe the same level of authority to the Scriptures. But the vast majority of Christians do value what the Bible says, and they believe it is authoritative for the church's belief and practice.

In other words, my assumption in this book is that most Christians make a sincere attempt to live a faith rooted in the Bible. Many of us share the theological conviction that the Bible contains a common Christian standard for faith, for truth, and for how we are to conduct our lives.

All of us face a critical question though. Just how biblical must we be?

Recently I was amused by a Chinese student's question after class. He pulled me aside and asked quietly, "Does the Bible say we can study in a university?" This was a sincere question coming from a person with minimal exposure to Christianity. Our discussion in class that day—how biblical must we be?—had piqued his curiosity. He was dumbfounded to find out that some Christians— including a few in that very class—try to anchor every aspect of their lives in this extremely old text. The questions triggered by such considerations are endless:

- Are we allowed to speak English in the church? The Bible does not say we can.
- Can we sit in pews?
- Can we sit down during worship? Many Eastern Orthodox Christians still stand up during church services. Should we?
- Does the Bible say we can have paid church secretaries?
- Can we have church buildings?
- Shall we baptize babies or adults?
- Can we invent songs to sing—even if they contain no Scripture in them?
- Is it better to live celibate lives as Jesus did?
- Must we wash people's feet as Jesus said we should . . . and as Jesus did?

This list could run on and on.

We Christians like to ask, "What would Jesus do?" when in fact he did many things that we do not. It's not always a matter of what *would* he do, when we know, in fact, what he *did*.

Let me expand one small point for a moment. I have always thought it curious to read how direct Jesus was about foot washing. He washed his disciples' feet and stated explicitly during the Last Supper: "Now that I, your Lord and Teacher, have washed your feet, you also should wash one another's feet. I have set you an example that you should do as I have done for you. . . . Now that you know these things, you will be blessed if you do them."[1] A few denominations of Christianity actually still do it. But not many. Especially in the United States. Our common excuse is that they used sandals and we don't. They had dirty, dusty feet. Our feet are clean, covered with socks. Therefore, washing each other's feet makes no sense today.

The problem with this reasoning is that any ritual or belief can be dismissed on the same grounds. Based on this, a person might argue:

- There's no point in getting baptized. We have showers.
- There's no point in eating the Lord's Supper together. We can eat in our homes.
- There's no point in greeting each other with a holy kiss. We could get sick.
- There's no need to obey the New Testament's sexual ethics. They were needed to preserve family lines and property inheritance. But that was two thousand years ago. We have evolved. We had a sexual revolution in the 1960s. We now have legal systems for divorce and inheritance. Biblical views are no longer relevant on such topics.

With this kind of reasoning, we would have an emaciated faith indeed. But that's precisely what has happened during the centuries of Christianity, and in every generation we keep repeating the process. People make decisions on whether or not to do something, and a tradition gets established . . . or thrown into the dustbin of history.

For example, the Lord's Supper—in the New Testament—is obviously a meal. There is little doubt about that. But how many churches actually celebrate it as a meal nowadays? If your church is like mine, we have a tiny cracker we eat, along with a measly amount of wine. Oh, but wait. Somewhere along the line in church history people said we shouldn't drink wine. Rather, we should use unfermented grape juice. Who decreed this? Most of us have heard the famous explanation: "In Jesus's day the only reason they drank wine was because the water was so polluted." Really? No one drank water in those days? That's odd, because all through the Bible we can find people drinking water.

My sincere hope is that this book will cause people to think about what they do in church, change what they feel they need to change, implement some things they might have neglected, and show a little grace to sisters and brothers who do things differently.

More truth-in-packaging. I write from an ecumenical perspective and from a conviction that Christians need to be more gracious to each other. But to do this we need to understand why we do things differently. We need some historical context. We need to realize that not everything we do is rooted in Scripture. Nor, in my view, *must* everything we do be explicitly sanctioned in Scripture. A simple but good example is speaking English in worship. I don't want to attend a church that only uses *Koine* Greek. My Greek Orthodox friends take great pride in the fact that they still use only biblical Greek in their worship services. That wouldn't work in my Protestant church. Are they more biblical than we are? Well, yes, they are in one sense. They use biblical Greek, and we don't. But I suggest that "being biblical" does not mean just following the letter of the text or the language of the text. To be biblical may require more than just trying to emulate exactly what we see in a biblical text. Sometimes we have to interpret, to contextualize, to adapt the Greek Scriptures to our English audiences, to bridge two cultures that stand millennia apart, and to make judgment calls about the Bible's teachings.

Showing My Cards

Readers of this book have the right to know where I am coming from. The answer is that I come from California, New Mexico, Texas, and Canada. I come from Protestantism. I come from Evangelicalism. I come from academia. I come from the Churches of Christ—a Christian fellowship of churches that rose up under the leadership of Alexander Campbell in the United States in the early nineteenth century. The university where I teach—Pepperdine—is associated with that movement.

After growing like wildfire in the nineteenth and twentieth centuries, our movement seems to have plateaued in the United States. However, it is a fine group to be associated with. I was baptized in a Church of Christ. I came to know the Lord in a Church of Christ. I am descended from generations of Church of Christ people. I will probably die in the Church of Christ. However, I don't repudiate other Christians. By no means! I am a friend to other forms of Christianity. I admire them. At times I have even been tempted to convert to them (or at least to adopt some of what they do). But I find it useful to have a history, to stay rooted in my church, and to know something about my heritage.

Today, many Christians say they are unaffiliated with any church. They claim to be the non-denominational people. But that's probably not true. The fact is that they just don't *know* what church they are associated with. Just because a pastor says, "We're non-denominational," doesn't mean that the church he leads has no roots. It does have roots. And an honest explanation would be more forthcoming than that. Many non-denominational churches are spin-offs from Baptist churches. A good litmus test is to ask someone if they baptize babies or believers. If they baptize believers, then they probably stem from the Baptists, Churches of Christ, or Pentecostal churches. If they baptize infants, then they are probably from one of Christianity's historic denominations such as Catholic, Orthodox, Anglican, Methodist, Presbyterian, Lutheran, Reformed, or Congregationalist. Another litmus test is to ask where the pastor went to seminary. How she/he answers that question will often reveal his/her denominational affiliation.

It is possible, of course, for a new church to start up and disassociate from other churches, but inevitably, if the church survives, it will have to institutionalize. People often critique wealthy churches by pointing out that the churches in the Bible did not have huge cathedrals and massive endowments. But the early churches were . . . early. They only had a few years of history behind them. Add three or four (or nineteen or twenty) centuries, and suddenly you have significant treasure that has been stored. And buildings. And traditions. And rituals. All churches go through this process. How does a church gather without any rituals or traditions? I don't want to be part of a church that says, "Okay, whatever we do, we have to make sure that we've never done it before." (Such a church would probably last three or four weeks.)

Digging a little deeper, it might help my readers for me to disclose a little more about myself from a theological and even a philosophical perspective. I am familiar with the various approaches to authority that exist in Christianity, so I am aware that many Protestants *think* they operate from a *sola scriptura* perspective. In reality, it is always much more complicated than that. All conservatives tend to think that "our" tradition is rooted in the Scriptures. In reality, however, most of us follow the Christian tradition we inherited from our parents. Those of us baptized as infants feel no need to get re-baptized as adults. Vice-versa, those of us who grew up hearing why we shouldn't get baptized as infants probably aren't going to have our children baptized at birth. We inherit most of these views. Typically, we don't arrive at them through careful scrutiny. We tend to believe the people who taught us when we were young and most impressionable. Some people do change their beliefs radically after they grow up, of course, but most humans do not. The philosopher John Hick once estimated that around 99 percent of humans will hold to a faith very similar to their parents'.[2]

All of us are products of our ecclesial environment. "Not that there's anything wrong with that," as Seinfeld quipped. We learn from our parents, our mentors, our teachers. What else *can* we do but to allow their influences to shape what we believe about the world, about people, about God, about our church and doctrine and rituals and practices? It takes great humility to realize that we probably don't have it all figured out when it comes to Christianity. As Isaac Newton wisely observed, we all stand on the shoulders of the giants who have come before us.

However—and this is where I have made a conscious choice—I have come to the conclusion that it is *more* important to allow the Bible a place of primacy in my thinking. Traditions play a major role, of course, but when Luther made the carefully reasoned decision that he must uphold the Bible as the central authority in his theology, not only did he make the Catholic hierarchy (especially Pope Leo X) livid, but he also created a huge divide in how Christians *approach* Christian belief and practice. In effect, he was denying the Pope his centuries-long place of spiritual authority in the life of believers. Luther was saying, "No! The Bible is my authority." However—and here is where Luther was obviously naïve—people read the Bible differently.

Contrary to numerous clichés, there is no such thing as plain reason. We all reason a little differently. Only two years after posting his 95 *Theses* in Wittenberg in 1517, Luther's colleagues understood "reform" very differently than he did. Andreas Karlstadt was a close colleague to Luther, but by 1519 "tensions were already arising between the two reformers. These tensions were rooted in alternative readings of the Bible."[3] One notable difference of opinion was that Karlstadt came to the conclusion that infant baptism was unbiblical.[4] Luther disagreed with him. In a very short time, the Reformation had split into multiple factions of people who read the same Bible but did not read it the same.

Thus, it is with eyes wide open that I claim the Bible is *more* important than inherited tradition. However, as we'll see shortly, both sides of this debate have their merits, and when all is said and done, we have to admit that even the biblicists among us rely on tradition, probably more than they'd like to admit.

Inheriting Furniture

We have inherited other people's furniture when it comes to faith. When a group of people bring us into their Christian realm—be they family, friends, or missionaries—we inherit much of their understanding. Our theological landscape is shaped by them. As we grow and mature in faith, we have to make decisions. And sometimes those decisions are tough, even as excruciating as when we decide the old couch must go to the dumpster.

But we must think twice before we toss that couch into the trash. Why are we getting rid of it? Is it simply because it needs to be replaced by a newer one? Or is there something more fundamental to the question? Perhaps what we really need is a new bookshelf, so the couch must be jettisoned to make room.

To reject part of our faith heritage and replace it with something else is a big decision, but it happens fairly often. It is quite common for people to adapt or update their faith to make it fit the current times. In previous centuries, for example, divorce was scandalous for Christians; today it is commonplace. Few people today would consider divorce to be a mortal sin, worthy of damnation. Formal church discipline toward divorcees is almost unheard of in American Christianity today. Sure, there is a stigma that divorcees have to deal with, but grace is the name of the game today. Forcing someone into a period of public repentance seems cruel and legalistic. Legalism is out. Forgiveness is in. Hallelujah! (I must admit, however, that sometimes I fear we're all becoming relativists. Anything goes. Let it be. Live and let live. Stop judging. We know all the clichés, probably because we use them.)

Back to furniture. Some people will decide that they need more than just a furniture change . . . so they simply abandon the house. Changing furniture doesn't work for them anymore. They move out and leave the furniture problem behind. They go somewhere else. This would be the person who decides to convert, perhaps from Catholic to "non-denominational." Or from Baptist to Anglican. These people reach a point of frustration that cannot be suppressed any longer. They see no point in moving furniture from one place to another, trying to make it all work.

One thing these people may not realize, however, is that when they move into another religious tradition, they simply inherit a different set of furniture. And, in time, that furniture may not sit so well with them either. All furniture grows uncomfortable or undesirable. Why? Because we change. Because other things in the room get changed. Because we go to the mall and see newer furniture that we like. And so the process begins anew. We start thinking about mixing things up again.

In previous generations, people rarely reacted like this. They were born Catholic and they died Catholic. They had Baptist blood in their veins. They were proud to call themselves fifth-generation Church of Christ.

But a free-agency mentality has moved into our churches, much as it has moved into every other aspect of our lives. We like options. We like short-term contracts. Why play for the Dallas Cowboys all of your life when you could play for the 49ers and make twice the money? We don't need to work for Xerox or Ford for forty years. We can switch, we can move around. Besides, why be loyal to Ford or to the Dallas Cowboys when they'll probably lay us off at some point? It's not like the good ole days when we all had a gentleman's agreement that we would commit to each other for the rest of our lives. Nothing works that way anymore. Marriage doesn't. Jobs don't. Not much of anything works that way. So why should churches remain stuck in the past on this approach to things? Christians have simply joined the spirit of the times. Why remain stuck in my terribly boring Lutheran church when I could join up with the megachurch down the street with all of its bells and whistles (and fog and totally awesome music and light shows and massive speakers)?

Jesus addresses these issues quite explicitly in Matthew 9:14–17. Jesus gets grilled here by the followers of John the Baptist. If these guys were anything like their leader, then they were truly deprived ascetics. They frequently fasted and ate meals that consisted of honey-coated insects. John the Baptist was known for wearing itchy clothes (camel hair), possibly because such a costume was a sign to everybody around that he was willing to sacrifice for his faith (Matt. 11:8). John's disciples call out Jesus's followers in Matt. 9:14: "How come your guys don't fast?" Jesus gives a cryptic response, basically saying that they'll have time for fasting once he's gone. Then Jesus gives two analogies to emphasize his point. First, he says it makes no sense to patch up an old garment with a new piece of cloth, because it will shrink and actually make the tear worse. Then he says, likewise, it makes no sense to pour new wine into old wineskins, because the old skins will burst open. You need new wineskins for new wine.

What in the world was he talking about? Every commentator who takes on these parables comes up with a slightly different interpretation. So what is the essence of it? The gist of it is obvious. Jesus was talking about change. He was talking about tradition.

"We've never done it that way." These are common words in churches that have been around for more than one generation.

Some people are completely opposed to change, whether good or bad, whatever the reason. I have a friend who likes to characterize himself as innately opposed to change. I think many of us are this way. We're the practical ones. In Texas, they say, "Why fix it if it ain't broke?" Good question. But some of the innovators among us love to change things up. "Let's change things. Everything. Everything must change! Or else we'll all go to hell in a handbasket!"

I am reminded of ultra-Orthodox Jews who wear traditional garb, long beards, locks on the sides of their heads, speaking the Yiddish of their great-grandparents' homeland because to change to English would be to compromise. And to compromise would entail having to leave the community. A similar example is the Amish community that refuses to drive motorized cars. Or the Eastern Orthodox Christians who still recite the Divine Liturgy that was drawn up by John Chrysostom in the year 400. Or the Sharia-devoted Muslims who want to go back to the days of Muhammad, regardless of what has happened over the last fourteen hundred years.

Jesus was basically saying, "It's time for change." He knew some people would resist: "We've never done it that way before. Never." So be it. In that case, I guess we need some new people for these new ideas. The traditionalists—the old wineskins—can't handle it. As Jack Nicholson's character said in *A Few Good Men*, "You can't handle the truth." Jesus seems to be saying that. Thus, we need new vessels. We need new cloth. We need new skins. We need new people who will accept these new teachings.

But what about today? Is Jesus implying that we must always be changing (some might say here, "Bingo!")? Why did he say we need new wineskins? How do we take his metaphor seriously? Who represents "new" wineskins? Who among us are "old" wineskins? I seriously doubt Jesus was trying to drive a wedge between the older people and the young twenty- and thirtysomethings. Isn't he supposed to be the Messiah for all of us, regardless of our age?

It is a little ironic that in Jesus's day his teachings were considered "the new thing." Today, however, the teachings of Jesus seem to be "the old thing." You know, the "old paths," the "old rugged cross," the solid rock of God's teachings. These things are old now. It seems as if many Christians want to move on to the new. Forget the old stuff. Let's reinterpret the Bible. Let's advance. Let's create. Let's do it our way, not the way of our ancestors. The obvious problem is that if we adopt the new today, then we can expect to be dismissed as "old wineskins" thirty years from now. Must we change all the time? All throughout our lives? Is this what Christianity is supposed to be all about? Change?

I would argue that Matthew 13 gives advice on what to do with the conundrums raised in the "wineskins" story in Matthew 9. In Matthew 13:51–53, Jesus says that a "disciple in the kingdom of heaven" is a discerning person; he knows which treasures to keep from the past and which ones to include from the present.

It's not rocket science. Keep the old teachings that are still relevant and still make sense. But be willing to part with the outdated teachings that no longer contribute. In other words, both the traditionalists and the "emerging church" types are right. Neither extreme is good. The guy who rejects every new idea stands condemned. Similarly, the pastor chasing every new Twitter post just to stay relevant needs to settle down. Some truth and goodness can be found in both approaches, but not in their extreme forms. Wisdom is finding the balance.

One Solution: An Evangelical Balance

I'm an Evangelical. There's no getting around that. At times I wish I were a member of the Orthodox Church with its line of succession, liturgies, and practices that go back to the early church fathers. At other times I feel drawn to the Catholic Church with its global and diverse presence. I am at times drawn to the Anglican tradition with its beautiful *Book of Common Prayer*.

Other days I wake up drawn to the Pentecostal zeal that emphasizes the powerful gifts of the Holy Spirit. Sometimes I get excited about the Mennonites with their laser-focus on peace and justice. Some days I am attracted to the black churches like the African Methodist Episcopal or the Church of God in Christ with their deep ties of fellowship and prophetic voice in society.

However, I was not raised Catholic. I've never been a member of a Pentecostal church. I am an Evangelical. And I like it because of its balance.

The Evangelical movement struggles to find that balance between a deep commitment to the truth of Scripture and a passion for bringing the message of Christ to the surrounding culture. I like this tension.

All Evangelicals are not the same, obviously. Just as all Catholics or Anglicans are not the same. There are different shades. Some lean right, some left. Some lean toward curmudgeonly fundamentalism, some lean toward "extreme" relevancy (don't deny it: we have all been a part of "extreme Bible Study," "out-of-this-world retreat," "harder, better, faster, stronger marriages," etc.).

But all in all, that's the risk we take by being Evangelicals. We can look curmudgeonly when we act like our first cousins in the book of Acts—the Bereans. The Bible tells us (17:11) that they "were of more noble character . . . for they received the message with great eagerness and examined the Scriptures every day to see if what Paul said was true." Ditto. As Evangelicals, this is exactly what we do. Still. We are the modern-day Bereans. But we also err on the side of relevance from time to time with our laser-light shows and hard-rock drummers who get amped up and zealous during the "How Great Thou Art" drum solo.

Even we Evangelicals notice, sometimes, that we're a little extreme in how we adapt the faith to the culture around us. We're both new wine and old wineskins. We make mistakes and the wine spills out. We sew the patch on and ruin the cloth completely . . .

especially in our movies and novels (although we are improving in these areas . . . slowly).

However, when we get that balance right, we're a great bunch. And we have some saints among us. Overall, we're a people who try to remain faithful to the things we need to stay faithful to, especially the Bible. But we also try to innovate, at the risk of spilling wine all over ourselves. Our main goal is to evangelize, hence the word "evangelical." We like to reach out to others and share with them the good news that we've experienced in our own lives. We believe that a life with Christ—a life lived according to his will—is a good life. It is a fulfilling life. And we want the people around us to share in that goodness and grace . . . both now and in the life to come.

This book is a rather brief historical exposé examining why we do what we do in church. I hope that by looking at our churches' collective roots, we can all understand each other better. And, perhaps, walk shoulder to shoulder as we head into the next phase of Christianity in our own era, under the banner of Jesus Christ.

Notes

[1] John 13:14–15, 17.

[2] See Hick's 2006 lecture "Believable Christianity" at http://www.johnhick.org.uk/article16.html#sthash.Ygpiqvel.dpuf.

[3] Carter Lindberg, *The European Reformations*, 2nd Edition (Oxford: Wiley-Blackwell, 2010), 90–91.

[4] Ibid., 131.

Chapter 1

The Bible

Our Primary Source

Francis Chan asks a question that surely nettled some of the Christians who first heard it.

> Think about it. If all you had was the Bible, would you come to the conclusion—after reading this—that to become a Christian you would pray a prayer and ask Jesus to come into your heart? I know I am totally stepping on some toes right now. I'm just asking: Is that really what you find in here? Or if you only had the Bible, would you come out thinking, "You know, I need to repent, be baptized, be filled with the Holy Spirit"? What would you believe if it were just the Bible?[1]

Chan challenges his viewers to rely solely on the Bible, resisting the temptation to be spoon-fed teachings that have no roots in the biblical text. He argues that if we rely solely on the Bible, we would probably have to transform much of what we believe. He draws a major distinction between what is "fed" to us by others and what actually comes from the Word of God. He urges his listeners to be discerning and to realize that all of us have inherited some unbiblical baggage. He concludes by challenging his viewers "to test everything we hear and see if it's really in this book."

By all accounts, Francis Chan is a deeply committed disciple of Jesus Christ. He is bold in his faith, unabashedly countering what he believes to be bad Christian teaching. He is a unique leader who commands respect because of his deep integrity.

But how can the average Christian possibly know exactly what the Bible says on issues such as Sunday School, church services, music, leadership, church architecture, creeds, communion, sermons, testimonies, speaking in tongues, weddings, funerals, and filing lawsuits against each other? Does the Bible address all of this? Is there any room for interpretation? Should each Christian determine the answers to these questions all on his or her own? By allowing ourselves to be taught—or, in Chan's words, "fed"—by a teacher, are we succumbing to the mistake of not thinking for ourselves?

Here I Stand: Why Catholics and Protestants Differ on So Much

Catholics and Protestants are very, very different in fundamental ways. I have a good friend who is a devout Catholic, and he says that the cardinal virtue in Catholicism is that each person must "obey." At the end of the day, no matter what they might think deep in the corners of their minds, Catholics should submit to official church teaching. This is what it means to be Catholic. One submits to the authority of someone else—including one's interpretation of the Bible. This might sound a bit hyperbolic, but the truth of the matter is that Catholics who push the boundaries too far risk censure. They certainly don't have the liberty to start another Catholic congregation down the street, as Protestants often do.

Protestants, however, are experts at protesting. That is precisely why we are called Protestants. Each of us looks (or is supposed to look) deep into the pages of the Bible and figures things out for himself. And if we find that the preacher is saying something we disagree with, we feel compelled to "protest." We can blame it on Luther. He's the one who started this way of thinking. In his famous speech at the Diet of Worms in 1521, Luther defied the massive and powerful institution of the Roman Catholic Church with these words:

> Unless I am convicted by Scripture and plain reason—I
> do not accept the authority of popes and councils, for
> they have contradicted each other—my conscience
> is captive to the Word of God. I cannot and I will not
> recant anything, for to go against conscience is neither
> right nor safe. God help me. Amen.[2]

The earliest printed version of the speech claimed Luther actually stated, "Here I stand, I cannot do otherwise." Those words—"Here I stand"—are iconic for all Protestants. By confronting authority when we feel authority is in the wrong, we follow Luther's lead. We refuse to submit. We follow our conscience which has been shaped by Scripture and, what he calls "plain reason." And we stand. We take a stand.

Is this the genius of Protestantism, or is it a perpetual failing? It depends on how we define success and failure. There are estimated to be thousands of Protestant movements and denominations in the world. Even tens of thousands.[3] And Roman Catholic Churches? There's still only one. Certainly submission to authority prevents division in the body of Christ, but at what cost? Can the Popes and councils be trusted to make the decisions for us? Obviously Luther thought not.

Clearly, Francis Chan thinks not. Chan's approach to Scripture is precisely the same approach adopted by Luther: *sola scriptura*

(Scripture alone). The safest path for Christians to take is to make their decisions using "Scripture and plain reason."

There is an obvious problem, however. How could so many people come to different conclusions by using "plain reason" and "Scripture alone?"

Answer? There is no such thing as plain reason.

Indeed, Scripture is basically the same. Yes, we have different versions of the Bible, and that does account for some of the differences. The big problem, however, is that we think differently. Each person comes to the table of discussion with a different background. Different preachers and teachers. Different families. Different experiences. Totally different track records.

And what happens when we broaden the conversation to those from other cultures? Chances are slim that a Protestant from Indonesia is going to think the same way as a Catholic from Texas. Culturally they are worlds apart. Who has the "plainest" reason, the Texan or the Indonesian? The problem is that reason differs from human to human. Every person reads the Bible a little differently from anybody else, each based on their accumulated experience.

Ultimate Authority: Tradition or Text?

As an Evangelical Christian, I read two texts with regularity: the Bible and *Christianity Today*. *CT*—as it is often known—published an article by Mark Galli in 2015 entitled "Why We Need the New Battle for the Bible: It's Time to Turn to Scripture as Our Final Authority."[4] I can freely admit that I agree entirely with the author's arguments as I understand them. Galli argues that we neglect the authority of Scripture for several reasons.

1. Sometimes we wish to preserve relationships rather than to obey the Bible.
2. Sometimes we feel the Lord is "leading us" a certain way that might conflict with Scripture.

3. Sometimes a "consensus" arises among Christians that contradicts the rather clear teaching of the Bible.

4. Sometimes the Bible is explained away as figurative, allegorical, or metaphorical ("Jesus rose from the grave only in spirit").

5. Sometimes we dismiss the Bible as being obsolete. It's an old book!

6. Sometimes we feel "the Holy Spirit is doing a new thing!" Thus the traditional teachings of the Bible must be jettisoned.

7. Sometimes we individualize the Scriptures; arguing "what it means to *me*" might be very different than what it says, at least ostensibly.

An Evangelical might think of this list as "The Seven Deadly Sins of Biblical Interpretation."

Deadly? Perhaps that's overstating it. But as one who takes Scripture seriously, even literally most of the time, this list offers me a sobering perspective. The Bible is pretty lucid. What did Paul mean when he pointed out that some were being "baptized for the dead" (1 Cor. 15:29)? I have no idea. That passage is not lucid. I had to write a huge paper on it in grad school, and I still don't know what it means. But, for the most part, it would be disingenuous to argue that the Bible is altogether cloudy, difficult, impenetrable. When I began to turn to the Bible for answers for why my life was falling apart at the age of eighteen, I found it to be quite clear.

In seminary, we have to wrestle with questions such as, "Do the church fathers stand in authority over the Bible since they are the ones who compiled the canon of Scripture?" Nonsense. That's like asking if Adam had authority over God because he realized it was God who made him. The church fathers don't stand in authority over the Bible. They certainly did their part to discern which of the biblical texts were authentic, written by apostles, and inspired.

But they didn't have authority over the Bible, or God, or the church, or the Christians seventeen hundred years later, as some of my Orthodox and Catholic brothers and sisters seem to argue (sorry, friends, we can debate this next time we get together).

The church fathers deserve our utmost respect, much as the esteemed, seasoned elders, pastors, and teachers of today do (think Billy Graham, Pope Francis, or Rick Warren). We respect them because they live the faith. They teach it. They invest themselves into it. Only a fool would disparage a wise church leader. However, that does not mean that the church fathers, pastors, elders, or teachers are infallible. They are not (sorry, Catholic friends . . . and, by the way, please repeal Vatican I), at least according to my reading of Romans 3.

So which is it?

#1. Is Scripture a revelation by God that was declared authoritative by the church fathers?

Or,

#2. Is it an already authoritative revelation by God that the church fathers happened to recognize?

I go with option #2.

Why? Because I believe it is important to realize that the earliest writings in our canon—probably Paul's letters—were already being called "Scripture" *during the time when the New Testament was still being written.* The author of 2 Peter—whoever it was—refers to Paul's writings as "Scripture" in 3:16. The "church fathers" had little to do with that recognition. Paul's authority was already being recognized in his own lifetime, if we are to trust the New Testament documents. It wasn't up to the church fathers of the fourth, third, or even second century to stamp his writings with the "seal of authority." Rather, they were considered authoritative when they were written. The church fathers were simply echoing a tradition that had already recognized Paul as the crucial figure that he was.

Yes, there are some vexing problems with our canon of Scripture today. Where are the other two letters to the Corinthians that were written by Paul?[5] Alas, they have never been found. What if we found them? (Dan Brown, take note!) Why don't we revere those apocryphal texts—the *Book of Enoch* and the *Assumption of Moses*—cited by Jude?[6] Where is the *Epistle to the Laodiceans* that Paul brings up in Colossians 4:16? What about the *Gospel of Thomas*, that shares so much material—much of it word-for-word—with our canonical Gospels? What exactly is Paul referring to in Acts 20:35 when he quotes the apparently well-known words of Jesus, "It is more blessed to give than to receive," that are not cited in the canonical Gospels? How did so many additions get into our text— the woman caught in adultery (John 8), the striking passage on the Trinity in 1 John 5:8, (skip to the next paragraph if you are a snake handler in Appalachia) and the long ending of Mark?[7]

As Christians who ascribe full authority to the Scriptures, we believe our canon is sufficient for helping a person to achieve salvation. Perfect? No. God is perfect. The Bible, while inspired, has so much man in it that it can't be perfect. However, it can guide us to perfection—to our God. How else could God have relayed his will to us, except by using human beings? Should he have spoken to us through an ass? Well, um, he did that too (see Numbers 22), but my point is this: How *else* was God to communicate his will to humankind *but* to use humans?

As those who believe in the sufficiency of the Scriptures to convey salvation, we believe that these earliest sources—the biblical texts—are true and inspired by God, regardless of what may have happened at the church councils in the fourth and fifth centuries. Would the Scriptures still be authoritative had the church fathers never existed? Obviously, as pointed out, long before the church fathers they *already were* considered authoritative. The church fathers did a tremendous service by sorting out the wheat (inspired texts) from the chaff (crazy stuff like the *Infancy Gospel of Thomas* where Jesus gets angry and kills a bunch of kids), but God's authority was not bound to the church fathers. It functioned separate and apart (and before) them.

Thus, as an Evangelical Christian, I have to believe that the authority of the Scriptures is not what is at stake here. Virtually all Christians recognize the veracity and authority of the Bible. The problems arise when we enter the arena of interpretation. And we have to interpret. *What else can we do?*

Biblical Interpretation

Biblical interpretation is a virtual science these days. Many PhDs are granted each year in this truly impressive academic discipline. And one of the first rules of biblical interpretation is that some things are more important than others. The apostles knew this. Paul talks about this at length in Romans 14. Some people eat meat; others (whom Paul calls weak, showing his carnivore cards) are vegetarian on principle. But these are not things considered "of first importance." Rather, those things "of first importance" are explicitly pointed out by Paul in 1 Corinthians 15:3–7:

> That Christ died for our sins according to the Scriptures,
> that he was buried, that he was raised on the third day
> according to the Scriptures, and that he appeared to
> Cephas, and then to the Twelve. After that, he appeared
> to more than five hundred of the brothers and sisters
> at the same time, most of whom are still living, though
> some have fallen asleep. Then he appeared to James, then
> to all of the apostles, and last of all he appeared to me also.

According to Paul, a hierarchy of importance certainly exists in our Christian teaching, but figuring out that hierarchy is about as easy as fourth-year calculus.

Even someone as authoritative as Paul had his share of challenges when it came to correctly interpreting God's revelation. In 1 Corinthians 1, it is clear that the church at Corinth was quarreling about authority and interpretation. The debate seems to have been about whether they should follow Paul, Apollos, Peter, or Jesus. In addition, Paul tells us of his heated conflict with Peter (Gal. 2:11). We know that Priscilla and Aquila heard Apollos preach on one occasion and "took him aside and explained to him the way of God more adequately" (Acts 18:26). A serious conflict arose between John and Diotrephes in 3 John 9, and the result was that John and his faction were apparently barred from visiting that church. He accused Diotrephes of "spreading malicious nonsense." I feel guilty admitting this, but it is refreshing to know that church conflict has been ongoing since the founding of the church. Our churches are not so bad. Actually they fit right in. Perhaps living in a faith community is not so easy . . . and never has been.

All of us are struggling to understand the truth of Christ better, more clearly, more faithfully. As an irenic and ecumenical Christian, I am not eager to condemn others in their interpretations, just as I would prefer not to be condemned. However, I do feel it is important to articulate truth as I understand it. And maybe God will put a Priscilla or an Aquila out there who can help me to understand the way of the Lord more adequately if I stray too far in this or that direction.

The bottom line is that each of us has to make a decision. We have to choose the Bible as our supreme authority, or else we put the hierarchy of our church in that place. If one is a member of Orthodox or Roman Catholic churches, the authority of the tradition is as high, or higher, than the Bible, because the tradition is responsible for calling out and canonizing the biblical texts. This might sound strange to Evangelical ears, but it is quite true.

Each of us Protestants must decide how much authority to give to the Bible in our own faith and practice. I would argue that, in reality, most Protestants take an approach to authority fairly similar to that of most Roman Catholic and Orthodox Christians— they trust the tradition they are a part of. They realize that the centuries of accumulated wisdom—often called the "magisterium"—have handed down to us a trustworthy body of teaching. And who are we to question the creeds, interpretations, doctrines, practices, and rituals? So, typically, we non-Catholics trust our parents, we trust our church leaders, we trust the body of teaching we've inherited, and we do the best we can. Is there a better way? I would be suspicious of the guy who comes along and says, "Forget everything you've ever heard and listen to me!" Kool-Aid anyone?

A (Very) Brief History of the Old Testament Canon

The word "canon" is a Greek word which came from a Hebrew word meaning "cane" or "reed." In biblical times, reeds were used to make straight lines or to take measurements. The word "canon" came to mean something that is straight or accurate. To the Christian, the canon contains the accurate writings given to humans by God.

This concept is not unique to Christianity. Most religions have canons. Some faiths have canons that are open, consisting of numerous (and growing) volumes. Some canons are closed, as in the cases of Judaism, Christianity, and Islam.

In Old Testament times, many prophets were understood by their hearers to be speaking the words, or at least the thoughts, of God. The faith community had to decide which individuals truly spoke for God and which should be rejected as false. This tension is found in the Bible itself. There is an ongoing battle for authority over how to understand God's will; it is laced throughout both testaments. As these decisions are sorted out over time, the victorious parties are preserved as being trustworthy and God-ordained. The others are openly rejected, often in humiliating ways. They are the losers in the battle for canonicity. For example, in Numbers 16, a prophet named Korah rose up to oppose Moses's leadership.

He lost. In fact, the ground split open and swallowed him, "and all those associated with Korah, together with their possessions. They went down alive into the realm of the dead, with everything they owned; the earth closed over them, and they perished and were gone from the community" (32–33).

Moses's teachings are preserved to the present day, and Korah is rejected as a heretic, the poster child of what happens when potential usurpers try to challenge the authority of the true prophets of God.

Obviously the Torah—the five books associated with Moses's authorship—was worth preserving in the minds of the Israelites throughout history. And Moses has gone down in history as a true prophet, a key figure of Israelite history. Among Jews, only a fool would challenge his canonical authority today. Besides, who wants to be swallowed by the earth?

By the second and third centuries before Christ, Jews had latched on to much of what we have in the Old Testament today as their Scriptures. For example, the Septuagint—the Greek translation of the Hebrew Old Testament—was put together during those centuries.[8] The Dead Sea Scrolls, many of which date back before the time of Christ, preserve most of what we consider today to be the Old Testament. The only Old Testament book not found in the Dead Sea Scrolls collection is the book of Esther.

One major source for understanding the development of the canonical Scriptures is a book known to us today as Sirach—also known as the Book of Ecclesiasticus. It is part of the Apocrypha and is thus included in many Bibles today, but in a section separate from the Old and New Testaments. It is recognized as Scripture by many Christians, including Roman Catholics and most Orthodox Christians. Many Protestants read it, although rarely do they consider it to be on the same level of authority as the Old and New Testaments.

The reason Sirach is so important is because it is one of the earliest texts that demonstrates what Jews thought to be Scripture. Sirach was written between 198 and 175 BC.[9] The author, Ben Sira, shows a reverence for and familiarity with the Laws of Moses (24:23), the prophets (24:33; 39:1), and the Wisdom literature (39:1–3). The Prologue to the book explicitly discusses what seems to be an established canon:

> Many great teachings have been given to us through the Law and the Prophets and the others that followed them, and for these we should praise Israel for instruction and wisdom. Now, those who read the scriptures must not only themselves understand them, but must also as lovers of learning be able through the spoken and written word to help the outsiders. So my grandfather Jesus [Ben Sira], who had devoted himself especially to the reading of the Law and the Prophets and the other books of our ancestors, and had acquired considerable proficiency in them, was himself also led to write something pertaining to instruction and wisdom, so that by becoming familiar also with his book those who love learning might make even greater progress in living according to the law.[10]

Chapters 44–50 of Sirach provide an illuminating discussion of Old Testament figures held in high esteem at his time. This long passage is known as "the hymn in praise of the Hebrew fathers."[11] What is perplexing is not what Sirach includes but what he excludes: Ruth, Ezra, Esther, and Daniel. These books may not have been available to him, but in the case of Ezra, it is a notable omission indeed, considering his important role in the rabbinic tradition. Ezra often gets credit in Judaism for leading a great revival of Torah study.

The important Jewish historian Josephus (AD 37–100) gives us another explicit reference to what he thought to be the Jewish canon.[12] He wrote,

For we have not an innumerable multitude of books among us, disagreeing from and contradicting one another, but only twenty-two books, which contain the records of all the past times; which are justly believed to be divine; and of them five belong to Moses, which contain his laws and the traditions of the origin of mankind till his death. This interval of time was little short of three thousand years.

The five books Josephus mentioned here is what we call today the Torah or the Pentateuch. Next, Josephus addresses the other seventeen books of the Hebrew Bible:

But as to the time from the death of Moses till the reign of Artaxerxes, king of Persia, who reigned after Xerxes, the prophets, who were after Moses, wrote down what was done in their times in thirteen books. The remaining four books contain hymns to God, and precepts for the conduct of human life.

Josephus then explains the extremely high reverence that the Jews had already developed for their Scriptures by this point in history:

How firmly we have given credit to those books of our own nation, is evident by what we do. For during so many ages as have already passed, no one has been so bold as either to add anything to them, to take anything from them, or to make any change in them. But it becomes natural to all Jews, immediately and from their very birth, to esteem those books to contain divine doctrines, and to persist in them, and, if occasion be, willingly to die for them.

It is fascinating how little has changed. Orthodox Jews would heartily agree with these ideas today. One visit to an Orthodox synagogue confirms the unshakable commitment that these faithful Jews have toward their texts.

A word should be said about Josephus's comments on the Hebrew canon. Jews numbered their canon differently than we do today. In Josephus's time, as today, there were three major collections in the Bible: the Torah, Nevi'im, and Ketuvim. The acronym *Tanakh* is created from the first letter of these three collections. The first collection is the Torah—"the Law"—which includes the books Genesis through Deuteronomy. The second collection, the Nevi'im, includes the prophets: the Former Prophets (Joshua, Judges, Samuel, Kings) and the Latter Prophets (Isaiah, Jeremiah, Ezekiel, and the Book of the Twelve Minor Prophets). The Minor Prophets (Hosea to Malachi) were written onto one scroll and were thus considered one book. The Ketuvim ("writings") comprises eleven books arranged into three sections: (1) Psalms, Proverbs, Job; (2) The Megillot (scrolls): Song of Songs, Ruth, Lamentations, Ecclesiastes, and Esther; (3) Daniel, Ezra-Nehemiah (one book), and the Chronicles.[13]

Scholars know that whereas Josephus refers to twenty-two books in the canon, today Jews typically refer to their canon as having twenty-four books. It should be pointed out that Christians count thirty-nine books in the Hebrew Bible, but the Christian counting is very different. In Josephus's counting of twenty-two books, in all likelihood he had in mind the same number of texts that we use today, but he counted them in a slightly different way. Biblical scholar F. F. Bruce thinks Josephus may have thought of Ruth as an appendix to Judges, and Lamentations as an appendix to Jeremiah.[14]

Other important developments around the time that Josephus was writing (roughly AD 70–100) substantiate a rather stable understanding of the Jewish canon. For example, 2 Esdras—a Jewish text written in the aftermath of the destruction of the Temple in AD 70—refers to the Jewish Scriptures as consisting of twenty-four books.[15] This may be the first time the official counting was reckoned as twenty-four, the number that has survived to the present in Judaism.

A (Very) Brief History of the New Testament Canon

A key moment in the history and development of the New Testament canon was in AD 367. In that year, Athanasius—the famous Bishop of Alexandria—penned his "Thirty-Ninth Easter Letter" that dealt with which writings belong in the New Testament canon. Athanasius's canon is *still* considered authoritative in most of Christianity. His ordering of the books is unfamiliar to us today: Matthew, Mark, Luke, John, Acts, James, 1 and 2 Peter, 1 and 2 and 3 John, Jude, Romans, 1 and 2 Corinthians, Galatians, Ephesians, Philippians, Colossians, 1 and 2 Thessalonians, Hebrews, 1 and 2 Timothy, Titus, Philemon, and Revelation. After listing the authoritative texts, Athanasius writes:

> These are the fountains of salvation at which they who
> thirst may be satisfied with the words they contain.
> Only in these is the teaching of piety proclaimed. Let
> no man add to these, nor take away from them. It was
> in respect to these that the Lord shamed the Sadducees
> when He said, "You err, because you do not know the
> Scriptures."[16]

Interestingly, Athanasius then lists several works he considered uncanonical, although he emphasized that they were "designated by the Fathers" as being profitable and instructive: Wisdom of Solomon, Wisdom of Sirach, Esther, Judith, Tobias (Tobit), the *Didache*, and the Shepherd of Hermas.[17]

However, it would be ridiculous to claim that the authority of the New Testament Scriptures dates to AD 367. Rather, as mentioned earlier, Paul's writings were considered authoritative *when he wrote them*. Thus, facile claims that somehow Constantine is the person who made the Bible authoritative can be safely dismissed as nonsensical.

So how did the Christian Scriptures evolve? How did Christians make these judgment calls as to what should be considered authoritative?

As delineated above, the Old Testament canon was fairly well-established by the time of Jesus. Both Jesus and his followers considered the "law and the prophets" to be important and authoritative. However, the early Christians quite clearly believed that a new revelation occurred with the life and teachings of Jesus. One of the great passages in the Hebrew Bible anticipating this "new covenant" was Jeremiah 31:31–34, "The days are coming, declares the Lord, when I will make a new covenant with the people of Israel." Jews held on to this hope and often connected it to Messianic expectations such as those expressed in the famous Isaiah 53 passage, "He was pierced for our transgressions, he was crushed for our iniquities; the punishment that brought us peace was on him, and by his wounds we are healed." Christians have certainly understood Isaiah 53 as having Messianic undertones.

Thus, in the minds of the earliest Christians, a new covenant had arrived. And it was spiritual, not physical, for Christ, the Lord, "is the Spirit" (2 Cor. 3:17). Paul unpacks this logic effectively in 2 Corinthians 3:6, "He has made us competent as ministers of a new covenant—not of the letter but of the Spirit; for the letter kills, but the Spirit gives life." Paul contrasts "the ministry that brought death, which was engraved in letters on stone" with "the ministry of the Spirit"—the new, spiritual covenant now established through Christ (2 Cor. 3:7–8). So, in a very real sense, the early Christians were ambivalent about Scripture. Should the exhilarating liberation from the "letters on stone" (2 Cor. 3:7) be compromised by a new set of writings? Or should Scripture—old or new—be relegated to second-class status in the new age of the Spirit? These issues are still with us today.

We do not have any writings from Jesus, so it was left to his disciples to write down his words. We have very little historical understanding of the precise chronology of this process. Were stories written down as Jesus spoke them? Or were they passed orally for a few decades before being compiled in a common source—something scholars often refer to as "the hypothetical document Q?"[18] Or, perhaps, the Gospel of Mark was the first Gospel to be written? The bottom line is that we just do not know. What is clear is that Jesus's teaching—especially his *style* of teaching—was impressive: "No one ever spoke the way this man does" (John 7:46). And his charismatic life gave birth to countless stories about him. "Jesus did many other things as well. If every one of them were written down, I suppose that even the whole world would not have room for the books that would be written" (John 21:25).

The life and teachings of Jesus were first and foremost *remembered*. And while it is very possible, even likely, that earlier Gospels were written down, the problem is that they are now lost to us. It is rather clear from analyzing the canonical Gospels of Matthew, Mark, and Luke that they borrowed material from earlier sources. Alas, we don't have access to those sources—at least not yet.

Biblical scholars today maintain the canonical Gospels were not systematized into their final forms until decades after the life of Jesus—probably the 60s, 70s, and 80s of that first century. Does this prove the Gospels to be false or unreliable? Of course not. If anything, it shows a rather diligent attempt to "get it right"—to ensure that the most important aspects of Jesus's life and teachings were passed on to future generations. The process would have unfolded in this way:

1. Jesus's teachings were preserved orally for some time.
2. Next, they were written down in earlier drafts—perhaps, for example, in a "Q" document, or similar kinds of documents.

3. Those earlier, piecemeal documents were used as sources by Matthew, Mark, Luke, and John to create the impressive, final drafts of the canonical Gospels that were eventually adopted as authoritative.

Matthew, Mark, Luke, and John did a tremendous service to the church by "investigating everything from the beginning" (Luke 1:3), organizing their material, and systematizing them into helpful biographical presentations of Jesus's life and teaching. It must have been painstaking work—trying to figure out what exactly to pass on to their readers and what to edit out, checking their sources, making decisions on how to present information, and trying to interpret the material faithfully. While not perfect, in the end their works definitely passed the early church's standards for orthodoxy, authenticity, and accuracy. They succeeded magnificently. Indeed, it would not be far-fetched to say that these four texts are probably the most widely read of any texts in the history of the world.

Since Paul became a Christian after Jesus's resurrection, it is perhaps a bit counterintuitive to realize that his letters are the earliest New Testament documents. In all likelihood, 1 Thessalonians "was written before any of the other books now found in our New Testament, which would make it the earliest surviving Christian writing of any kind."[19] At the end of that letter, Paul shows great authority and writes, "I charge you before the Lord to have this letter read to all the brothers and sisters" (1 Thess. 5:27). Similarly, in Colossians 4:16, Paul charges the congregation to read his letter publicly and requests them to make sure it is read to another congregation, in the great city of Laodicea.[20]

It is difficult to fully comprehend Paul's rather meteoric rise to apostolic authority in the early Christian community, but his authority cannot be denied. He was esteemed in the early church, ministering side by side with the original, chosen apostles of the Lord. After his sudden conversion to Christ while traveling to

Damascus in search of Christians to persecute, he immediately started to "preach in the synagogues that Jesus is the Son of God" (Acts 9:20). Some Jews conspired to kill him, but he was smuggled out of the city by "his followers" (Acts 9:25).

Paul's evangelistic efforts and apologetic work in the synagogues began to bear fruit early on. He traveled to Jerusalem where he befriended Barnabas, who introduced him to the apostles. Paul began preaching and debating with Hellenized Jews, but once again they conspired to kill him. The Christian community came to the rescue and whisked him off to another city to do his work.

It is clear that Paul was a great asset, and Christians went to great lengths to keep him alive. Paul had become their greatest convert, probably their most capable defender, and in due course became their greatest missionary. Adopted into the circle of apostles, his teachings and writings were treated as authoritative very early on.

Paul's authority is obvious in the New Testament documents, and, as we noted earlier, "all his letters" are explicitly referred to as "Scripture" in 2 Peter 3:16. In the first two centuries of the faith, virtually all of the church fathers show a familiarity with and reverence for Paul's writings. Between AD 80–98, Clement of Rome wrote: "Let us set before our eyes the good Apostles," whom he names Peter and Paul. He continued,

> Paul showed the way to the prize for endurance. Seven times he was in chains, he was exiled, he was stoned; he became a herald in the East and in the West, and he won splendid renown through his faith. He taught righteousness to all the world, and after reaching the boundaries of the West and giving his testimony before the rulers, he passed from the world and was taken up to the holy place. Thus he became our greatest example of perseverance.[21]

Another important early Christian, St. Ignatius of Antioch, wrote the following around AD 110: "Not as Peter and Paul did, do I command you. They were Apostles, and I am a convict."[22] And the famous martyr, St. Polycarp of Smyrna, a disciple of the apostle John, wrote the following:

> For neither can I nor anyone like me match the wisdom of the blessed and glorious Paul. When he was among you, face to face with the men of that time, he expounded the word of truth accurately and authoritatively; and when he was absent he wrote letters to you, the study of which will enable you to build yourselves up in the faith which was given to you, a faith which is the mother of us all.[23]

Comments such as these illustrate the great regard the early church had for Paul, his ministry, and his writings.

Around AD 200, a literary "New Testament" or "New Covenant" had emerged. Second and third-century fathers Clement of Alexandria, Tertullian, Origen, and Irenaeus were all acquainted with this body of writing, although they may have differed ever so slightly in their precise lists of texts.[24]

An important document known as the Muratorian Fragment marks a great milestone in the history of the New Testament canon. The document, named after an Italian historian, contains a list of Scriptures recognized by the entire church as being fit for public reading in the church. The traditional date suggested for the fragment is late second century, perhaps AD 170.[25] While that year is disputed, no one doubts that what it offers is an important, early list of what Christians considered to be Scripture. Twenty-two of our twenty-seven New Testament documents are included in the list. Excluded are Hebrews, 1 and 2 Peter, 3 John, and James. Since the fragment is an incomplete text, however, there is no way of knowing whether the original document included these other texts.[26]

Thus, it is clear that a New Testament was well on its way of coming together by AD 200. Everett Ferguson writes:

> By the end of the second century there was a core canon recognized virtually everywhere in the great church: four Gospels, the Acts of the Apostles, thirteen letters of Paul, and varying other apostolic writings. In general, Revelation was accepted in the West but not in the East; Hebrews was accepted in the East as a writing by Paul, but not in the West. Of the general epistles, the widest acceptance was given to 1 Peter and 1 John; the others were less well known.[27]

Over time, however, these discrepancies would smooth out, and the church would reach a strong consensus.

Around the year AD 300, Eusebius (who lived AD 260–339) published books 1–7 of his illustrious work *Church History*—perhaps *the* vital source for understanding early Christianity.[28] Eusebius was a towering scholar. He was bishop of Caesarea, he served as one of the chief contributors to the Council of Nicaea in AD 325, and he became a close confidant to Emperor Constantine. Eusebius gives us a snapshot of what elite Christians thought about the canon in the early AD 300s.[29] He used four categories to distinguish which books should be considered canonical and which should be questioned (or even rejected):

- Canonical everywhere:
  - The "holy quartet" of the Gospels
  - Acts of the Apostles
  - Paul's epistles (Romans through Hebrews)
  - 1 John
  - 1 Peter
  - Revelation of John (although Eusebius had some misgivings; see below)

- Disputed but used commonly in the churches:
  - James
  - Jude
  - 2 Peter
  - 2 and 3 John

- Spurious (doubted, but not heretical):
  - Acts of Paul
  - Shepherd of Hermas
  - Revelation of Peter
  - Epistle of Barnabas
  - The *Didache* (so-called "teaching of the apostles")
  - Revelation of John (Eusebius placed John's Revelation in both lists due to his uncertainty about it)

- Heretical, Impious, and Absurd:
  - Gospel of Peter
  - Gospel of Thomas
  - Gospel of Matthias
  - Acts of Andrew
  - Acts of John

Thus, we see that on the eve of the great Council of Nicaea, all twenty-seven of our current New Testament books were included by Eusebius as being profitable. Indeed, the top two categories used by Eusebius include precisely what we have in our Bibles today.

In the latter half of the fourth century, the New Testament canon became finally and firmly established. The great bishop of Alexandria, Athanasius, issued his Thirty-Ninth Easter Letter in AD 367, effectively putting any lingering debates to rest. In AD 397, the Third Council of Carthage officially ratified the twenty-seven books of the New Testament that we acknowledge today. Around the year 400, Jerome's Vulgate—his Latin translation of the Bible—simply *assumed* the twenty-seven-book canon in use today. "Jerome treated the New Testament canon as a 'given' not subject to modification."[30]

After Jerome, the Christian Bible began its long journey of translation into languages far and wide.[31] Around the year 350 the Gothic version appeared. The fifth century was a remarkably fertile century for Bible translation: Persian, Syriac, Armenian, Ethiopic/Geʿez, and Georgian versions all appeared. Between the sixth and the ninth centuries several more versions were created: Nubian (Sudanese), Sogdian (Uzbekistan/Tajikistan), Chinese (by Nestorians), Anglo-Saxon (by Caedmon and Bede), Slavonic, and Arabic.

The important Paris Bible appeared in the thirteenth century (although it was not the first French version). After the advent of Gutenberg's printing press in the fifteenth century, there was no stopping the rapid proliferation of Bible versions. In the sixteenth century, several new versions appeared: Swedish, Aztec/Nahuatl (only portions of the Bible), German (Luther's Bible), Polish, and Spanish.

The famous King James Version appeared in 1611. Later that century, portions of the Bible appeared in Malay, Algonquin (by John Eliot, it was the first complete American language Bible), and Celtic.

In the eighteenth century, the Bible began to appear in Tamil (by Ziegenbalg, in South India) and Inuktitut (Greenland).

In the nineteenth century, Bible translation work really blossomed alongside Protestant missionary work, with new versions appearing in Bullom (the first Sub-Saharan African translation), Tahitian (first Oceanic language), Chinese (Robert Morrison's version), Inuit (Labrador, Canada), Aymara (first South American indigenous language), Malagasy (Madagascar), Amharic (Ethiopia), Tswana (Niger-Congo-Botswana), Maori (New Zealand), Cree (Saskatchewan-Alberta), Mongolian, Japanese, Yoruba (Nigeria-Benin), Korean, and Mabuiag (first Australian Aboriginal translation).

In the twentieth century, more and more versions of the Bible appeared in a wide array of languages. In addition, many new English versions appeared, battling to supplant the old King James Version that had dominated for over three hundred years.

Before closing this section we should mention how the chapters and verses came to be inserted into the Bible. The chapter system used in virtually all Bibles today was created in the late 1100s and early 1200s by an Archbishop of Canterbury named Stephen Langton (1150–1228). Langton's *chapter* divisions have been applied far and wide: to the Greek New Testament, the Septuagint, and the Eastern Orthodox Bibles. Remarkably, even many Jewish Bibles incorporate his chapter system.[32]

The numbering system for *verses* in the Bible is traced to a Calvinist named Robert Estienne, the "former official printer to the King of France."[33] Estienne converted to Protestantism and fled France in 1551 to join up with John Calvin, where he applied his verse-numbering system to the Greek New Testament. The best-selling Geneva Bible integrated it into the text, and it caught on from there. Within a very short time, even the Catholic Bibles had adopted his verse-numbering system.

How Do We Know the Bible Is from God?

This is a tough question, but it is asked often. The short answer is that we have faith it is from God. With deep humility, we trust that God has revealed himself through Christ, and that the testimony of the early Christians is trustworthy and true. The Bible's contents have been put to the test for two thousand years and still survive, indeed they thrive. No other piece of writing in all of history has endured the scrutiny applied to the Bible.

But is it from God?

First of all, that depends on what one means by "from God." Christians disagree on which books of the Bible are most significant. For example, few people would argue that 2 John is as important as the Gospels. If you were sent to a remote mission field and had to choose a text to bring, would it be Philemon or Romans? Do you reckon that Paul thought Romans and Philemon were equal in weight? I seriously doubt it.

Throughout history, Christians have debated these issues. And they still do. Some people prefer the synoptic Gospels (Matthew, Mark, and Luke) to John. Others, however, prefer John. Martin Luther is a good example here. He thought most highly of the Gospel of John, considering it preferable to the other three because it will "show you Christ and teach you all that is necessary and salutary for you to know, even if you were never to see or hear any other book or doctrine."[34] However, Luther "relegated certain books (Hebrews, James, Jude, Revelation) to a distinctly inferior place."[35] Famously, Luther detested the "faith without works is dead" teaching of the book of James, causing him to make the now-famous critique, "St. James's epistle is really an epistle of straw . . . for it has nothing of the nature of the gospel about it."[36]

In addition to preferences within the canon, Christians have different understandings of the concept of inspiration as well. Some Christians, like Luther, see certain parts of the Bible as more inspired than others. Others take a very high view of inspiration, to the point that they view the whole Bible as coming down from God. This view is similar to the way Muslims understand the inspiration of the Quran. Muslims believe there was a very precise way that the Quran was passed down from God to humanity: God spoke to the archangel Gabriel, then Gabriel recited the words to Muhammad, then Muhammad recited the words to his scribe Zayd, and then Zayd wrote down the words. Muslims claim there is an unbroken chain of authority from God to the written word, without any meddling by humans.

Christians tend to approach the "inspiration" conversation a little differently than Muslims do. Most Christians argue that the Scriptures are inspired but not unmitigated by the thoughts or cultures of humans. Muslims differ here; they believe God speaks Arabic. Christians hold the view that God cannot be characterized as speaking one preferred language. This is one reason why the Bible is commonly translated into other languages. Christians don't have to learn Greek and Hebrew in order to understand God's intentions. Muslims, however, must be familiar with Arabic. They typically pray in Arabic and do not consider translations of the Quran to be the actual Quran at all. A translation of the Quran is something of an oxymoron. Once it assumes the clothing of another language, it ceases to be the Quran. Translations of the Quran are not from God—only the Arabic version is inspired. Christians, however, believe the Bible is inspired whether translated into English or Spanish, or left alone in Hebrew and Greek versions. The *message* is what is inspired by God, the medium is rather immaterial.

These reasons illustrate why Christians worship Jesus, not the Bible. The text is helpful and authoritative insofar as it gets us to God—who revealed himself in Jesus Christ. Can a person become a Christian without having the Bible? Of course! Many Christians throughout history were illiterate. The earliest Christians did not even have a New Testament! All they had was the Old Testament and stories of Jesus that were circulating. Paul's writings eventually came onto the scene, but in the earliest days of the church they were certainly not known universally among Christians. They were passed from church to church and eventually found their way into a canon. But in the earliest days the Bible was not necessary. The gospel was necessary, not the Bible.

Christians must rejoice that the Bible came into being. Christians should be thankful that the New Testament writers—Paul, Peter, Luke, and John—wrote these things down for us. However, our faith in Christ is not dependent upon texts. Jesus is divine, according to Trinitarian theology. In Christianity, it would be theologically problematic to argue that the Bible is divine. The Bible is a major source of information, but it is not *the same thing* as the gospel. It *contains* the gospel. It is an *account* of the gospel according to faithful and committed disciples. *The gospel* transcends these esteemed individuals, as important as they are to the faith. The gospel is its own authority. It does not require authorization of a council or of the church fathers. It is not reliant on the stamp of approval from ecclesial authorities in any time or place. The gospel is living, active, organic, and rooted first and foremost in the life and teaching of Jesus. It cannot be reduced to mere pen and paper.

Conclusion: The Bible . . . Our Roots

Throughout this book, we will be referring back to our Bibles. Thus, it is important to spend significant time thinking through the importance of the textual witness.

In this conclusion, however, I want to emphasize again that, as an Evangelical Christian, I try to strike a balance between two extremes: 1. An extremely high view of the Bible that seems fairly close to the way Muslims understand the Quran, and 2. The Catholic-Orthodox view of the Bible that sees it as essentially called into being by the church fathers. Let me unpack, briefly, what I mean.

As we saw in the opening quotation by Francis Chan, some Christians cling to the Bible as a complete, precise, and essentially word-for-word instruction from God. I would argue that this is too high a view. It puts the Bible on the throne. It doesn't account for inconsistencies in the text. It takes the focus off of Jesus and puts it onto a material object—even if that object is a text *about* Jesus.

The Roman Catholic and Orthodox Churches also make a similar mistake, yet in the opposite direction. They do not give the biblical text enough credit. They see the biblical text as a part of the magisterium of faith, but not the core or foundation of it. The institution of the church is foundational in this view, and the church is responsible for calling the text to its canonical status.

I studied church history under Professor Everett Ferguson, and I must say that in my case the apple did not fall far from the tree. Ferguson makes some careful distinctions here that I find tremendously helpful for making my central point:

> The organized church did not create the canon, but recognized it. . . . The canon was in a sense "inherited." Writers from the second century on repeatedly referred to the canonical writings as the books "handed down to us." . . . Succeeding centuries ratified a situation already established. The church, therefore, functioned as a witness, not as the judge in the process of canonization.[37]

Some readers may not fully realize what is at stake here. What is at stake is whether we should see the *Bible* or the *church* as our authority. And this is where Ferguson's seasoned conclusions are careful and extremely helpful:

> Instead of being an indication that the church has authority over the Scriptures, the church's role in recognizing the canon of Scripture is a testimony against the authority of the church. *Recognizing a canon was an act of placing herself under another authority.* If the church wanted to have unlimited authority, it would not have said, "These books are our authority in doctrine and life." The act of canonization was an act of declaring that the church was not her own authority, but that she was submitting to another authority.[38]

For these reasons, this book will call its readers back to the authority and authenticity of the text over and above the traditions of the church. Make no mistake; we will certainly look at what Christians have done over the course of its two thousand-year history. But when it comes time to discuss our earliest roots, we will look carefully at the seeds—the sacred Scriptures. The seed of the gospel not only pre-dates the balance of history, but is the wellspring.

That being said, we realize that the Scriptures are not divine in themselves. They help us to comprehend the fullness of the divine. They *point us toward* the divine. Granting the text too high an authority would be to commit the sin of bibliolatry: worshiping a text. And that is something Christians should reject.

As Christians, we can have great confidence that our sacred texts are "God-breathed . . . useful for teaching, rebuking, correcting and training in righteousness, so that the servant of God may be thoroughly equipped for every good work" (2 Tim. 3:16). The Scriptures are not God. They reveal the story of God's activity to us. As Paul states, they are useful. They are inspired. God's "breath" is in them, to borrow Paul's metaphor. It is important for us to acknowledge that these texts have been preserved to assist us in the Christian path. However, we also must understand that God transcends text. He will never be utterly and absolutely contained in texts. We must leave room for his mystery, his omnipotent power, and his supremacy over anything and over all things.

Notes

[1] The quotation is from a video entitled, "Francis Chan: Are Your Beliefs Biblical? (Crazy Love Chapter 5)," located at https://www.youtube.com/watch?v=5Is8QnxviOI.

[2] Quoted in Roland Bainton, *Here I Stand: A Life of Martin Luther* (New York: Meridian, 1955), 144.

[3] To get a sense of the number and variety of Protestant denominations only in America, see Pew Research Center, "America's Changing Religious Landscape." See "Appendix B: Classification of Protestant Denominations." See: http://www.pewforum.org/2015/05/12/appendix-b-classification-of-protestant-denominations/. Bear in mind this particular study is for America alone.

[4] The date of the article is 24 September 2015. It is located at: http://www.christianitytoday.com/ct/2015/october/why-we-need-new-battle-for-bible.html.

[5] In 1 Corinthians 5:9 Paul writes of an earlier letter he wrote dealing with how to treat the sexually immoral. Also, 2 Corinthians 2:3–4 and 7:8 seem to refer to a lost letter written by Paul, since his description of that letter in 2 Corinthians does not match the tenor of 1 Corinthians.

[6] See Jude 14–15 and Jude 9.

[7] Biblical scholars believe that the three passages mentioned here are later additions to the text.

[8] It should be pointed out that the Septuagint also included numerous other texts, known to scholars as "Deuterocanonical books." Christian traditions vary on how seriously to take these other texts. For example, Roman Catholics generally recognize the following as deuterocanonical: Tobit, Judith, Additions to Esther, Wisdom of Solomon, Sirach, Baruch, 1 and 2 Maccabees, and several other "additions" to Old Testament books such as the Letter of Jeremiah, Prayer of Azariah, Susanna, and Bel and the Dragon.

[9] A. J. Couch, "Sirach," in *International Standard Bible Encyclopedia* (Grand Rapids: Eerdmans, 1988).

[10] See Sirach, "The Prologue." *New Oxford Annotated Bible*, New Revised Standard Version (New York: Oxford University Press, 1994).

[11] Couch, 531.

[12] For the Josephus quotations, see William Whiston, trans., *The Works of Josephus* (Peabody, MA: Hendrickson Publishers, 1987), 776. The quotations all come from Josephus's *Flavius Josephus Against Apion* or *Antiquity of the Jews*, Book 1, Section 8.

[13] For an excellent study of the canon, see F. F. Bruce, *The Canon of Scripture* (Downers Grove, IL: InterVarsity Press, 1988), 28–33.

[14] Ibid., 33.

[15] It should be noted that 2 Esdras is known by several other names in biblical scholarship: Jewish Apocalypse of Ezra, 4 Esdras, Latin Esdras, or Latin Ezra.

[16] St. Athanasius, "The Thirty-Ninth Festal Letter [A.D. 367]," in William A. Jurgens, *The Faith of the Early Fathers*, Vol. 1 (Collegeville, MN: Order of Saint Benedict, 1970), 342.

[17] Ibid.

[18] The "Q" may refer to the German word *Quelle*, which means "source."

[19] Mark Allan Powell, *Introducing the New Testament* (Grand Rapids: Baker Academic, 2009), 371.

[20] Pauline authorship of Colossians is sometimes disputed.

[21] St. Clement of Rome, Pope, "Letter to the Corinthians [ca. AD 80 (96/98?)]" in Jurgens, 7–8.

[22] St. Ignatius of Antioch, "Letter to the Romans [ca AD 110]," in Jurgens, 22.

[23] St. Polycarp of Smyrna, "[Second] Letter to the Philippians [ca AD 135]," in Jurgens, 29.

[24] Everett Ferguson, *Church History*, Vol. 1 (Grand Rapids: Zondervan, 2013), 115.

[25] The *Diatessaron* by Tatian should be mentioned here since it too is usually dated to the year 170. It is a harmony of the four Gospels and "became for two centuries the standard form of the Gospels in Syriac-speaking areas." See Ferguson, 71.

[26] See "The Muratorian Fragment [inter AD 155/200]" in Jurgens, 107–108. We should note that the Muratorian Fragment approves of "The Wisdom of Solomon." It is cautious with "The Shepherd of Hermas," an important early Christian work considered Scripture by some. The fragment clarifies, however, that Hermas was written "quite recently in our time, in the city of Rome; and, therefore, it too should certainly be read. But it cannot be read publicly to the people in church."

[27] Ferguson, 116.

[28] Paul Maier argues that volumes 1–7 of *The Church History* were most likely published *before* the year 300. The final edition of the work was published just before the Council of Nicaea commenced. My discussion of Eusebius is based on Maier's *Eusebius, The Church History* (Grand Rapids: Kregel, 1999).

[29] The following list comes from *The Church History* 3:25. See Meier, 115.

[30] Interestingly, the Syriac church did not recognize 2 Peter, 2 and 3 John, Jude, and Revelation until the sixth century, and the Church of the East (Nestorian) has never recognized those books as being canonical, even up to the present. See Ferguson, 117.

[31] For this section, I am using the helpful chart "Milestones in the Worldwide Spread of the Sacred Scriptures" in the *Encyclopedia of the Bible and Its Reception*, Vol. 11 (Berlin: De Gruyter, 2015), 1204.

[32] W. H. Kent, "Langton, Stephen," in *Catholic Encyclopedia*, Vol. 8 (New York: The Encyclopedia Press, 1913), 791.

[33] See Diarmaid MacCulloch, *The Reformation: A History* (New York: Penguin, 2003), 247.

[34] Martin Luther, "Preface to the New Testament (1522, Revised 1546)," in *Martin Luther's Basic Theological Writings*, 3rd Edition (Minneapolis: Fortress Press, 2012), ed. by William Russell and Timothy Lull, 96.

[35] R. P. Meye, "Canon of the New Testament" in *International Standard Bible Encyclopedia* (Grand Rapids: Eerdmans, 1988), 605.

[36] Luther, "Preface to the New Testament," 96.

[37] Ferguson, 120.

[38] Ibid.

Chapter 2

Baptism

Becoming "Little Fishes"

"We, little fishes, are born in water after the manner of our IXΘΥΣ (fish), Jesus Christ; nor can we be otherwise saved, except by abiding permanently in the water."[1]

—*Tertullian*, c. 200 AD

The quotation above comes from Tertullian's work "Baptism." This writing is one of the earliest treatments of what has become known as a "sacrament" in Christian parlance: an outward sign of inward grace.

Tertullian and the Jesus Fish

Tertullian holds a special place in the history of the Western/Latin church as "he was the first to write in Latin, the new vernacular, when Greek was beginning to pass away as a common language in the West."[2] Despite his highly esteemed status—then and now—Tertullian eventually fell out of favor with the church hierarchy as he began to embrace teachings contrary to what most in the institution's hierarchy seemed to believe at the time.

What concerned and irritated Tertullian's colleagues most was that he adopted a rather anti-clerical outlook later in life.

Protestants would be quite proud of this move. It sounds similar to Luther's "priesthood of all believers" idea—just about thirteen hundred years before Luther! Also, later in life, Tertullian joined up with an early Christian movement known as Montanism—a Pentecostalism-like ideology that took the Christian world by storm, emphasizing prophecy and hard-core asceticism.[3]

Tertullian's "little fishes" quotation is fascinating on a number of fronts. First, it shows us that by the year AD 200, baptism was an assumed practice. By Tertullian's time, Christians were defined by this ritual. Tertullian's play on words is telling. Christians— "little fishes"—all submitted to it. It was the ritual of baptism that essentially changed one's identity from non-Christian to Christian. Once baptized, a person was expected to live a new, baptized life.

Secondly, Tertullian is careful to point out that no person can be "saved" without baptism, and "abiding permanently in the water." The Christian can be likened to a land animal who transitions into a sea-creature. We used to live a "dry" life, yet now we live a "baptized" life, abiding in Jesus Christ.

Yet there is more. Tertullian's use of the term ΙΧΘΥΣ (ichthus) is critical to the entire analogy. ΙΧΘΥΣ was perhaps the most important image associated with Christianity early in its history. It is the Greek word for *fish*. Although Tertullian is the celebrated early Latin Church father, he tellingly wrote this specific word in Greek. Why? Because it only made sense in Greek. ΙΧΘΥΣ was a famous mnemonic to trigger the basic tenants of Christian faith, that "Jesus is the Christ, the Son of God, the Savior." Thus, ΙΧΘΥΣ was an acrostic. Each of the Greek letters in the word has great potency:

Ιησους = Jesus
Χριστος = Christ ("anointed")
Θεου = God
Υιος = Son
Σωτηρ = Savior

Perhaps no other image was more important for early Christians than the fish. Jesus fed thousands with several loaves of bread and a few fish. Jesus ate fish with some disciples on the shore of the Sea of Galilee after his resurrection (John 21). Jesus promised his disciples that he would be in the earth for three days, as Jonah was in the belly of the fish for three nights (Matt. 12:40). The Jonah analogy may have something to do with Christians using the fish as a common funerary inscription on their tombs and sarcophagi.[4] By the time of Augustine, fish were still closely connected to Christianity. In his masterpiece work *The City of God* (published around AD 426), he provided a more elaborate explanation of why the fish was an apt symbol: ". . . because Christ was able to live, that is, to exist, without sin in the abyss of this mortality as in the depth of waters."[5]

Even today the widespread Christian practice of displaying the "Jesus fish" on the back of one's vehicle signifies to everyone around that this car belongs to a follower of Christ; this driver is a "little fish." When the Darwin fish came along—with legs—some competitive Creationists simply swallowed up "Darwin" with a larger "Truth" fish. And so it goes—and likely will go—probably as long as we continue to send messages on the backs of our vehicles.

My point here is that for centuries the fish symbol has been linked to Christianity, specifically to *joining* Christianity through water baptism. No Christian rite is as important to becoming a Christian. It is telling that when Luther trimmed the list of sacraments from seven to two, he held on to baptism and Eucharist. However, today, while some Protestant Christians downplay Eucharist—sometimes offering it but a few times per year—baptism continues to be the most fundamental rite. Christianity without baptism is almost non-existent.

When Jesus invited his earliest disciples to become "fishers of men," he made them a promise: "Come, follow me, and I will send you out to fish for people" (Matt. 4:19). After his death and

resurrection, he made good on that promise, explicitly command-
ing them to baptize new recruits. We know Jesus's words here as
"the Great Commission" (Matt. 28:18–20):

> All authority in heaven and on earth has been given to
> me. Therefore go and make disciples of all nations, bap-
> tizing them in the name of the Father and of the Son
> and of the Holy Spirit, and teaching them to obey every-
> thing I have commanded you. And surely I am with you
> always, to the very end of the age.

It is fascinating to see how Matthew provided two bookends for his
story of Jesus's mentorship of the apostles. First, when Jesus calls
them into his ministry, he promises he will enable them to become
"fishers of people." Later, in his final words to them, he commands
them to go out into the world and baptize, using the Trinitarian
formula: "in the name of the Father and of the Son and of the Holy
Spirit." We still use this formula to the present day.

Where did Jesus get all of this? Was he drawing from his Jewish
roots? Indeed, in many ways he was.

The Jewish Background of Water Baptism

The roots of Christian baptism are found within Judaism. However,
by no means did Judaism have a monopoly on baptism. Water
purification rituals such as baths are found in many religious
movements and in many societies. The "pagan" religions and
Hellenistic mystery religions in the Greco-Roman world regularly
practiced different forms of baptism. Ritual initiatory baths were
common in that era. Baths were used often to purify individuals
from sins or crimes. They were also used in initiation ceremonies.
For example, the devotees of the Egyptian goddess Isis as well as
members of the cult of Mithras both practiced initiatory baptism.[6]
Centuries later, Christian missionaries encountered baptism-like
rituals in the societies they tried to win to Christ. For example,

before Christianity came to Scandinavia during the medieval ages, it was common for babies to have water poured over them during a naming ceremony.[7]

Judaism was obviously a part of the larger religious context of the Ancient Near East and the Greco-Roman world. However, it put its own stamp on the rituals it shared with other civilizations, including baptism. In Leviticus 14, ritual baths are prescribed for people who have skin diseases. They had to be washed before they are able to participate in community-wide religious rituals. In Leviticus 15, the Lord tells Moses and Aaron that any man who has "an unusual bodily discharge" should be considered unclean until he is bathed and his clothes are cleaned. Similarly, when a man "has an emission of semen, he must bathe his whole body with water" (15:16). Similar rules are established for menstruating women. Even the priests are commanded to bathe and wash their clothes before an appearance before the Lord. Stiff penalties were imposed on those who "defiled the sanctuary of the LORD" by not first bathing with water: "They must be cut off from the community" (Num. 19:19–20).

The story of Naaman's healing in 2 Kings 5 has been used by Christians to emphasize the cleansing value of baptism. Naaman was a Gentile army commander who fought for the king of Aram near Damascus, Syria. He was a leper facing death, but he heard through the grapevine that he could be healed by the Jewish prophet Elisha. Naaman went to Elisha for help but was insulted when the prophet did not even come outside to see him. Rather, Elisha sent a messenger to tell Naaman to simply wash seven times in the Jordan River. Angry Naaman stomped off: "I thought that he would surely come out to me and stand and call on the name of the LORD his God, wave his hand over the spot and cure me of my leprosy." Finally, Naaman conceded and washed in the Jordan. He was instantly cleansed. Perhaps the whole point of the story, however, is that Naaman changed his religion and began to be a follower of Yahweh: "Now I know that there is no God in all the world except in Israel." Naaman declared publicly that he would "never again make burnt offerings and sacrifices to any other god but the LORD."

Naaman may have experienced a unique grafting into the Jewish faith through water baptism, but by the time of Jesus it was a relatively common practice. "Proselyte baptism" was required for both women and men who wanted to join Judaism. By the end of the first century AD water baptism was an extremely important practice amongst Jews, even to the point that rabbis questioned whether it had become more vital than circumcision.[8] This controversy seems to have spilled over into the early Christian community (Acts 15; Gal. 2).

The key difference between Jewish proselyte baptism and Christian baptism was that Jews self-administered. These converts, known as "God-fearers," typically immersed themselves in a Jewish *mikveh*—a pool constructed for ritual cleansing.[9] The Mishnah (Jewish rabbinic text) prescribed total bodily immersion as the method to be employed.[10] When Gentiles converted to Judaism, their children were typically baptized into the faith as well. However, once a family was baptized into Judaism, their future children did not have to be baptized. The family line had already become sanctified. This idea may have a parallel in 1 Corinthians 7:14 when Paul writes: "For the unbelieving husband has been sanctified through his wife, and the unbelieving wife has been sanctified through her believing husband. Otherwise your children would be unclean, but as it is, they are holy."

Baptism in the New Testament

Early in the Gospels readers are introduced to Jesus's cousin, John the Baptizer. The baptism he administered was not exactly a Jewish baptism, nor was it a Christian baptism. Rather, it was "a baptism of repentance for the forgiveness of sins" (Mark 1:4). We are told that people confessed their sins and were then "baptized *by* him" in the Jordan River. This was different from the common Jewish baptisms, because converts to Judaism typically self-administered baptism in order to join the faith.

In addition, all three of the synoptic Gospels explain that John's central message was that someone was to come after him, one "more powerful," one who would baptize "with [or *in*] the Holy Spirit" (Mark 1:8). Great crowds came to be baptized by John. Even Jesus himself showed up one day to be immersed. While the Gospels make much of the baptism of Jesus, the ritual is down-played for much of the rest of Jesus's ministry. One notable exception here is in the Gospel of John, chapter 3, where Jesus explains to a Jewish leader named Nicodemus that "no one can enter the kingdom of God unless they are born of water and the Spirit" (v. 5). Shortly after this famous section (which includes John 3:16), we are told that both Jesus's and John's followers were baptizing people in the Judean countryside "because there was plenty of water."

Another notable exception is at the end of the Gospels (Matt. 28 and Mark 16), where we encounter the "Great Commission" that we quoted earlier. You may recall that in Matthew 28:19–20, Jesus instructs his disciples to go out into "all nations, baptizing them in the name of the Father and of the Son and of the Holy Spirit, and teaching them to obey everything I have commanded you. And surely I am with you always, to the very end of the age."

The ritual of baptism is quite prominent during the early days of the Christian church. The Acts of the Apostles makes it clear that those grafted into the Jesus movement always were baptized immediately upon evidence of their devotion to Christ:

- After the apostle Peter preached the first gospel sermon, the crowds—reportedly three thousand in number— accepted the message, repented, and were baptized "for the forgiveness of [their] sins." Peter promised them that they would "receive the gift of the Holy Spirit" (Acts 2).

- The evangelist Philip converted a sorcerer to Christianity and immediately baptized him. Later in that same chapter (Acts 8), when Philip explained the meaning of Jesus to an Ethiopian official who was on pilgrimage to Jerusalem, the man saw water and asked to be baptized. Philip consented and immersed the man.

- When the apostle Paul—known early in life as Saul—converted to Christ, he was baptized (Acts 9).

- At Cornelius's house, Peter baptized "a large gathering" in the name of Jesus Christ after he realized that they had "received the Holy Spirit" (Acts 10).

- In Acts 16 and 18 we see the interesting phenomenon of entire households being baptized. First, Lydia, a business woman, was baptized along with "the members of her household." Then a jailer whose life was saved by Paul and Silas was baptized along with his entire household. Third, in Corinth we see a leading Jewish man named Crispus being baptized, along with "his entire household."

When Luke (the author of Acts) mentions households, he probably has in mind multiple generations from the family as well as servants living there.

Baptism is mentioned repeatedly in the New Testament epistles. Many different contexts provide richness and depth for the practice, which still is used regularly by Christians today. Some of the more notable references to baptism are in the form of imagery and analogy:

- *Burial.* "All of us who were baptized into Christ Jesus were baptized into his death" (Rom. 6:3; see also Col. 2:12).

- *A sign of unity and equality.* "We were all baptized by one Spirit so as to form one body—whether Jews or Gentiles, slave or free" (1 Cor. 12:13; see also Gal. 3:27–28).
- *As fundamental to Christianity as the doctrine of the Trinity, the holy faith, and the church.* "There is one body and one Spirit, just as you were called to one hope when you were called; one Lord, one faith, one baptism; one God and Father of all" (Eph. 4:4–5).
- *A new circumcision.* "Your whole self, ruled by the flesh, was put off when you were circumcised by Christ, having been buried with him in baptism" (Col. 2:11–12).
- *Cleansing.* "He saved us through the washing of rebirth and renewal by the Holy Spirit" (Tit. 3:5; see also Heb. 10:22).
- *Like Noah's ark, a vessel for salvation.* "This water symbolizes baptism that now saves you also" (1 Pet. 3:21).
- *Closely attached to Jesus's identity.* "This is the one who came by water and blood—Jesus Christ" (1 John 5:6).

Finally, baptism is probably what is being referred to in Revelation when the author writes of "those who wash their robes, that they may have the right to the tree of life and may go through the gates into the city" (Rev. 22:14; 7:14).

It is clear that baptism in the New Testament is linked to salvation. However, I have talked with people who emphasize that the thief on the cross was granted Paradise by Jesus without having been baptized. I suppose the point being made is that while baptism is an important ritual, it is not absolutely necessary for salvation. But given the ubiquitous—and crucial—place of baptism in the New Testament, one has to wonder why a convert to Christianity would want to avoid or downplay this rite.

- Jesus was baptized.
- The apostles baptized their converts.

- Jesus commanded his disciples to baptize.
- Baptism is linked repeatedly to salvation.
- Baptism is linked to the forgiveness of sins and the gift of the Holy Spirit.
- Perhaps Jesus's most explicit statement on the subject is in John 3:5, "Very truly I tell you, no one can enter the kingdom of God unless they are born of water and the Spirit."

With all of this biblical support, why would someone want to contend that baptism is somehow unnecessary for a Christian? If I were converting to Christianity, yet was dissuaded from baptism, I would have to question the motives of the evangelist!

Baptism in the Early Church

Baptism is well attested in the early church.[11] The rich metaphors from the New Testament were drawn upon frequently by early Christians. By the end of the second century, baptismal ceremonies were highly developed. One of the earliest Christian documents, the *Didache* (the "teaching"), provides a snapshot of how Christians were institutionalizing water baptism around the year AD 100:

> Concerning baptism, baptize in this way. After you have spoken all these things, "baptize in the name of the Father, and of the Son, and of the Holy Spirit," in running water. If you do not have running water, baptize in other water. If you are not able in cold, then in warm. If you do not have either, pour out water three times on the head "in the name of the Father, and of the Son, and of the Holy Spirit." Before the baptism the one baptizing and the one being baptized are to fast, and any others who are able. Command the one being baptized to fast beforehand a day or two.[12]

It should be pointed out that the Greek word for baptize, βαπτίζω (*baptizo*), is properly translated into English as "immerse."[13] "Baptism" is simply a transliteration of the Greek word. Threefold pouring was advised only if "baptism" or "immersion" was impossible due to lack of water.

If we were to witness a baptismal ceremony in the second century, we would see just how solemnly Christians approached the act.[14] First, the baptismal candidate would undergo teaching, intense prayer, and a period of fasting before ever entering the baptismal pool. The period of instruction would last about three years. Typically, preparations culminated with water baptism on the night before Easter. Later, baptismal ceremonies were commonly held on Easter Sunday.

During the ceremony, the Holy Spirit was invoked onto the water. The candidate would disrobe and renounce Satan and all evil. Oil of exorcism was applied to the candidate. While standing in the water, the candidate confessed belief in each member of the Trinity and was immersed each time. The candidate was asked if he or she believed in God, Jesus, and the Holy Spirit. These confessions form some of our earliest sources for the Christian creeds. One early church document, "The Apostolic Tradition," dated to around AD 215 records the following:

- *Do you believe* in God, the Father Almighty?
- *Do you believe* in Christ Jesus, the Son of God, who was born of the Holy Spirit, of the Virgin Mary, and was crucified under Pontius Pilate and died and was buried, and rose up again on the third day, alive from the dead, and ascended into heaven, and sat at the right hand of the Father, about to come to judge the living and the dead?
- *Do you believe* in the Holy Spirit and the holy Church and the resurrection of the flesh?[15]

After each question the person answered, "I believe," and was immersed.

The administrator of the baptism kept his hand on the candidate's head in order to help plunge his or her head under the water as he or she kneeled down. After the immersions, the person was anointed with oil and re-clothed. Laying on of hands then took place, with oil. The congregation exchanged the kiss of peace, and a Eucharistic service followed.

This basic order continued throughout the centuries of the church, both in the East and in the West. Minor variations and innovations crept into the ritual, but there is remarkable consistency from the second century onward to the time of the Protestant Reformation. The Eastern Orthodox churches continue to practice a very similar order when welcoming an adult into their church. Infant baptism is quite different, of course; no confession of faith is possible, and the baby is held while passively undergoing the rite. Let's quickly explore the roots of infant baptism.

Infant Baptism

Infant baptism today is by far the most common method for Christians worldwide. It has a long history that goes back to at least the time of Cyprian (AD 200–258). Pedobaptists (those who practice infant baptism) argue that their stance is not only historical but biblical as well.[16] They use the following Scriptures to validate the practice:

- The Holy Spirit is conferred upon a child "even from his mother's womb" (Luke 1:15).
- Jesus claims the Kingdom of heaven belongs to "little children" (Matt. 19:14).
- The offspring of believers in Christ are considered holy (1 Cor. 7:14).

- Baptism, forgiveness, and the gift of the Holy Spirit were promises extended by the apostle Peter to "you and your children" (Acts 2:38–39).

A Christian who practices believer's baptism will say that these texts are far from conclusive. None of these Scriptures says explicitly that Christian baptism is a practice for infants. Thus, Christians in the early days of the church were rather ambivalent for some time about whether to practice infant baptism or believer's baptism, but the consensus was moving in the direction of infant baptism when Augustine came along. And Augustine pretty much ended the conversation—until the era of the Protestant Reformation a millennium later.

Saint Augustine (354–430) is perhaps the most esteemed theologian in Western church history. His theology was rooted in the notion of original sin. Historian Peter Brown explains that, until the time of Augustine, questions about original sin and the consequential teaching of infant baptism had remained "open to disagreement among experts." However, Augustine represents a turning point. He left no room for dissent. Augustine and his colleagues taught these doctrines "with peremptory certitude." Original sin was not up for debate. It was settled. Obvious. Not open to challenge.[17]

Why was Augustine so obstinate on the matter? The answer is clear: Pelagius. Born in the British Isles, Pelagius was the greatest threat to Augustine's system of thought during his lifetime. Pelagius lived from roughly 360 to 418 and was Augustine's archenemy. By all accounts he was a deeply committed Christian man, even saintly. He was certainly a competent scholar. Whereas Augustine never mastered Greek, Pelagius was fully functional in the language of the New Testament. Nevertheless, Augustine launched a broadside at Pelagius's teachings, attacking him with such fury that everybody who was anybody during that time was forced to pick a side. Popes and emperors became embroiled in the controversy. Pope Innocent I excommunicated Pelagius, only to have his successor—Pope Zosimus—reinstate him. However, due to pressure from the emperor at the time, Zosimus changed his tune and also condemned Pelagius as a heretic. If that wasn't enough, he banished him from the entire Italian peninsula. Thereafter, Augustine was finally satisfied that his greatest theological challenger had been publicly humiliated and roundly condemned.[18]

In an era fixated on the precise, almost mathematical understanding of the Trinity, Pelagius's Christology was not the issue. Rather, it was his anthropology that got him into trouble. Simply put, he believed in free will. He thought humans were born sinless; people only became sinners *after* they reached an age of accountability. He did not approve of the doctrine of inherited guilt—that everybody *inherits* sin and guilt from Adam, even upon conception. However—and herein lays the problem—inherited guilt was the cornerstone of Augustine's theological system. He thought humans were born into sin because of their lust—which Augustine called concupiscence. In other words, since each human being is conceived in lust, every single human being therefore stands condemned, even at conception. This is original sin. Blame it on Adam and Eve, but Augustine's point is that we all inherit it. We've all been tainted. It's in our spiritual DNA. When we produce children, we pass it on to them.

Pelagius disagreed with all of that. It goes beyond the scope of this chapter to detail the theological nuances, but in essence Pelagius thought free will was a grace given to human beings by God. Augustine thought the human will was in bondage—a theme that Luther would capitalize upon in the sixteenth century. The "touchstone" of Augustine's entire system was the words of Jesus in the Lord's Prayer, "Forgive us our sins." For Augustine, humans were unable to get rid of sin. Sin pulsates through us without our knowledge. Thus, we must constantly pray those words: "Forgive us our sins." We must always work on our "tiny little sins." The goal of Christian life is to "expunge these tiny sins," although in fact it is impossible to completely accomplish the task. The Christian life is a life of "continual penance." Especially as concerns the Eucharist, we are to be mindful of our sinfulness. Pelagius was wrong, railed Augustine. We exist in "a daily state of sinfulness."[19]

Did Augustine think a person had to be baptized to be saved? He has certainly been interpreted that way throughout history, but he does give a glimmer of hope that God might possibly have mercy on the Christian couple whose children are not baptized in time. His argument hinges on Matthew 12 where Jesus says, "How can anyone enter a strong man's house and carry off his possessions unless he first ties up the strong man? Then he can plunder his house." In a strange and vague passage in *The City of God*, Augustine struggles with whether a non-baptized child can manage to get his or her name written into the book of life.[20] His conclusion is opaque, but he seems to say that God has the power to snatch the unbaptized children from the devil's possession, even if the devil appears to be unbound. God can do all things—even something as difficult as saving an unbaptized baby.

The larger point here is this: Augustine *assumed* infant baptism was the correct way to go for Christians. Any idea that God might save a non-baptized person was, in the best case, doubtful. In Augustine's view, Christian parents should feel compelled to have their children baptized into the church as soon as possible, placing them safely underneath the banner of Christ.

How did Augustine get to this point? Which of the early church fathers influenced him? What happened during the three centuries between Paul and Augustine? In the New Testament we can find no clear evidence of infant baptism, but by the early 400s virtually all baptisms were infant baptisms. How did this transition occur?

Everett Ferguson writes, "The circumstance of emergency baptism may provide the clue for the actual origin of infant baptism."[21]

Christians were afraid that their children might die without this powerful rite. After all, Jesus appears unequivocal in his statement about baptism: "Unless one be born of water and the Spirit he cannot enter the kingdom of heaven" (John 3:5). No baptism, then no heaven. The other important statement from Jesus comes from Matthew 19:14, "Let the little children come to me, and do not hinder them." Do not prevent a child from being baptized.

Most of the first Christian converts were Jewish. From a Jewish perspective, it would have been natural for baptism to be seen as a new version of circumcision. And according to Leviticus 12:3, Jews were to administer circumcision to newborn boys on the eighth day. However, the earliest Christians seemed not to make this connection, in spite of the fact that Paul did make the parallel between baptism and circumcision in Colossians 2:11–12. Infant baptism did not catch on until much later.

It is difficult indeed to assign a precise date to the origin of infant baptism. Some have argued that the "households" of Lydia and Crispus—which were baptized in Acts 16 and 18—must have included infants. That is possible, but not certain.

Tertullian (AD 200) is "the writer who makes the first explicit reference to infant baptism in Christian history."[22] However, he opposed it.[23] The doctrine of original sin was not widespread by the early second century. Therefore, baptism was not thought to be a mechanism for removing guilt in a baby. Infants were considered to be in a state of innocence. Indeed, "The whole language of 'rebirth' in connection with baptism implies the guiltlessness of the infant."[24] Infants were considered pure, and therefore saved.

Irenaeus of Lyon (AD 140–202) was an early church father who alluded to infant baptism but did not speak out against it.[25] Origen and Hippolytus were two church fathers who lived around the year AD 200, and both of them believed infant baptism was sanctioned by the apostles. Another church father, Cyprian, came along a little later, and he found infant baptism to be valid.

Baptism at a young age was not mandatory, however. Several of the great church fathers famously put off baptism until "the end of their student days."[26] Waiting until the end of their studies seemed to be the popular way of doing it in the fourth century. Basil the Great, Gregory of Nyssa, Gregory of Nazianzus (more on him later), John Chrysostom, Ephrem the Syrian, Jerome, Rufinus, Augustine—they all put off baptism until the end of their education.[27] Augustine was about thirty-three years old when he was baptized into Christ in the year 387.

Presumably, these saintly individuals figured the more sins they could wash away, the better. In that era, baptism was thought to be an extremely powerful act, perfectly efficacious in the removal of sin. However, sins *after* baptism were much more difficult to remove. It made sense for these heroic Christian fathers to delay their baptism in order to have more of their past sins washed away. The great emperor Constantine (who died AD 337) put off baptism until the end of his life.[28] Was he simply outsmarting the system—allowing himself to sin boldly throughout life and receive absolution in the baptismal waters? Or was he nervous about what his pagan subjects might think if he joined Christianity? We'll probably never know.

Infant baptism seems to have been associated with a child who might not thrive after birth. In this case, "infant baptism was not routine but occurred as a precaution against death."[29] The fear of death drove parents to baptize their child when any sign of illness appeared. Baptism was a rite that was so closely associated with salvation that parents did not want to risk their child not making it into heaven.

We must be cautious with our history here, however. Augustine reasoned that because Christians commonly practiced infant baptism in his day, then original sin must be true. But the historical development of the sacrament of baptism seems to have followed the reverse sequence. In other words, first came infant baptism, then came the notion of original sin and original guilt. Augustine was probably unaware of the earliest history—that "the early Christian documents, in contrast, contain frequent reference to the sinlessness of children."[30]

Ironically, the great church father Gregory of Nazianzus preached strongly in favor of early baptism, but he himself waited to be baptized until he was at the end of his studies. He advised that children should be baptized around the age of three. He felt that delaying baptism in order to wash away more sin was "a specious argument of the devil."[31]

Gregory held an extremely high view of baptism, most evident in his famous "Oration on Holy Baptism," preached in Constantinople on January 6, 381.[32] In that sermon he described baptism as "that which quenches fire," meaning that it held the power to save us from hell. He argued strongly against postponing the sacrament. Some of Gregory's readers were prone to "wait for a fever" prior to getting baptized. Their extremely high view of the cleansing power of baptism caused them to delay the sacrament until they felt they were close to death. Therefore Gregory urged infant baptism at the "tenderest age" so the child would be "sanctified" from his infancy and "consecrated by the Spirit" while in his youth. He exclaimed, "Give your child the Trinity, that great and noble Guard!"

Interestingly, in Gregory's view, baptism led to social equality as well: "You who are in slavery, be made of equal rank."[33] Presumably a slave could become his master's equal through the practice, at least in a spiritual sense.

Gregory's most severe criticism was aimed at people who wanted to indulge in the flesh and therefore put off baptism until much later in life. By delaying baptism, they could relish the sweet fruits that this world had to offer, and then have all of their sins suddenly washed away at the end of life. It was certainly strategic, but those who took this route were haunted by the possibility that they might die suddenly before they received the salvation that only baptism could offer. Gregory's sermon was intended to heighten their angst so that they would submit to the sacrament and start living pure lives for God.

Most certainly Gregory understood that these individuals were playing the system. He himself had taken this approach in his youth. All the while, he and everyone else knew that this was cheating. Nevertheless, they believed that Christ had indeed set it up this way. In Gregory's sermon, he repeatedly referred to the "laborers in the vineyard" parable in Matthew 20. In that parable, the people who worked only one hour received the same pay as those who worked all day. It seemed unfair to human ears, but Jesus corrected them, "I am not being unfair to you, friend. . . . Don't I have the right to do what I want with my own money? Or are you envious because I am generous? The last will be first and the first will be last."

Gregory knew his audience was familiar with the Parable of the Laborers, and it frustrated him. He also knew that his audience had a clear understanding of God's grace. In Gregory's time, one of the main reasons people chose not to get baptized was because they thought God would have mercy on unbaptized sinners, allowing them to be baptized *by their desire*. The Catholic Church refers to this doctrine as *Baptismus flaminis*, or, "Baptism of desire." In Gregory's day, this notion was already well-established, yet he cautioned against it. He thought it was tantamount to being contemptuous of baptism and could lead to more suffering and punishment in the afterlife.[34]

The great Byzantine Emperor Justinian I (who reigned 527–565) made infant baptism compulsory for his subjects in the sixth century, and the issue of believer's baptism was scarcely raised again until the Protestant Reformation. In reality, however, it was Augustine of Hippo in the 400s who contributed the decisive turning point, because he "secured the triumph of the doctrine of original sin."[35] Once that doctrine was the established teaching, infant baptism seemed to make great sense for the masses. After Augustine, infant baptism was rarely questioned as the dominant mode for this sacrament.

Medieval Baptism

In the medieval world, baptism retained its privileged status as an exceptionally important sacrament that all should follow, babes and new converts alike. When Clovis, King of the Franks, converted to Catholic Christianity around the year 497, virtually all of his subjects were baptized *en masse*. The Franks became officially Catholic, and very soon the rest of the Germanic kings would follow.[36]

A similar process occurred in Russia in 988 when Vladimir the Great "was converted to Christianity and married Anna, the sister of the Byzantine Emperor."[37] His subjects in Kiev went down to the Dnieper River for a mass baptism; suddenly Orthodox Christianity became the state religion of the Russian Empire from that year until 1917, when the Bolsheviks rose up. Now that the Soviet oppression has lifted, the Orthodox Church is once again thriving, and baptism in the former Soviet Union is again widespread.

Baptism was typically a mass event throughout the medieval era. It was often the case that large districts only had one baptistery, since the parish system was not refined until the thirteenth and fourteenth centuries. For example, in Florence, Italy, even up to modern times, there was only one baptistery for virtually all Florentines—the octagonal Baptistery of Saint John (San Giovanni).[38] Similarly, in most districts people were baptized at one designated church—often a cathedral or important basilica. These mass baptisms were usually carried out on Easter Sunday, the day of the Resurrection.

We must frankly admit that the mass baptisms throughout the medieval era were not full-blown conversions as we understand them today. Scholars debate how "Christian" these societies became at these mass baptisms. It is quite clear that in many cases pagan worship continued unabated. Mass baptisms often were tied to politics. When Russia's Vladimir required his subjects to dip into the river, they had little choice but to obey.

On the other hand, to think that there was no change in the hearts of people would be presumptuous on our part hundreds of years after the fact. Whether it was years or even generations later, it seems that these societies did indeed turn to Christ in an authentic way. In all likelihood, the seriousness of conversion varied greatly from person to person, much as it does today. People get baptized, or they baptize their children, for a variety of reasons: marriage, for refugee status, to join up with a particular church, because their family expects it of them, because they had a spiritual experience, and so on.

Whatever the case, "by the end of the sixth century the vast majority of the inhabitants of Western Europe were in fact baptized Christians" although "there is little consensus regarding the degree to which they had adopted Christianity."[39]

As Christianity began to go global in the age of Catholic missions, a similar course of action was followed. Entire civilizations were baptized both in Europe and overseas. Conquistadors took great pride in claiming subjects for the crown back home and for the church in Rome. Jews were forced to convert to the Catholic Church regularly, perhaps most notably in Spain, although they often became Christians in name only. These Jews became known as "conversos." Andres Bernaldez, a fifteenth-century Spanish church historian, wrote:

> The baptized Jews who stayed were called conversos
> . . . which means those converted to the Holy Catholic
> Faith. The conversos observed the Faith very badly. . . .
> for the most part they were secret Jews. In fact, they

were neither Jews nor Christians, since they were baptized, but were heretics, and [yet] without the Law [of Moses].[40]

It should be noted that the only reason these Jews became Christians was because these were the days of the Spanish Inquisition, when "people spitefully put the Jews in Castile to the sword and killed many, and this occurred all over Castile in a single day."[41] With persecution of this scale, it made sense to submit to baptism. Many did. Or, the other option was to move, which many other Jews also did.

The Spanish and Portuguese took this same zeal with them to the Americas, to the parts of Africa that they conquered—such as the Portuguese Kingdom of Kongo, and to Asia. Indeed, the Philippines were conquered in much the same way that Columbus, Cortez, and Pizarro and company conquered the New World— by force. In South India, the Portuguese implemented the Goa Inquisition. However, far and away the most profound of these events was the sacking of the Aztecs and the Incas and the taking of the Americas from indigenous hands in the early sixteenth century. Inevitably, as with the Jews in Spain, the survivors were offered few options but to submit to the sacrament of baptism and become Christians. Latin America—by far the most Christianized region of the entire world—has remained very Catholic ever since.

Anabaptism . . . Baptized Again

The early waves of Protestants—Luther, Zwingli, Calvin—maintained much of the Catholic ethos in baptism, albeit with their own distinct emphases. It was with the Anabaptists, however, that Christianity experienced a major crisis surrounding the sacrament of baptism. The Anabaptists—which simply means "rebaptizers"— are the forefathers of what we know as the "Baptist" traditions, meaning those who baptize believers rather than babies. In the 1520s, only a few years after Luther had launched his reforms, a radical group of disciples rose up primarily in Switzerland. They thought Luther had not gone far enough in his reforms. They assumed pacifism to be the correct way for a Christian. They took the teachings of Jesus at face value. They followed the Sermon on the Mount with great care. This reasoning led them to examine what the Scriptures had to say on all manner of church practices.

On January 21, 1525, one of the radicals in Zurich, Conrad Grebel, began to baptize adults. Obviously, these were Christian people who had already undergone baptism in their infancy. That is why they were ridiculed by everybody as being "Anabaptists." The term was not quite accurate, because Grebel and his crew decided that infant baptism was invalid. In other words, he taught that these people had not really been baptized at all when they were young. Both Protestants and Catholics were furious at him for such sacrilege. How dare he insult the entire Christian world by arguing that nobody's baptism was valid, except for his little group of "rebaptizers"?

For the first time in history, it seemed that Protestants and Catholics were united on one thing: the Anabaptists must be punished and put down, even eliminated. They were often killed by drowning in order to make a cruel point crystal clear to them: you will be baptized until dead. Thousands of Anabaptists were tortured and killed, hunted as heretics from the 1520s onward. Even into the twentieth century they endured persecution due to their refusal to serve in national militaries. While the Anabaptists were brutally suppressed, it was too little, too late. Their teachings carried on.

In spite of these vicious rounds of persecution, the Anabaptists became one of the major strands of the Reformation and are still very much with us. The Mennonites, Hutterites, and Amish are their direct posterity, as are some of the Brethren churches. The Anabaptist belief about the sacrament of baptism lives on in many denominations and movements today, such as the huge and global

Pentecostal movement which practices immersion for believers. As mentioned previously, the Baptists—the United States' largest denomination—adopted their stance that baptism should only be administered to a believer who could offer a public profession of faith. My own fellowship—the Restoration churches, launched by Alexander Campbell and Barton Stone in the nineteenth century—has also adopted the Anabaptist approach to the sacrament of baptism.

As Christianity continues its global expansion, believer's baptism has established itself firmly across the array of world Christianities. While it will surely never be practiced by the majority of Christians, it is today by a respectable minority. Perhaps 15 percent of all Christians baptize in this way.[42]

A Defiant Baptism . . . Getting Back to Our Roots

Why do we practice baptism? We practice it because Jesus practiced it. Because the apostles practiced it. Because it has been faithfully applied to Christians since the inception of the faith. At the same time, we still practice it today because we believe it is a powerful rite. It is a sacrament full of imagery. We are cleansed. We die to our old selves and are raised up with Christ. We come out of the water as he came out of the tomb. We are reborn, of water and Spirit.

Perhaps it is time for Christians to rediscover the full potency of baptism again. This chapter shows how Christians from all eras have emphasized baptism as perhaps the most important entry point into living a Christian life.

In the earliest years of Christianity, baptism was an act of defiance. By entering the baptismal waters, Gentile Christians in particular were rejecting the ways of the world. They were turning their backs on the standards of their society such as violence, immorality, and materialism. And they knew when they entered the water that it could cost them. Sometimes it could result in persecution, marginalization, or even death.

When we are baptized, we join a new order—that of Christ, with all of his demands: loving our enemy, blessing those who persecute us, protecting children and others who are vulnerable, restoring the disgraced, valuing those who have no societal value. Christ's teachings ran contrary to Greco-Roman society, yet they proved to be vital and attractive for people. The church grew dramatically because of its countercultural beliefs.

In our society today—a society that is theoretically Christian—perhaps we can rediscover the power of baptismal disassociation. By this we mean that we can begin again to view baptism as a time of renouncing our association with the world's standards and aligning ourselves with Christ. To early Christians, the price of Christian baptism was steep. They could lose everything by following Christ, but they were empowered by the promise that in reality what they were gaining was far superior to what the world could provide. I wonder if the price of baptism has been cheapened by the close alliance of Christianity and culture. Following Jesus Christ as Lord should be utterly transformative. The baptized life should not be the same as the unbaptized one. Being "in Christ" should not be the same thing as living life without Christ. Most certainly, baptism must entail a commitment to living one way and disassociating with other ways. Jesus exhorts his followers: "I am the way, the truth, and the life" (John 14:6). Presumably Jesus's way precludes other ways.

In Galatians 3, the apostle Paul explains that when we are baptized, we "clothe ourselves with Christ." We are no longer Jew or Gentile. We surrender our ethnic identity for an identity built around our beliefs and behaviors. We become "Christians," people who take their identity from Christ. The world may understand us by our pigment or our ancestral connections, but Christ does not. Christians who are able to make this transition into an identity founded upon Christ should be praised, for they have grasped one of the core tenets of the gospel.

Similarly, we are no longer "slave or free" when we submit to baptism. The Guatemalan woman who cleans the hotel room is no better than the CEO who slept in that Marriott bed that she made up. The recent immigrants in the basement who washed the sheets are no different from the executives who divide the spoils of annual profits. When they come to the baptismal font, or to the baptistery, they are equals. To submit to the world's values is to depart from Christ. In Christ, we resist human hierarchy. We are one people, one church, united by our one baptism.

When we descend into the purifying waters of baptism, we abandon our gender biases and preferences. The apostle said, "Nor is there male and female." Men and women must look beyond their physicality. Gender characteristics are not eternal. In Christ, our bodies are frail. Our bodies are vessels, jars of clay (2 Cor. 4:7). What is important is the treasure inside. Outwardly we are wasting away, but inwardly we are being renewed by God's grace. This renewal process should be the cause of great joy and *profound thanksgiving*. The Greek word for thanksgiving is εὐχαριστια, or, in English, *Eucharist*. And Eucharist—thanksgiving—is the subject of the next chapter, because a baptized life should be a most thankful life.

Notes

[1] Tertullian, "Baptism," dated sometime between AD 200 and 206. See William Jurgens, *The Faith of the Early Fathers*, Vol. 1 (Collegeville, MN: The Liturgical Press, 1970), 126.

[2] Jurgens, 111.

[3] Montanism, also known as the "Phrygian heresy," emphasized ecstatic revelations, prophecy (from both men and women), and more rigorous practices than the mainstream churches. For example, they could be very harsh in their fasting, sexual ethics, proscription of second marriages, church discipline, and conservative habits of dress (precise lengths of veils to be worn by women). Montanists did not allow their members to flee during times of persecution, but rather expected their members to exhibit a willingness to die for their Christian beliefs. See Dennis Groh, "Montanism," in *Encyclopedia of Early Christianity*, 2nd Edition (New York: Routledge, 1999), ed. by Everett Ferguson.

[4] See Everett Ferguson, "Fish," in *Encyclopedia of Early Christianity*, 432.

[5] Saint Augustine, *The City of God* (New York: The Modern Library, 1950), trans. by Marcus Dods, 630.

[6] Everett Ferguson, "Baptism," in *Encyclopedia of Early Christianity*, 2nd Edition, 160. The most authoritative and comprehensive treatment of the history of Christian baptism is Everett Ferguson, *Baptism in the Early Church: History, Theology, and Liturgy in the First Five Centuries* (Grand Rapids: Eerdmans, 2013).

[7] T. M. Lindsay, "Baptism: Reformed View," in *International Standard Bible Encyclopedia, Rev. ed.* (Grand Rapids: Eerdmans, 1979), 418–419.

[8] See Everett Ferguson, *Backgrounds of Early Christianity*, 3rd Edition (Grand Rapids: Eerdmans, 2003), 547.

[9] The book of Acts mentions this class of "God- fearing" Gentiles in several places. See for example 10:2; 13:16; 13:26; and 13:50.

[10] See Ferguson, *Backgrounds*, 549.

[11] My main source here is Everett Ferguson, *Early Christians Speak*, 3rd Edition (Abilene, TX: Abilene Christian University Press, 1999). See chapter three, "Baptism in the Second Century." Ferguson does his own translating.

[12] Ferguson, *Early Christians Speak*, 30. Scholars are reluctant to assign a precise date to the *Didache*, but most estimates fall between AD 70 and 150.

[13] For example, see the *Didache* specialist Aaron Milavec's translation in his book *The Didache: Text, Translation, Analysis, and Commentary* (Collegeville, MN: Liturgical Press, 2003), 19–20.

[14] In this section I am drawing from Everett Ferguson, "Baptism," in *Encyclopedia of Early Christianity*, 160f. Ferguson uses Hippolytus's "The Apostolic Tradition" (c. 215) as his main source to reconstruct a ceremony.

[15] The translation here is from Jurgens, 169–170.

[16] Ferguson, *Early Christians Speak*, 59. Cyprian seems to have been "the first clear theological exponent of the baptism of new-born babes." Indeed, Cyprian spoke of infants taking Communion too.

[17] Peter Brown, *Through the Eye of a Needle: Wealth, the Fall of Rome, and the Making of Christianity in the West, 350–550 AD* (Princeton: Princeton University Press, 2012), 369.

[18] See Joanne McWilliam, "Pelagius, Pelagianism" in the *Encyclopedia of Early Christianity*.

[19] In this paragraph I have repeatedly cited Brown, 362.

[20] See Augustine, *The City of God*, Book 20, section 8.

[21] Ferguson, *Early Christians Speak*, 61.

[22] Ibid., 57.

[23] Ferguson, "Baptism," in *Encyclopedia of Early Christianity*, 162.

[24] Ferguson, *Early Christians Speak*, 57.

[25] Ibid., 58.

[26] Ferguson, "Baptism," in *Encyclopedia of Early Christianity*, 162.

[27] Vasiliki Limberis, "The Cult of the Martyrs and the Cappadocian Fathers," in *A People's History of Christianity*, Vol. 3 (Minneapolis: Fortress Press, 2006), ed. by Derek Krueger, 50.

[28] See Eusebius, *Life of Constantine*, Book 4, Chapters 61–63.

[29] Ferguson, "Baptism," in *Encyclopedia of Early Christianity*, 162.

[30] Ibid.

[31] Vasiliki Limberis, "The Cult of the Martyrs and the Cappadocian Fathers," 51.

[32] See a translation of the sermon online at "New Advent," located at http://www.newadvent.org/fathers/310240.htm.

[33] See "Oration on Holy Baptism," paragraphs 17 and 18.

[34] Ibid., paragraphs 20–23.

[35] Ferguson, *Early Christians Speak*, 59.

[36] Daniel Bornstein, "Living Christianity," in *Medieval Christianity* (Minneapolis: Fortress Press), ed. by Bornstein, 5.

[37] Timothy Ware, *The Orthodox Church* (London: Penguin, 1997), 78.

[38] Bornstein, 24.

[39] Yitzhak Hen, "Converting the Barbarian West," in *Medieval Christianity*, 35. Scandinavia was not Christianized until much later, perhaps as late as the twelfth century.

[40] Cited in Teofilo Ruiz, "Jews, Muslims, and Christians," in *Medieval Christianity*, 285.

[41] Ibid.

[42] For the statistical breakdown see Dyron Daughrity, *To Whom Does Christianity Belong?* (Minneapolis: Fortress Press, 2015), 157.

Chapter 3

Eucharist
The Giving of Thanks

"Love is not a meal, but let the banquet depend on love."[1]
—*Clement of Alexandria*, c. AD 200

Gratitude. it is a popular concept these days. The clichés are many: "Have an attitude of gratitude." "Count your blessings." "Happiness isn't getting what you want; it is being grateful for what you have."

Gratitude was critical to the newfound faith of the early Christians. It was central to their assemblies. It was essential for the individual Christian's life, whether the new believer was living in slavery, in a difficult marriage, or in a state of persecution. Christians were thankful people. Paul's earliest letter, 1 Thessalonians, contains a most concise exhortation: "Rejoice always, pray continually, give thanks in all circumstances; for this is God's will for you in Christ Jesus" (1 Thes. 5:16–18).

It is no wonder, then, that the most sacred component of Christian worship, from the very earliest days until now, is the giving of thanks. In Greek, the word is ευχαριστια, or Eucharist, a word that is commonly translated "thanksgiving." Unfortunately, in American society when we hear the word "thanksgiving," we almost automatically picture a turkey or a pilgrim hat. Perhaps it is more reverent and even more accurate to translate the word "the giving of thanks."[2]

In some ways the Eucharist is a sad topic. Over the centuries it has been the subject of endless debate, violence, and a means of keeping control over people. By denying someone the Eucharist, the church could punish them severely, especially in a worldview that saw the Lord's Supper as deeply nourishing to the individual believer. Whether we call it Holy Communion, Lord's Supper, Eucharist, the Agape, or the Love Feast, one thing is certain: the misuse of this sacrament has caused much pain.[3]

Still Divided

Before unpacking the unsettling history of the Eucharist, I can share a few anecdotes from my own life. I suspect most Christians will be able to relate all too well.

In 2006, I served as an elected delegate to the Ninth Assembly of the World Council of Churches, held in Porto Alegre, Brazil. It was one of the great experiences of my life. Thousands of Christians from all stripes gathered under a massive tent to celebrate our unity, our common witness in the world, and our shared commitments to Jesus Christ as Lord.

The opening plenary was exuberant: choirs from Africa, dancers from Latin America, icons from the Orthodox churches, speeches from notable Christians. There was no dominant ethnicity. It was an almost perfect balance: black, Hispanic, indigenous, white, Western, Eastern, Islander, Asian, rich, and poor. For the first time in my life, I realized just how global the Christian faith had become. When it came time for the thousands of attendees to say the Lord's Prayer together in our various "mother tongues," I was amazed that I could not hear anyone else speaking in English, other than my own voice. African languages, Asian, Swedish, Spanish, Portuguese—it was a cacophony of sound that brought me to tears. I was a small part of a global church: two and a half billion people. And they each had their own connection to God through their own language, their own culture, their own social group. I still get chills thinking of that pivotal moment—that crucial realization—in my own understanding of Christianity. It is no longer just a Western thing. It is so, so much bigger.

Then, rather suddenly, the music stopped. A man walked onto the stage, starkly. Behind him was a table with a cross on it, a chalice, and a loaf of bread. He then began speaking clearly into the microphone: "We are still divided. Therefore, let us proceed to the proper venues for the taking of the Eucharist." He then listed where different faith traditions needed to go in order to take the Lord's Supper. Eastern Orthodox here, Oriental Orthodox there, Roman Catholics behind this building, Lutherans over there in Room 200, and so on.

In a matter of seconds, the joyful and global throngs of Christians hushed. Smiles turned serious. Eyes were darting around, almost in disbelief. Do we really have to go to separate places to partake? Can we not take Communion together, even after all these years of division and heartache? Are we actually so set in our layers of tradition that we can't simply fellowship with one another in the way Jesus taught us on the night before his death?

What was so ironic to me was that the World Council of Churches is supposed to be the world's leading ecumenical institution. This is the one place where Christians can come to realize that we all share something incredibly deep. In spite of clergy disputes, wars, and painful histories, we are the ones who are beyond that. Right?

Apparently not. Heads hung, we all shuffled to our separate places. The singing was over. It was business as usual. Back to reality. Christians are not united. Not even close. They cannot even acknowledge one another at the Table.

Cross Yourselves Out

While living in Canada, my wife and I were enthusiastic ecumenists. Let me explain what I mean. First of all, an ecumenist is someone who recognizes the profound unity of the body of Christ, in spite of the man-made denominations that exist. An ecumenist is one who sees beyond the ecclesiastical divisions. An ecumenist treasures Jesus's famous High Priestly Prayer in John 17, the night before his crucifixion:

> I pray also for those who will believe in me . . . that all
> of them may be one, Father, just as you are in me and I
> am in you. May they also be in us so that the world may
> believe . . . I in them and you in me—so that they may
> be brought to complete unity. Then the world will know
> that you sent me and have loved them even as you have
> loved me.

An ecumenist is able to see that although fallible humans erect walls between our various Christian groups, there are things of higher importance. Our unity in Christ is profound, whether or not our priests and pastors recognize it.

My wife and I were born and bred in the Churches of Christ, but both of us were ecumenical in our orientation. We hold our heritage in high regard, but we realize that like any tradition it has a history. So we enthusiastically befriended other Christians. My wife taught fourth grade at a Mennonite school. I pastored a local church that had merged in past years. It was a combination of a Disciples of Christ church with a United Church of Canada congregation. The United Church of Canada formed in 1925 with the merger of Canadian Methodists, Presbyterians, and Congregationalists. However, our little church—Campbell Stone

United Church—ministered to anybody regardless of denominational bent. In fact, on one Sunday we took a straw poll to figure out which denomination had the most adherents in our church, and the result showed that we had more Anglicans than anything else.

During our Canadian years we also befriended several Roman Catholics. I had never known before just how high the walls stand between Protestants and Catholics. I realized that in church history there had been much bloodshed, but I believed we should let bygones be bygones. However, two experiences made me realize that in some ways the walls are still there.

One evening we were invited to an Ash Wednesday service, the first day of Lent. Lent is intended to be a forty-day preparation for Easter, reminiscent of Jesus's fasting in the wilderness. It is typical that a cross of ashes is marked onto the forehead of participants who come forward for Communion during the Ash Wednesday service. However, as my wife and I were rising from our pews, our friends directed us to do something that I had never done before, nor did I even understand what they meant: "When you get up to the priest, you have to cross yourselves out." We were confused, but we saw someone else stand in front of the priest and cross their arms over the chest. It was a signal to the priest not to administer Communion to us. But, we were assured, we would receive the ash cross on our forehead as a sign of repentance.

Crossing ourselves out was unsettling, even distressing. We did not fully understand the context at the time. Had we known, we never would have gone to the Ash Wednesday service. It is demeaning to join with a group of Christians for worship and prayer, only to be chastised publicly for being somehow unworthy. We are not non-Christians. We are part of the Body of Christ. Who gets to make these decisions?

A second experience in Canada also reminded us of the broken nature of the Lord's church. This time, it was on me. I screwed up.

It was an honest mistake, but as a church historian I should have known better. And it has to do with that word "transubstantiation."

Again, we were with a Roman Catholic family, eating dinner at their house. We were close friends and could speak about anything . . . except the Eucharist. At some point in the conversation, I asked my friend whether Catholics today still believe that the bread and the wine *actually* turn into flesh and blood. My friend answered yes, of course. They're Catholics. And why would I ask this question in such a flippant way as to cause offense?

I was truly sorry. How could I have made such an elementary mistake? I guess somehow I had gotten the impression that my friend would turn to me quietly and say, "Yeah, they believed all of that stuff in the medieval world, but we're much more scientifically aware now." He didn't. He was hurt. I still fear that our friendship was permanently affected by that moment. No, we didn't "break up" or anything, but I got the sense that I had crossed a line. And I could not go back. It was one of those moments that you cannot undo. We all have them, especially when it comes to religion. And we usually regret them. Thankfully, our friendship continued and is still strong. They have not given up hope that we might convert to Catholicism one day, as they send us "Come home to Rome—the Mother Church" books from time to time. But the obvious lesson I learned was that I need to be much more careful when discussing doctrinal differences with other Christians.

Was It First a Meal?

Historians typically assert that the Eucharist, "the giving of thanks," was first a meal. Some of the key New Testament texts certainly seem to frame it that way. We will briefly review those texts below. But first, let's look at some historical background.

The "Last Supper" story in the Gospels is situated during an important Jewish festival, the Passover, when the Jews remember their liberation from slavery in Egypt. In Exodus 23, the

Israelites are told to celebrate three annual festivals: Unleavened Bread, Harvest, and Ingathering. These are called pilgrimage festivals, because Israelites were to "appear before the Sovereign LORD" (Ex. 23:17). Throughout Jewish history, these three festivals evolved and become known as:

- Passover (also known as *Pesach*, the Feast of Unleavened Bread, or *Matzos*—named after the bread),
- *Shavuot* (also known as Pentecost or Feast of Weeks), and
- *Sukkot* (also known as Feast of Tabernacles, Feast of Booths, or Feast of Ingathering).

Passover, the setting for the Last Supper, begins with a Seder—a meal that requires several ritualistic elements, including prescribed foods such as lamb, a hard-boiled egg, bitter herbs, and one other vegetable (usually parsley, potato, or celery). The family gathers around the table and recounts the Exodus story, as instructed in Exodus 13:8: "You shall tell your son on that day, 'It is because of what the LORD did for me when I came out of Egypt.'" Songs are sung and important texts are read. Unleavened bread—*matza*—is eaten, wine is drunk, and the liberation of the Jews from Egyptian captivity is recounted.

The darker side of the story—where we get the word "Passover"—is told in Exodus 12. In that chapter, the Israelites are told to slaughter animals and paint blood on the sides and tops of their door-frames. God would then "pass over" Egypt and "strike down every firstborn of both people and animals" who did not have the protection of the blood. "The blood will be a sign for you on the houses where you are, and when I see the blood, I will *pass over* you" (Ex. 12:12–13).

In the Gospels, Jesus was celebrating this same Passover. The biblical writers Matthew, Mark, Luke, John, and Paul (in 1 Corinthians 11) record the Last Supper, but each has his own way of interpreting it. While there are differences in each of their accounts, we can safely assume that all of them were commenting on the same event.

We are told that Jesus and his apostles were celebrating on the first day of the Passover feast. The centerpiece of the meal—the lamb—was explicitly mentioned by Mark and Luke. The disciples knew the feast required fairly elaborate preparations, and they asked Jesus about it (Mark 14:12). Jesus reserved an upper room in Jerusalem for the preparing of the meal. All twelve of the apostles were there. We know it was a full-meal setting because of the reclining and lengthy program of events celebrated by them. In other words, this was not a simple *Kiddush* ceremony where Jews recite a blessing over wine in preparation for *Shabbat* or for Jewish holidays. Jesus and the twelve enjoyed a full and elaborate meal that took hours to prepare and celebrate.

At some point in the evening—writers vary on the details—Jesus took bread, gave thanks ("eucharist"), broke the bread, distributed it to the disciples, and said, "This is my body." He also took a cup of wine, gave thanks ("eucharist"), and everyone present drank from it.

The mood became decidedly sullen at some point in the evening, probably around the time when Jesus equated his body and blood with the bread and wine. There were more cheerful moments, however, such as Jesus's prediction that he would drink wine once again "in the kingdom of God" (Mark 14:25). Matthew points out that Jesus said he would drink wine "with you"—with the apostles—"in my Father's kingdom" in a future time. Jesus and his apostles also did some singing together that night, which would have brought a glimmer of encouragement to what was otherwise a depressing sequence of events.

It must have been deflating for the entire group when Jesus shared his conviction that Judas was going to betray him soon. Further, Jesus predicted they would all forsake him, but he explicitly mentioned Peter in the context of the three denials.

Matthew and Mark both agree that the breaking of the bread and the consecration of the wine took place "while they were eating." Matthew connects the cup of wine with the forgiveness of sins (26:28). Luke introduces the idea that Jesus wanted the apostles to "divide" the cup (Luke 22:17), leading many Christians through the years to prefer "cups" to "a cup" in the taking of the wine. Luke also introduced a second novel idea—that Jesus consecrated the cup *before and after* the consecration of the bread. In Luke, Jesus says "Do this in remembrance of me" (22:19).

The synoptics (Matthew, Mark, and Luke), as well as Paul, note that Jesus explicitly mentioned this entire ritual as being covenantal. A new covenant was being established. It was likely unclear to the apostles what exactly was happening, but in hindsight the new covenant was clear. No longer was escaping Egypt the centerpiece of faith, as in the Passover. From now on, according to this "new covenant" (Luke 22:20), the central event in the history of God's people was the life, death, and resurrection of Jesus—the new sacrificial Lamb who offers forgiveness of sin.

Luke introduced yet another unfortunate event that took place within the sacred context of the Passover meal. The disciples broke out in a dispute over who was the greatest. Jesus corrected them, pointing out that servanthood is what he is after: "I am among you as one who serves" (22:27). Luke also raised the stakes by pointing to a future meal. Not only would Jesus eat and drink with his apostles one day, but the apostles would eventually become rulers; they would "sit on thrones, judging the twelve tribes of Israel" (22:30).

The apostle Paul's rendition of what he calls "the Lord's Supper" is slightly different. In his discussion, he chastises church members for overeating and getting drunk while celebrating this sacred event. He urges them to "examine" themselves before participating, otherwise they "will be guilty of sinning against the body and blood of the Lord" (1 Cor. 11:27). Paul also connects the Lord's Supper to the death of Jesus, "Whenever you eat this bread and drink this cup, you proclaim the Lord's death until he comes" (11:26). Paul explicitly mentions the Lord's Supper as a "new covenant" (11:25). In addition, Paul offers up a strange statement about how many individuals have become ill or even died because of their taking the Lord's Supper in an unworthy way (11:30). He surmises that this weakening of their bodies was "discipline" from the Lord that would help them avoid condemnation with the rest of the unbelieving world. There is no doubt that Paul's words struck fear into the hearts of early Christians and made the Eucharist that much more holy. There were harsh—even tragic—consequences for those who did not approach the Eucharist with the greatest amount of seriousness. In the medieval world, these warnings would take on a life of their own. Christians trembled when presented with the "host"—the bread—which they understood to be from the literal body of Christ.

We should note that Paul also situates his discussion of the Lord's Supper within the context of a meal. However, he advises people against showing up at the assembly with ravenous hunger. If they are really hungry, they should eat beforehand. Nevertheless, the context of a meal is assumed by Paul.

John's account of the Last Supper is unique. During the meal, Jesus wraps a towel around his waist and washes the feet of his disciples, drying them with the towel around him. Jesus makes the point that a life of service is what is required of his followers. Jesus also emphasizes the centrality of loving one another, "By this everyone will know that you are my disciples, if you love one another" (13:35). John also depicts the betrayal of Judas and the prediction of Peter's denials of Jesus within the Supper.

The original Last Supper was certainly a meal. It was a Jewish Passover feast. The mood was subdued, as if Jesus was aware of what was about to happen. There were moments of good cheer such as the prayers of thanksgiving and the hymn-singing. However, there was a definite seriousness; something important was happening. A new covenant was being established, although there is no way the apostles would have known the reality of that covenant at the time.

The Eucharist and the Church Fathers

The Sunday assembly of Christians virtually always included the breaking of bread, which means they shared a meal together (Acts 20:7). It is easy to superimpose our current Eucharistic practices onto the early church, so it is important that we are careful when trying to understand exactly what those early Christians did during their gatherings. The book of Acts mentions that they devoted themselves to apostolic teaching, fellowship, breaking bread, praying, giving, sharing, praising God, and performing signs and wonders. And they experienced rapid growth (Acts 2:42–47).

In Acts 2, Luke mentions that the disciples met together in the Temple courts, but "broke bread in their homes." Thus, while today's house-church movement rightly emphasizes the early church gathering regularly in homes, we have ample evidence that the Christians met outside of their homes as well. Presumably, though, the breaking of bread would have taken place in a location that offered facilities conducive to preparing a meal. Thus, the Eucharist was probably celebrated inside homes in the earliest years of the church.

One important early Christian document that may date to the first century, the *Didache,* has several things to say about the Eucharist, but it is hard to tell what exactly is being communicated in that text. In the Eucharistic service described in chapter 9, the blessing of the cup comes before the blessing of the loaf, as Luke spells out in his Gospel—except that Luke includes the blessing of the cup before *and after* the bread, as we noted earlier. This same chapter of the *Didache* also specifies that the Eucharist was a ritual designed to emphasize the unity of the believers: "Just as this broken loaf was scattered over the hills as grain, and, having been gathered together, became one; in like fashion, may your church be gathered together from the ends of the earth into your kingdom" (9:4).[4]

Chapter 9 of the *Didache* also specifies that only "those baptized in the name of the Lord" are able to partake, because the elements are holy, and the Lord said, "Do not give what is holy to the dogs."

Chapter 10 of the *Didache* assumes that the Eucharist takes place within a meal: "Both food and drink you have given to people for enjoyment in order that they might give thanks." The word "Eucharist" is actually used here in verb form. The text goes on to state that the elements of the Eucharist are "Spirit-sent food and drink for life forever through your servant [Jesus]."

Chapter 14 of the *Didache* contains more details about the Eucharist:

> According to the divinely instituted day of the Lord,
> having been gathered together, break a loaf. And give
> thanks [Eucharist], having beforehand confessed your
> failings, so that your sacrifice may be pure. Everyone, on
> the other hand, having a conflict with a companion, do
> not let him/her come together with you until they have
> been reconciled, in order that your sacrifice may not
> be defiled.

These passages are not entirely clear on whether the Eucharist was simply a meal, a love-feast (Agape), a ritual within a meal, or something else.[5]

A word should be interjected here on the meaning of Agape, the love-feast. The Greek term *agape* means "love," but the word came to signify a meal in the early church. See, for example, Jude 12: "These people [the ungodly] are blemishes at your love feasts, eating with you without the slightest qualm—shepherds who feed only themselves." Several early church fathers, for example, Ignatius (AD 50–117), try to draw a distinction between the Eucharist and the love-feast. Others, such as Justin Martyr (AD 100–165) and Clement of Alexandria (AD 150–215), seem to blend the two. One thing is clear, however. The Agape emphasized the feeding of the poor and destitute. It was a meal that was intended to help people in distress or those living on the margins, such as widows. "Tertullian is quite clear about its social purpose: it is for the relief of the poor."[6]

Around AD 250 the love-feast and Eucharist seem to separate, leaving the Eucharist to develop outside the context of a shared meal. Over time, the popularity of the Agape meal declined, and "by the end of the patristic age [fifth century] . . . the agape had fallen into disuse."[7] Many Christians through the years have bemoaned the de-linking of the Eucharist from the context of a meal. Something was lost when the Eucharist lost its original association with a fellowship gathering where like-minded people enjoyed food together. Perhaps Paul's admonition to those who were overindulging set the stage for the decline of the Agape, but whatever the case, few churches today still keep the Eucharist linked to a meal.

In the time of Jesus, it was common for Jews to have a ceremonial breaking of bread and blessing of wine accompanied by prayer before a meal.[8] Thus it is entirely reasonable to assume that it was taking place in the early Christian context as well. Indeed, Everett Ferguson writes: "The early rabbinic directions for the Passover meal instruct that a benediction be said over a cup of wine before the meal begins, a benediction be pronounced on the unleavened bread, and at the close of the meal a benediction over another cup."[9] This is precisely the same formula adopted by Luke in his description of the Last Supper.

Thus, in the Bible as well as in the *Didache*, the Eucharist seems to be closely linked to table fellowship. Hippolytus's *Apostolic Tradition*—another important text on early Christian services and practices—presents a similar perspective. Dated to around AD 215, the *Apostolic Tradition* has a lot to say about the Eucharist. In one curious passage, Hippolytus writes, "When they dine, the faithful present shall take from the hand of the bishop a small piece of bread before taking their own bread, because it is blessed. Yet it is not the Eucharist, like the body of the Lord."[10] This text indicates that a fellowship meal, even when presided over by the bishop, was not necessarily a Eucharist. The Eucharistic service required something more.

Hippolytus demands that Christians hold their cups and give thanks when they are about to eat, so that "they will eat and drink in purity" (26:2). The catechumens—those preparing to join the church—are not allowed to sit with those partaking of the Lord's Supper. However, they are given exorcised (purified from evil) cups and bread so as not to eat and drink judgment upon themselves, as cautioned by the apostle Paul. All Christians present at the meal are to pay attention to the propriety outlined by Paul in 1 Corinthians 11; they are to eat and drink in moderation so that disorderly conduct does not invite ridicule. Hippolytus also encourages those assembled to keep some food as leftovers so that it can be sent to other Christians who were not able to attend (26:3).

Hippolytus declares that if the bishop is not present for a supper, then the meal should continue. However, an elder (presbyter) or a deacon should bless a particular loaf of bread, and the people should take it from that leader's hand. Presumably, this is the consecrated bread of Eucharist, or of Thanksgiving. Apparently, this bread was special due to its being blessed. It was to be given straight from the church leader (bishop, elder, or deacon) to the people gathered. Interestingly, if only laypeople are assembled—without a bishop, elder, or deacon—then the blessing of the bread should not take place. This is in all likelihood an early reference to the notion that a clergyman should be present for the consecration of the elements of the Eucharist.

According to the *Apostolic Tradition*, the meal was to be taken "in the name of the Lord." Older widows were to be invited to fellowship meals, but they were instructed to leave the house before sunset, probably so as not to incur moral suspicion by outsiders. If it was not wise for widows to come inside, then they were to be given food and wine and sent away to eat in their own homes.

Hippolytus specifies that the Eucharistic bread and wine should be taken "before eating anything else. For if they eat with faith, even though some deadly poison is given to them, after this it will not be able to harm them" (36:1). This passage seems to contain some of the same ideas in 1 Corinthians 11:27–32, where Paul cautions that some had fallen weak and ill—and some had even died—due to taking the Lord's Supper in an unworthy manner.

Great care was to be taken with the Eucharistic elements. Hippolytus urges that "no unbeliever tastes of the Eucharist, nor a mouse or other animal, nor that any of it falls and is lost. For it is the Body of Christ, to be eaten by those who believe, and not to be scorned" (37:1). Similarly, the blessed cup was not to be spilled, otherwise, "You will become as one who scorns the Blood, the price with which you have been bought" (38:1).

In the early centuries of Christianity, other important rituals often took place at the Eucharistic services. In the *Apostolic Tradition*, Hippolytus outlines a Eucharistic service that immediately follows a baptism.[11] After the individual confessed full belief in God, Christ, and the Spirit, he or she was baptized and anointed with oil. The person then dried and put on clothes and proceeded into the assembly to receive the laying on of hands and public pronouncement of remission of sins. Next, there were prayers and the kiss of peace amongst all present. Thereafter followed a Eucharist.

In the post-baptismal Eucharist, the deacons brought the elements to the bishop for consecration. In this case, consecration was called "eucharistizing." In other words, the giving of thanks was what made the elements particularly sacred. The wine used was called "mixed wine," which may have been two types of wine mixed together, or else wine diluted with water and certain spices. Next, the deacons would bring out cups of milk mixed with honey, representing "the promise made to the fathers . . . a land flowing with milk and honey." Finally, cups of water were brought out which signified "the washing, so that the inner part of the man, which is of the soul, may receive the same as the body." In other words, now that the body had just been baptized (washed), the cup of water was symbolic of the final rinsing of the soul.

After the cups were brought out, the bishop would break the Eucharistic bread into individual pieces and say, "Heavenly Bread in Christ Jesus," and the people would respond, "Amen." While standing reverently, the elders and deacons would hold the cups— of water, milk mixed with honey, and wine. The newly baptized believers would partake of each cup three times, while an elder or deacon would invoke the three members of the Trinity—Father, Son, and Holy Ghost.

Everett Ferguson writes, "For many of the average Christians, the central point of their Christian experience was the common meal."[12] He observes that the earliest catacomb paintings suggest that the Christians reflected deeply and often on the table fellowship that they shared. It is terribly difficult for us to discern whether these paintings depict a love-feast, a Eucharistic blessing, the Last Supper scene, or a heavenly banquet. But one thing they understood well: sharing bread and wine together was holy. It was something their Jewish predecessors did. It was what Jesus taught his disciples to do. It was practiced by the earliest Christians. And it was a foretaste of what they would experience in heaven.

While it may be impractical to share a meal every Lord's Day, it is still crucial that we do it. Christian faith and practice can be inconvenient at times, but table fellowship is one practice that should not die out. While the Eucharist is certainly a wonderful ritual, it was intended to be so much more than a mere bread crumb and a taste of wine. What enlivens the mystery of the Eucharist—the giving of thanks—is not so much an ordained clergyman or even a properly recited prayer. The mystery of Christ is preserved in the radical fellowship of the saints. The mystery of God's new covenant is preserved in the fact that this community has gathered together to remember Jesus, to reject social barriers about who can eat with whom, and to share all things in common. Yes, even food. It is a proclamation. We proclaim Jesus, even in something as ordinary as eating, until he comes.

Transubstantiation, Real Presence, and the Sacrifice of the Mass

The medieval (roughly 500 to 1500) understanding of the Eucharist became extremely complex. The Eucharist grew into something very different from what it was in the New Testament, or even in the era of the early church fathers. For example, the Eucharist began to take on "a utilitarian character." It was offered to ask God for special favors such as "a good harvest or a fruitful marriage."[13] Some women took Communion at the first sign of labor pains so God would help them through the ordeal.[14] However, "Menstruating women . . . could not receive communion."[15]

Viewing the Eucharist as a personal benefit was not an entirely new way of understanding it. As we saw earlier, in 1 Corinthians 11, the apostle Paul may have been arguing that by profaning the Eucharist some had died or had become weak and sick. This idea persisted into succeeding generations. For example, Ignatius of Antioch (died AD 110)—the important first-century bishop who knew the apostle John—described the bread of the Eucharist as the "medicine of immortality, the antidote against death, enabling us to live forever in Jesus Christ."[16]

A later example of this perspective can be seen in a woman named Gorgonia, the sister of Gregory of Nazianzus (329–390), the gifted preacher who became Archbishop of Constantinople.

On one occasion, Gorgonia was injured in a carriage accident. She refused medical care because she trusted in the power of the Eucharistic elements to heal her. She entered a church and cried on the altar for healing. Then she took the bread and the wine and rubbed them on her body as if applying salve.

A similar event happened with Macrina, the sister to Gregory of Nyssa, another important church father. She had a tumor on her breast and took dirt, moistened it with her tears, and applied the mixture to the growth. Her mother then made the sign of the cross over the tumor, and Macrina was healed; only a small scar remained.[17]

Medieval Christians, both in the West and in the East, varied greatly in how they practiced the Eucharist, which elements were allowed, how frequently they communed, and so on. No uniform characterization can be cited for how the Eucharist was practiced. For example, in the late Byzantine Empire (1200–1453) it was common for Orthodox Christians to take Communion only during Holy Week. However, if the person had not fasted, he or she was considered spiritually impure, and thus received only the "antidoron"—unconsecrated bread that has been cut away from the consecrated loaf. The word *antidoron* means "gift in place of the gift." In the Orthodox Churches, the "prosphoron" is the consecrated bread which is used for Eucharist. It is important to note that Orthodox Christians use leavened bread rather than unleavened. In their interpretation, the Gospel of John (as opposed to the synoptic Gospels, which are unclear) specifies that the Last Supper took place *before* the Passover. Therefore, Orthodox Christians assume Jesus used leavened bread on the night he was betrayed.

A certain ambivalence about the Eucharist can be seen in the medieval world. People embraced the sacrament, but they also feared it. Some people feared taking it when they were extremely ill because they thought that taking it in the wrong way might hasten their death. Others, as we saw above, thought of the Eucharistic elements as healing agents. Sometimes the dying would take the Eucharist just before death, believing that having the body of Christ in their mouth might guarantee them an entrance into Paradise.[18]

Being refused the Eucharist could be a punishing sentence to undergo in an age where the Eucharistic elements were seen to be powerful. Church hierarchs often worked with civil magistrates to reduce crime by forbidding the Eucharist to certain criminals. For example, grave robbers—a despised and feared subset of criminals who wreaked havoc on medieval society—were prohibited from the Eucharist for two years.[19]

In medieval times, the power of the Eucharistic elements of bread and wine stemmed from the fact that people believed it was the literal body and blood of Jesus. The elements were considered to be sacred relics, except these were relics that the faith declared should be ingested by the faithful. Relics were treated with extreme reverence in those times and could become big business. Pilgrimages to relics could prove highly profitable for the holder of the relics. Important medieval statesman would often display their collections to show their power and piety. The body and blood of Jesus, however, was the relic that demanded the greatest attention due to the importance it had in common life. For example, judicial proceedings performed before the body and blood were particularly solemn. To make an oath in front of the host—from the Latin word *hostia* meaning "sacrificial victim"—meant that the utmost seriousness and conviction must be observed.[20]

The term "transubstantiation" was officially introduced at the Fourth Lateran Council in Rome in the year 1215, although it was being used informally for over a century already. That council declared:

> . . . the same Jesus Christ is both the priest and the sacrifice, whose body and blood are truly contained in the sacrament of the altar under the species of bread and

wine, the bread being transubstantiated into the body
and the wine into the blood by the divine power, in order
that, to accomplish the mystery of unity, we ourselves
may receive of His that which He received of ours.[21]

When the priest pronounced the consecration: "This is my body," it
was believed that a transformation of substance took place, changing the bread and wine into the flesh and blood of Jesus. This is
what is meant by the "real presence" of Christ in the Eucharist.

The Fourth Lateran Council did not specify exactly how this
transformation happened; however, later theologians asserted
that while the "accidents" (bread and wine) remain unaltered, the
"substances" (or essences) change into Christ. Catholic historian
Daniel Bornstein writes: "The Eucharist might still look like bread,
feel like bread, smell like bread, sound like bread as the priest broke
it, and taste like bread as the believer received it, but once the priest
spoke those four simple words, it no longer was bread: it was the
body of Christ."[22] While early Christianity certainly took the sym-
bolism of the Eucharist seriously, it began to reach new heights
around the time of this council.

The leading theologians during the Eucharistic debates were
Berengar of Tours and Lanfranc of Pavia. They debated these
issues in the late eleventh century and relied heavily on Aristotle's
distinction between an object ("*substantia*") and its external features ("*accidentia*"). Lanfranc won the debate, because the Fourth
Lateran Council dogmatized his position: "The change of bread
and wine was indeed essential (of substance) but not outward visible (accidental)."[23]

Medieval writings are full of stories geared to convince people
of the truth of transubstantiation and the real presence of Christ
in the Eucharist. For example, a laywoman who made the bread
once doubted that this was the actual body of Jesus only to look
down at the wafer, shocked to see that it had become "bloody flesh

in the shape of a finger." Indeed, "bleeding host" stories—where the consecrated bread bleeds copiously during the Eucharist—are not uncommon in medieval history.[24]

One unfortunate story about a Jew in Paris emerged in the thirteenth century. It recounted how he cut and stabbed a consecrated host to prove it was only bread. The more he manhandled it, the more it bled. He was unable to conceal the bleeding and was found out by church officials. He was promptly executed, and his family converted to Christianity because of the miracle. This story inspired many others and added to an already heightened antisemitism, which resulted in "a number of . . . legal condemnations or extralegal massacres of local Jewish communities."[25] Various, local renditions of this story are preserved in paintings across Western Europe.

Most Christians in the world hold to some version of the "real presence" of Christ in the Communion elements. The Divine Liturgy of Saint John Chrysostom—the most common liturgy among Eastern Orthodox churches—upholds the notion throughout. The Catholic Mass, of course, still adheres to the dogma of transubstantiation and the real presence. Several Protestant denominations hold to a modified version of the real presence, some even hint at transubstantiation. We will review Protestant stances on the Eucharist in the next section. It is important to point out that these ideas were honed throughout the medieval era and were reaffirmed at the Council of Trent (1545–1563), the important council that transitioned the Catholic Church from the medieval into the modern world.

Before we move on from the medieval era, though, something must be said about the notion of the Eucharist Mass being a sacrifice. Many Protestants struggle to understand what the "sacrifice of the Mass" means, since the sacrifice of Jesus already took place. Protestants are deeply impacted by Martin Luther's critique here.

He argued that the book of Hebrews makes it clear that Christ's sacrifice is "once for all"; therefore, no more sacrifices are necessary.

First of all, the term "Mass" probably stems from the dismissal of the Latin Eucharistic service: "*Ite, missa est,*" which translates into English as, "Go; it is the dismissal." The word "Mass" may have evolved out of that word *missa*. It has also been argued that the term "Mass" may come from the word *matzah*, the Hebrew word for unleavened bread. This would explain why Orthodox Christians do not use the term "Mass" but instead use "Divine Liturgy" for the Eucharistic service.

The notion of the sacrifice of the Mass comes from antiquity. The Israelites made sacrifices of animals to God to remove their sins. This is the origin. In early Christianity, however, Christ came to be seen as a new high priest, an idea put forth most strongly in the book of Hebrews. Clement of Rome, who died in AD 99, made the argument that elders should present the Eucharistic gifts much as the Levites did among the Israelites. This sacrificial understanding "was the universal language of worship in the ancient world (Jewish and pagan), [and] no other imagery was so readily understood or suitable."[26]

Likewise, the *Didache* describes Christian worship as a sacrifice. In the second century, Justin Martyr (AD 100–165) wrote that the Jewish sacrifices had been rendered obsolete by the coming of Christ. Now "the only sacrifices perfect and well pleasing to God" are "the Eucharist of the bread and of the cup, the sacrifices which are done in all the earth by Christians."[27] Subsequent church fathers maintained this notion that the Eucharist had somehow supplanted the Jewish sacrificial system.

Both the Orthodox Church and the Catholic Church keep this sacrificial motif intact, but it is a bloodless sacrifice. It is a sacrifice offered by the priest to God. The sacrifice itself is Christ, present (real presence) in the Eucharistic elements. When the elements are consecrated, they become the host (Latin *hostia*), the sacrificial

victim. Christian believers are the ones who are the primary beneficiaries of the sacrifice. The sacrifice of Christ today functions in
much the same way as animal sacrifices did for Jews:

- Only a properly ordained priest may offer it.
- An altar is used for the presentation of the sacrifice.
- Blood is presented to God since life is in the blood.
- God's wrath is removed (propitiated) by the act
  of sacrifice.
- Each person's sins are blotted out.

Therefore, a proper observance of the Mass should lead to an
absolved conscience in the believer.

Protestantism and Its Discontents

Martin Luther did not want to abolish the Mass altogether, although
he was accused of that. Rather, he wanted it to conform to his ideas
of what it should be. While Luther was in hiding in the Wartburg
Castle in late 1521 and 1522, however, his colleague at the University
of Wittenberg, Andreas von Karlstadt, beat him to the punch and
initiated radical Eucharist changes that irked Luther terribly.

The Protestant Reformation made a huge and sudden impact
on virtually every church practice. The rapidity of change was
shockingly profane, or liberating and exhilarating, depending on
one's point of view. The gaping chasm that separated clergy from
laity in the medieval world was bridged. The Protestant pastor conducted services while facing the congregation, as opposed to the
ancient, Roman-Catholic practice of the priest speaking in Latin
toward the altar, with his back to the people.

Furthermore, the Protestant pastor conducted services in the
local language of the parishioners, like a teacher. They jettisoned
the medieval rood screen—an elaborate screen that separated the
altar from the laity (that screen is still used in Orthodoxy and is
called the "iconostasis"). Anything that was not promoted in the

New Testament—pilgrimage, relic worship, veneration of Mary, reverence toward statues and paintings, cult of the saints, memorial Masses, extensive religious feasts and fasts, special clerical robes, clerical celibacy . . . these all came under intense scrutiny, if they were not scrapped altogether. It all depended on how dramatically and rapidly the Reformation was instituted in a particular locale.

Perhaps the most important change that came with the Protestant revolution had to do with the Eucharist—the centerpiece of Christian worship and liturgy. The Protestants preferred the term "Lord's Supper" to the unscriptural "Mass." Latin was, of course, quickly abandoned, since few even understood the language. The notion of a "sacrifice" was removed from the Eucharist. Everyone was welcomed to the Table to partake of the "blood"— although many refused since they had been raised to think they were forbidden from drinking it.

The Protestant changes were not integrated smoothly anywhere. Protest—that great definer of Protestantism—emerged almost the moment Luther uttered the phrase, "Here I stand," in 1521. Luther protested, but other leaders protested against Luther, and each of those protesters had people protesting against them, and on and on. The genie found its way out of the bottle early on in the Reformation, and there was no way to stuff it back in.

The first major disagreement of the Reformation was between colleagues at the University of Wittenberg, Luther and Karlstadt, the first two reformers. One would think that they should have considered each other valuable allies, since Pope Leo X viciously struck out at them in his famous 1520 papal bull *Exsurge Domine* ("Rise up, O Lord"). However, Luther and Karlstadt ended up turning against each other and became the worst of enemies.

While Luther was in hiding in the Wartburg Castle, Karlstadt took charge of the Reforms in the city of Wittenberg. Everyone was shocked when, on Christmas Day 1521, Karlstadt officially instituted his reforms during a church service. He broke many medieval taboos. Although a priest, he presided over the Eucharist in plain secular clothing, indeed, "in his shirt sleeves."[28] This act alone would have traumatized most of the people. However, he went much further. He offered the chalice to the people to drink, a practice that was forbidden by the Catholic Church. The blood was only for clergy. He pronounced the words of institution ("This is my body") in German, not in Latin. The people were able to hold the bread and chalice with their own hands, rather than having the "host" get placed directly on the tongue by the priest. No mention was made of a "sacrifice" during the service.

This was only the beginning. Luther found out about this some weeks later and immediately came out of hiding and began denouncing Karlstadt. A few weeks after that, Karlstadt shocked the late medieval world when he renounced celibacy and promptly married. A few years later, in 1525, Luther also married. Luther thought Karlstadt was integrating reform with a haste that was unwise, even diabolical.

Both Karlstadt and Luther rejected transubstantiation. However, Karlstadt opened up "the most fateful intra-Protestant controversy in the sixteenth century—and beyond—over the real presence of Christ in bread and wine" when he began to focus on the words of institution and what Jesus actually meant when he said them.[29] Karlstadt's theory shook the medieval world and caused Roman Catholics extreme distress. He said that when Jesus spoke the words, "This is my body," he pointed at himself—rather than at the bread. Karlstadt was promptly expelled from Saxony because of this and was branded a troublemaker by the Protestants and a heretic by the Catholics for the rest of his days.

Luther was incensed. Why? It is clear that Karlstadt and Luther were colleagues, friends, and theologically quite similar in so many ways. How did this one issue cause such deep theological division and eventually split the Protestant Reformation into a hundred different pieces . . . and later into tens of thousands of fragments?

Reformation historian Hans Hillerbrand put it this way: "Luther was profoundly upset by Karlstadt's notions because they suggested that Scripture, the new locus of authority, *could be interpreted differently*."[30]

Luther thought his great principle of *sola scriptura* would vindicate his views, provide a tool for correctly interpreting Christian doctrine, and perhaps even one day unite the Christian world. But Luther was wrong. And this was painfully clear early in the Reformation. There was no such thing as "sola" scriptura. There had to be an interpreter. And interpretations are profoundly subjective. In the twenty-first century, we see this dilemma clearly. Luther did not see it. Nor did he ever acknowledge it. In his view, interpretations that matched his own were correct. Deviations were not. Ironically, the other reformers, the Roman Catholic Church, and even the Orthodox Church each held a view similar to Luther's: it's our way or the highway. None of them could understand how people could possibly reach conclusions different from their own.

In the early days of the Reformation, the only reformer who could be considered an intellectual equal to Luther was Ulrich Zwingli of Zurich. These two heavyweights—who otherwise agreed on just about everything else—went round and round and ultimately fell out of favor with each other over a hairsplitting aspect of the Eucharist. In 1529, the two leaders met in what has become known as the Marburg Colloquy. They reached agreement on fourteen of fifteen crucial points of doctrine. The issue that kept them divided was whether Christ is really present in the Eucharist or just symbolically present. Luther argued for a "sacramental union"—that Christ *really* was in the Eucharistic elements, thus divine grace was bestowed when one partook.

Zwingli, however, argued that the elements were simply signs of fellowship, and the presence of Christ in the Eucharist was merely symbolic. Luther upheld something near to the Catholic notions on this issue. During the debate, Luther continually emphasized the words of Jesus: "This *is* my body." Zwingli argued that in this context, the word "is" simply means "signifies." To Zwingli, Jesus was not saying the bread was *actually* his flesh and the wine *actually* his blood. That seemed patently absurd to him. The two men refused to reconcile on this matter, so two forms of Protestantism emerged early on—Lutheran and Reformed.

In general, the medieval Catholic laity celebrated the Eucharist only once per year, which often took place at Easter. Otherwise, Masses were performed for special reasons, for example, to help someone in their journey through purgatory. Luther critiqued this system as being corrupt, a mere fundraiser for the church. With the rise of the Reformation, virtually all aspects of the Eucharist were called into question, and the changes varied from place to place and from group to group. The Reformed Christians, for example, taking their cues from Geneva and the great John Calvin, took Communion quarterly, and they partook of both bread and wine. They also segregated according to gender.[31]

The Scots, however, sat at tables, in an apparent move to replicate the Last Supper. The Scots also practiced a fairly common Reformed approach to the Communion wherein people had to submit a Communion token made of lead—distributed by the elders in the church—in order to demonstrate their approved worthiness of participation. The elders guarded carefully who was given a token and kept watch over the flock to ensure that a token was submitted by any communicant. This was very different from the medieval system, chiefly in the sense that now lay elders were distributing the holy elements. In the medieval world, the Eucharist was the exclusive domain of the ordained clergy.

Changes to the Eucharist were replete in the aftermath of the Reformation. As in all aspects of Protestant Christianity, on this matter there is no authority greater than the Bible. Thus, today, the Eucharist is one of the most notable examples of how the New Testament is read so differently by Christians. Many Christians, such as Baptists, have completely abandoned any notion of "real presence" in the Lord's Supper. It is a time of remembering. After all, Jesus said, "Do this in remembrance of me."

Some Protestant groups—notably several Brethren movements—retain the biblical practice of the Agape meal as well as the foot washing in their Eucharistic celebrations.

Frequency of the Eucharist varies widely across the Christian spectrum. Some celebrate quarterly. Others such as Methodists and Reformed Christians typically celebrate monthly. A few Protestant movements such as the Disciples, Christian Churches, Churches of Christ, as well as Anglicans, take Communion weekly, as do Roman Catholics and Orthodox Christians. Some groups, such as Quakers and Salvation Army Christians, typically do not observe Eucharist, since what they deem to be more important is daily living the Christian life.

The elements of the Eucharist vary a bit as well. Instead of wine, grape juice is common, particularly in the United States, where consuming alcohol was at one time unlawful. Breads of all kinds have been used throughout history, particularly today in global Christianity. Asian Christians may use rice or coconut for bread and coconut water in place of wine.[32] I know of one occasion where a youth group used Oreo cookies and Coca Cola in order to be more relevant to younger people.

The Roots of the Eucharist

This chapter has shown just how far we have come in the history of the celebration of the Eucharist: from a required Jewish ritual celebration to cookies and soda. I would venture to say that no other Christian doctrine has been as fractious as this one. However, it could likewise be argued that no other doctrine unites Christians quite as profoundly as this one. For each Sunday across the world millions of people partake of the elements in order to somehow commune with God and to affirm fellowship with one another.

However, perhaps way down in our roots, we can perceive the meaning of the Eucharist—ευχαριστια—"the giving of thanks." The Jews gave thanks to God for rescuing them from Egyptian domination. Jesus gave thanks for the bread and wine. The church has for two millennia given thanks for Jesus.

I wonder what God would want us to give thanks for today. For being rescued from sin? For our daily bread and wine? For Jesus?

Perhaps the spirit of the Eucharist is precisely what it means: "the giving of thanks." Each of us has different ideas of what we are thankful for. Some of us who struggle to make ends meet might—indeed—be thankful for the fact that we have food. Others of us may be thankful for being rescued from a life of darkness, a life condemned, or an overwhelming fear of meaninglessness. Some of us might be thankful for the children sitting to our left and to our right when we put that cup to our lips.

All of us who confess Christ are thankful for his life, death, and resurrection. We are all thankful for the meaning he has infused into us.

But perhaps what Christ was seeking was not that we think specifically of this or that during Eucharist. Perhaps what he wanted from his followers was that they practice Eucharist itself—"the giving of thanks."

Ultimately, a Eucharistic heart is one that pumps gratitude. And this is something we should venture to share with the world. This is what is often missing in our lives, and in our communities. This is precisely where Christians can exercise their faith most openly, most lovingly, and most convincingly.

The Eucharistic heart is the thankful heart. And the frequency of the Eucharist? The great apostle Paul said it best in his earliest letter: "Give thanks [he actually uses the word *Eucharist* here] in all circumstances; for this is God's will for you in Christ Jesus" (1 Thess. 5:18).

Notes

[1] Quoted in Everett Ferguson, *Early Christians Speak,* 3rd Edition (Abilene, TX: Abilene Christian University Press, 1999), 125.

[2] Ibid., 94.

[3] The designation "Communion" comes from the Greek word *koinonia*, which is often translated "fellowship." The designation "Lord's Supper" is used by Paul in 1 Corinthians 11, his most important passage on the topic. The Agape, or love feast, is discussed later in this chapter.

[4] I am using Aaron Milavec, *The Didache: Text, Translation, Analysis, and Commentary* (Collegeville, MN: Liturgical Press, 2003).

[5] Ferguson, 95.

[6] Thomas Finn, "Agape (Love Feast)," in *Encyclopedia of Early Christianity*, ed. by Everett Ferguson, 2nd ed. (New York: Routledge, 1999), 25.

[7] Ibid.

[8] Ferguson, *Early Christians Speak,* 95.

[9] Ibid.

[10] I am using Kevin Edgecomb's excellent translation: *The Apostolic Tradition of Hippolytus,* located at: http://www.bombaxo.com/hippolytus.html. See 26:1.

[11] See Hippolytus's *Apostolic Tradition,* section 21.

[12] Ferguson, 128.

[13] See Wim Blockmans and Peter Hoppenbrouwers, *Introduction to Medieval Europe, 300–1500,* 2nd Edition (London: Routledge, 2014), 58.

[14] Alice-Mary Talbot, "The Devotional Life of Laywomen," chapter ten in *A People's History of Christianity: Byzantine Christianity,* Vol. 3, ed. by Derek Krueger (Minneapolis: Fortress Press, 2006), 206.

[15] Ibid., 209.

[16] William Jurgens, *The Faith of the Early Fathers,* Vol. 1 (Collegeville, MN: The Liturgical Press, 1970), 19.

[17] These two stories about Gorgonia and Macrina are in Vasiliki Limberis, "The Cult of the Martyrs and The Cappadocian Fathers," chapter two in Krueger, ed., 48–50.

[18] Nicholas Constas, "Death and Dying in Byzantium," chapter six in Krueger, ed., 125.

[19] Ibid., 138, Costas writes that grave robbing was "a major social problem."

[20] See Daniel Bornstein, "Relics, Ascetics, Living Saints," chapter three in *A People's History of Christianity: Medieval Christianity,* Vol. 4, ed. by Daniel Bornstein (Minneapolis: Fortress Press, 2009), 89.

[21] Ibid., 91.

[22] Ibid., 92.

[23] Blockmans and Hoppenbrouwers, 274.

[24] Bornstein, 92–93.

[25] Ibid., 95.

[26] Ferguson, *Early Christians Speak,* 117.

[27] Ibid., 116.

[28] To recount the Luther-Karlstadt disagreements, I relied on Hans Hillerbrand's introduction to "Against the Heavenly Prophets in the Matter of Images and Sacraments 1525." See *The Annotated Luther*, Vol. 2: *Word and Faith* (Minneapolis: Fortress Press, 2015), ed. by Kirsi I. Stjerna. The quotation here is from page 41.

[29] Hillerbrand, 46.

[30] Ibid., 50. Italics are mine.

[31] For the varieties of Eucharistic practices in the Protestant churches, see Raymond Mentzer, "The Piety of Townspeople and City Folk," in *A People's History of Christianity*, Vol. 5, *Reformation Christianity* (Minneapolis: Fortress Press, 2007), 32–36.

[32] See for example Paul Collins, *Christian Inculturation in India* (Burlington, VT: Ashgate, 2007), 161–162.

Chapter 4

The Church Building
Where the Saints Meet

"You don't need to go to church to be a Christian.
If you go to Taco Bell, that doesn't make you a taco."[1]

—Justin Bieber

"Established 33 AD." These are the words emblazoned on many Church of Christ buildings throughout the United States. As a member of that group of Christians, I was exposed, early on, to the very clear distinction between the *church building* and the *church*. We were taught we should never conflate these two ideas. A church building is built with human hands and is a place where the saints—those who follow Jesus—can gather comfortably.

The *church*, however, is a more spiritual term meaning something akin to "the disciples of Jesus," or, as we used to call it in the Churches of Christ, "the saints." So convinced were we of this message that our fellowship's national address and phone book took the title *Where the Saints Meet: A Directory of Churches of Christ.* We had ditties and clichés to help us remember this important distinction: "You can't go to church, 'cause the church is you."[2] Yet even the prestigious *Oxford English Dictionary* fails to understand this distinction, for their lead definition for the term "church" reads: "A building used for public Christian worship."[3]

We were convinced of this point, and we knew we had it right. A cursory glance at the Bible made it clear: the Jews worshiped at the Temple, but God wants to be worshiped in the heart. For some reason, we reasoned, the Jews never figured this out. Their own texts made the point clear, however:

> "The multitude of your sacrifices, what are they to me?" says the LORD. "I have more than enough of burnt offer-ings, of rams and the fat of fattened animals; I have no pleasure in the blood of bulls and lambs and goats. When you come to appear before me, who has asked this of you, this trampling of my courts? Stop bring-ing meaningless offerings! Your incense is detestable to me. . . . I cannot bear your worthless assemblies. Your New Moon feasts and your appointed festivals I hate with all my being. They have become a burden to me. . . . When you spread out your hands in prayer, I hide my eyes from you; even when you offer many prayers I am not listening." (Isa. 1:11–15)

In the rather sectarian, Evangelical, Protestant world of my youth, these were condemnations of Temple ritual. Actually, they were condemnations of any kind of ritual at all, except, of course, our rituals—which we dared not call rituals. Nevertheless, the prophets had condemned the "Old Law" as opposed to the "New Law" that was clearly prophesied, even in the Old Testament: "I desire mercy, not sacrifice, and acknowledgment of God rather than burnt offer-ings" (Hos. 6:6).

We were confident in our arguments, especially since they had plenty of New Testament support as well. Jesus himself spoke of this coming age, when the old covenant would be rendered obso-lete and a new spiritual covenant would prevail: "A time is coming and has now come when the true worshippers will worship the Father in the Spirit and in truth, for they are the kind of worshippers the Father seeks. God is spirit, and his worshippers must worship in the Spirit and in truth" (John 4:23–24).

We were often reminded of the proof text in Acts (17:24) that made this teaching most explicit: "The God who made the world and everything in it is the Lord of heaven and earth and does not live in temples built by human hands." Boom. There it was. Temples were no longer necessary.

The only problem, however, was that we Christians have church buildings. Are church buildings simply a modern version of the Temple, albeit scaled down? Could we worship in spirit and in truth inside a building? Indeed, why were we having these very discussions *inside a church building*, yes, *one made with human hands*?

This is where our theology was rescued by that fine distinction between "spirit of the law" and "letter of the law." We reasoned that God did not detest buildings. That would be patently absurd. What God detested was too much emphasis on the church building. Therefore, church buildings should be modest. Ideally, Christians would meet in homes, as they did for the first few centuries. But since our churches were always "growing"—at least presumably (it would be anathema to argue otherwise)—we needed to relieve the pressure from the homes and from the ladies who would have to cook for everybody, and establish buildings where we could worship "in spirit and in truth" (that was often code language for worshiping in the Church of Christ way).

The Meaning of Church

Looking back, I now realize that not only was our theology far from perfect, but we had glossed over the meaning of that English word "church." The word has a long history that predates Christianity. It stems from the Greek adjective *kyriakos*, or, "belonging to the

Lord." Many languages, however, prefer to use the Greek word *ekklesia*, which means "called out" (*ek* = "out"; *kalein* = "to call"). Thus, in the Spanish language the word *ekklesia* gets transliterated into *iglesia*. However, in the Greek New Testament, any time we see that word *ekklesia*, our English translators—oddly—have chosen to use "church" or "belonging to the Lord."[4]

Put another way, our understanding of the word "church" comes from a conflation of two concepts: "called out" (*ekklesia*) and "belonging to the Lord" (*kyriakos*). Perhaps we could say that the church consists of people who have been called out from the rest of society, people who now belong to the Lord.

Over the last two centuries of the movement, many Churches of Christ struggled mightily over what objects could be included in the church building. Were crosses allowed on the walls? Could we have classrooms for teaching children? Is it appropriate to serve coffee and donuts in the church building? And what about an attached gymnasium for kids to play basketball after school?

A somewhat crude story was once told to me by a colleague, shedding light on how seriously our movement has thought about such things. He told me that when he was growing up in Alabama, his congregation once held a "men's business meeting" that dealt with whether a kitchen should be added to the church building. Some churches were adding kitchens, while others refused. This dispute gave rise to the "anti-kitchen" Churches of Christ.

On this particular occasion, the men sat together after church services, perplexed about what they should do. They needed to make a decision. Arguments were made, both pro and con, with apparently little progress, when one elderly gentleman, a farmer, rose to speak. He said, "Brothers, is it lawful to have a toilet in the church?" Several of the men looked at each other and nodded in agreement: "Yes, yes. It is fine to have a toilet in the church. That's why we have them in the church already." So far, so good. The farmer was making good sense. But then, he clinched his argument with the following: "Well, if we can have a toilet for pushing out the food, then why can't we have a kitchen to prepare the food we put into our mouths?" Brilliant. If there was any disagreement, then presumably they'd have to remove the toilets. The argument broke the gridlock, and construction on the new kitchen commenced shortly thereafter.

I must admit that I have been impacted by some of the most conservative arguments of the Protestant world. For example, there are good arguments out there supporting a return to house-churches. Any good Protestant knows that if we use *sola scriptura* as our guide, then we really do not have any business at all meeting in church buildings. The early Christians met in homes, outdoors, or in public places. Should we emulate the early Christians or not?

Many of us Evangelicals who lean toward *sola scriptura* approach this topic with ambivalence. We do not want to be legalistic. But we also don't want to lift the floodgates and allow every random or even pagan idea into our precious Christian faith.

Thus, on one hand, church buildings make good sense. They give us a place to gather in large numbers, to fellowship in a meal together, to teach our children in classrooms, and, yes, to use the bathroom. However, on the other hand, could we not do all of these things in homes? Perhaps in a rich man's home? Or perhaps in a public place, or in an outdoor setting, like the early Christians did? For example, while staying in Ephesus, Paul held church meetings— daily—in "the lecture hall of Tyrannus" for two years (Acts 19:9).

In my church tradition, we have the idea that we should "speak where the Bible speaks, and keep silent where the Bible is silent." We are told that our fellowship's founders tried to operate by that principle in the nineteenth century. Ironically we have treated that maxim as if it were Scripture. It is perhaps a little more precise than Luther's expression of the same idea: *sola scriptura*, but how far do we take this principle? As we discussed in the first chapter, this logic can lead to ridiculous arguments. Must we speak only biblical words and ideas? Must we worship without electricity? Must our women cover their heads? Must we greet each other with a kiss and wash each other's feet? Must we be pacifists?

I have fond memories of the church building in the town where I was raised. As a teenager I was employed as the church janitor, so I knew every corridor, closet, and square foot of carpet— indeed I had to vacuum that carpet twice each week. I grew to love that little building. I still do. I pop in each year when I travel to New Mexico to visit my parents. That church building has special meaning for me. I was baptized there. I came to know the Lord there. Now I take my own children there when I visit. My kids are learning to love the place where their daddy spent so much of his youth. A church building can bring back so many powerful memories; it can pull at the heart strings and cause us to re-evaluate life. In some ways, that little church in New Mexico is a sacred place for me, yes, even for an Evangelical who realizes the church is not the brick and mortar but the believers who gather.

However, on the other end of the spectrum, I have also seen the liberation that can come from *not* having a church. When I pastored a church in Calgary, Canada, we rented a facility. We did not have to worry about leaks or mortgages. Occasionally we wished we had a nice, big kitchen to prepare food, but overall, we were comfortable in our space. We were thankful we could focus our financial offerings on ministry and mission rather than on heating and pesticides. We watched with relief as church buildings were being closed in the city due to declining church memberships. There simply was not enough money to keep these large buildings going. Canada is secularizing rapidly. Surely there are more church closures and consolidations to come. These discussions can be painful, even uncivil.

In one unfortunate incident, the United Church of Canada's Calgary Presbytery closed a church building and locked it one Sunday morning without warning the congregation. Tension had been building for months, but the sudden closure was unexpected. The members of the congregation showed up to a locked door, and instead of sheepishly walking away, they boldly held services in the snow![5] The incident was all over the local news. A lot of money is tied up in church buildings, and some members give small fortunes to sustain them. When that building is closed or deserted, it can become a deep wound.

The *Wall Street Journal* reported on one very odd case in the Episcopal Church. After disagreeing with the denomination on "what the Bible says about sexuality," a specific congregation in New York made an offer to purchase the church property from the diocese so that they could become an independent church. The denomination, however, seized the building in court and then sold it for a fraction of the previously offered price "to someone who turned it into a mosque."[6] Tens of millions of dollars have been spent in litigation in the Episcopal Church, but *hundreds* of millions of dollars are at stake. For example, the breakaway Diocese of South Carolina is fighting to keep its buildings and grounds, which are estimated to be worth five hundred million dollars.[7]

The Roots of the Church Building

The notion of a *church building* is foreign to the New Testament. When the word *ekklesia* is used in the New Testament—well over one hundred times—it always refers to a gathering, an assembly, or a group. Obviously church buildings came much later. The earliest Christians thought of the church as the people. Typically they met in homes or in public places such as the Temple courts in Jerusalem.

In Acts 2:46 we read, "Every day they continued to meet together in the temple courts. They broke bread in their homes and ate together with glad and sincere hearts." Wow, the money they must have saved by not purchasing land and buildings! Indeed, Luke also informs us in verse 45 that "they sold property and possessions to give to anyone who had need." So *that's* where their money went.

Similarly, in Acts 5:42, we are told, "Day after day, in the temple courts and from house to house, they never stopped teaching and proclaiming the good news that Jesus is the Messiah." Is this an unequivocal endorsement for the house-church movement that is catching on today? Yes. Well, yes and no. Nothing in these passages prohibits constructing a church building. The earliest Christians also met in synagogues (the first Christians were Jews), in the Temple courts in Jerusalem, and in members' homes. And, as we noted earlier, when in Ephesus, Paul arranged gatherings in the lecture hall of Tyrannus.

Other snippets of information in the New Testament show where Christians met. For example, in Acts 21 a group of believers met on the beach of Tyre—in modern Lebanon—to pray together before a sea voyage. All of the data seems to point to the fact that Christians met virtually anywhere. As if any place could be a holy place. Thus, while the house-church idea is certainly a good one, it is not the only good one. And if we follow Jesus's example, we'll find him and his followers gathering on mountains, in gardens, in boats, in homes, in synagogues, and elsewhere.

Thus, the biblical evidence is clear: early Christians gathered and prayed wherever it was convenient. The place was never an issue, unless they were pressured and forced out, as happened in synagogues when Jewish-Christian differences became increasingly irreconcilable.

By the third century, a common place for Christians to gather was in subterranean cemeteries—better known as catacombs. In order to avoid interference from the Roman authorities, Christians spent considerable time underground visiting their deceased and worshiping Christ. These burial chambers were built outside the city walls, usually along the major roads that proceeded out of cities like Rome. Catacombs were certainly not limited to Rome, but those have been well-preserved and well-excavated. Jews and Christians commonly used catacombs due to their preference for burial rather than the Roman custom of cremation. By the third century, however, even non-Christian Romans seem to have begun preferring burial for reasons that are not fully understood.[8]

The earliest known example of a Christian using the expression "go to church" is Clement of Alexandria. Around AD 202, he wrote the treatise "The Instructor," also known as the *Paidagogos*. In a fascinating passage, mainly about how women should dress in church, he wrote the following:

> Woman and man are to *go to church* decently attired,
> with natural step, embracing silence, possessing
> unfeigned love, pure in body, pure in heart, fit to pray
> to God. Let the woman observe this, further. Let her be
> entirely covered, unless she happens to be at home. For
> that style of dress is grave, and protects from being gazed
> at. And she will never fall, who puts before her eyes
> modesty, and her shawl; nor will she invite another to
> fall into sin by uncovering her face. For this is the wish
> of the Word, since it is becoming for her to pray veiled.[9]

However, when Clement wrote this passage, there was no such thing as a church building. These were still the days of house churches and shared facilities.

Sadly, the world's oldest known church building, located in the ancient city of Dura-Europos, on the border of modern-day Syria and Iraq, was destroyed by the Islamic terrorist group ISIS in 2014.[10] This church was extremely important in the history of Christianity. Its architectural layout and artistic images were tremendously useful in understanding how Christians worshiped in the third century. The looting and pillaging of this precious site is one of the greatest tragedies to befall the scholarly study of Christian history.

The famous Dura-Europos church building is located on the Euphrates River, and is dated around AD 240. It was discovered by British soldiers in 1920 and excavated by the French two years later. Eventually, Yale University took a leading role in the discovery.

Dura-Europos was cosmopolitan and religiously diverse. Archaeologists were pleased to find that the city had been buried during the destruction of the region by the Sassanians in AD 256. Many religious sites were preserved by dust and sand, including thirteen temples devoted to Greek, Roman, Parthian, and Palmyrene deities.[11] A Mithraeum—devoted to worshipers of Mithras, a Jewish synagogue, and the famous Dura-Europos church were also found in extremely good condition. Both the synagogue and the church were—before ISIS's destruction—the "oldest known surviving synagogue and oldest known surviving Christian church building."[12]

The Christian church was smaller than the synagogue. It was a house that had been converted to exclusive use for church functions. On the outside it remained a house, but on the inside it had clearly been transformed into a church building. It included a rectangular assembly hall—formed by the combining of two rooms, a room with a baptistery tub in it (the earliest known baptistery), a small courtyard, and another significant room that was probably used for the instruction of new converts (the catechumens).

The frescos found on the walls of the Dura-Europos church are the earliest known examples of Christian art aside from the Roman catacombs. Portrayed on the walls are the women at Jesus's tomb, the good shepherd, the healing of the paralytic, Christ and Peter walking on water, the woman at the well, David and Goliath, and nude images of Adam and Eve with the serpent. The "Healing of the Paralytic" fresco may be the earliest known representation of Jesus. Jesus is depicted in the standard attire of a Greek philosopher—the tunic and pallium—and is wearing sandals. His hair is close-cropped in the Roman way, and his face is youthful and clean shaven. In reality, however, it is very likely that Jesus wore a beard in conformity to Jewish custom. Thankfully, these precious pieces of art were removed and are housed and preserved at Yale University.[13]

Was the house-church at Dura-Europos Christianity's first church building? The answer to that question is "most certainly not." For example, the *Chronicle of Arbela* discusses a church building at Edessa, the capital of Osrhoene—an ancient kingdom located in modern Turkey—that was built around AD 130. This Syriac text says that the church building was destroyed by flooding in AD 202.[14] Nevertheless, while written records may point to various church buildings, the facility at Dura-Europos is the earliest church building uncovered by archaeologists.

Proper church buildings did not exist until the time of Constantine in the 300s. Christians typically met in homes, outdoors, or in public spaces. Sometimes homes would be transformed into sites specifically for Christian activity. Presumably, in the years 250 to 313, Christians abandoned the use of public space, since Roman persecution could become intense during that period.

With Constantine's rise, all of that changed. In AD 313, Christians were given a new lease on life that was outright unimaginable in previous decades. In the eyes of the Roman Empire, Christianity went from being a despised superstition to a bona fide, even preferred, religion. Indeed, even Constantine himself would eventually submit himself to the rule of Jesus Christ. And Christians were the great beneficiaries of this most momentous shift in the history of Western civilization. Not all Christians are happy with this surprising development, though. Some of them despise the Roman-Christian merger. They see it as the moment when Christianity lost all authenticity and became, basically, an arm of the state. Whatever one's view, it is a historical fact that in AD 300 it was illegal to be a Christian. It was dangerous. By AD 400 the opposite had happened. Indeed, it could be dangerous *not* to be a

Christian. And while Constantine's reign can best be described as a pluralistic one—open to many interpretations of religion—some of his successors late in the fourth century were outright hostile toward non-Christian faiths. This is what is commonly known as the Constantinianization of Christianity.

The Constantinianization of Church Architecture

It is a myth to assume that Christians were severely persecuted from Emperor Nero (in the AD 60s) until Constantine's Edict of Milan in AD 313. It is more accurate to say that Constantine represents a major shift in policy. It is wrong to think that all of the Roman emperors before Constantine persecuted Christians. In fact, the early church historian Eusebius (AD 260–340) writes of the fair treatment of Christians immediately prior to Diocletian's murderous reign from AD 284 to 305.[15]

The Edict of Milan was issued in the aftermath of the Battle of the Milvian Bridge on October 28, AD 312. That battle has been described as "one of the most momentous events in church or secular history."[16] The night before the battle, Constantine had a dream in which he saw the *chi* and *rho*, the first two letters for Christ in the Greek language. He then heard a voice say in Latin, "In this sign you will conquer" (*In hoc signo vinces*). The next morning Constantine had his soldiers paint the *chi* and *rho* on their shields, and he put the sign on his helmet. When Constantine won that battle, Christianity's fortunes changed dramatically.

Constantine was probably a convert already, but after that battle he "deemed himself the servant of God, chosen to convert the Roman Empire to the Christian faith."[17] The following year, Constantine and his co-ruler Licinius—whom he later had killed—issued the famous Edict of Milan which offered full toleration for people of all religions. Importantly, it offered reparations for Christians who had suffered terribly in the previous two decades. It was plain for all to see, Christianity was now privileged.

The restitutions were lavish. Churches were given huge dona-
tions. Clergymen were granted immunities, rights, and payments
unimaginable only months before.

What follows is some of the more notable parts of the famous
Edict:[18]

> We have long intended that freedom of worship should
> not be denied but that everyone should have the right
> to practice his religion as he chose. Accordingly, we had
> given orders that both Christians and [all others] should
> be permitted to keep the faith of their own sect and
> worship. . . . As issues of highest priority, we decided
> to issue such decrees as would assure respect and rev-
> erence for the Deity; namely, to grant the Christians
> and all others the freedom to follow whatever form of
> worship they pleased, so that all the divine and heav-
> enly powers that exist might be favorable to us and all
> those living under our authority. . . . Everyone desiring
> to observe the Christians' form of worship should be
> permitted to do so without any hindrance. . . . We have
> granted to these same Christians free and limitless per-
> mission to practice their own form of worship.

Many Christians had been put to death, their homes confiscated,
and their possessions seized by the state during the persecutions.
To them, the Edict offered relief: "All this property must be handed
over to the body of the Christians immediately, through zealous
action on your part and without delay."[19] The Edict of Milan con-
veys an unmistakable preference for Christianity. The bishops
are told that they can ask for whatever they need, any amount
of money, and Constantine will ensure that it gets handed over
"without question."[20]

The emperors were concerned about divisions in the church,
due mainly to the Arian and Donatist controversies. Thus, they

announced an upcoming gathering that would smooth over the differences. This announcement led directly to the Council of Nicaea in AD 325. Constantine made it clear that he wanted unity. He referred to schismatics as "persisting in madness." He advised the bishops to report schismatics to the judges, that "they may turn these people from their error."[21]

In closing, the Edict announced that "clergymen should once and for all be kept entirely free from all public duties. Then they will not be drawn away from the worship owed to the Divinity by any error or sacrilege but instead strictly serve their own law unencumbered."[22] It was a new day for Christianity. With the Constantinian shift, the period of church architecture began with gusto.

It is hard to overemphasize what Constantine did for Christianity. This religious group that had been suppressed—sometimes harshly—suddenly became legal and clearly favored. Some of Constantine's predecessors such as Decius (AD 249–251), Valerian (AD 253–260), and most especially Diocletian (AD 284–305) resented Christianity and went to great lengths to keep the faith illegal. Diocletian's most intense persecution—beginning in 303—is remembered as one of the most punishing Christian persecutions in history.

Not only did Constantine eradicate any vestiges of Christian persecution, but by the end of his reign he was effectively suppressing traditional Roman religion. It was an obvious reversal of fortune. Christians were now on the good side of the Empire, while the decline of Roman religion accelerated quickly. One historian put it this way:

> On the pagan side, things were different. Money
> was hard to find. . . . A once glorious non-Christian
> Establishment—with all the claims of temples on local
> taxes, the temple-estates, the investments set aside by
> devoted or boastful donors to pay the priests and cover

the costs of worship—all this accumulated fat of centuries of piety was essentially torn away. There can have been nothing much left by A.D. 400.[23]

And where did all of that money go? It went to the churches. More specifically, it was used to build Christian basilicas. Constantine believed that . . .

> no harm could be done in requiring Christianity's rivals, wicked and misguided folk that they were, to foot the bill. Best known are the extraordinary number, size, and grandeur of the basilicas with which Constantine enriched the church in Rome, many of them also assigned great endowments of land and other wealth.[24]

Constantine's massive building project was not limited to Rome, however. He invested tremendous resources in the church in all corners of his empire. The amount of money he spent on the church in Constantinople—when he built his capital there in the years AD 324 to 330—was breathtaking. It was a gargantuan windfall for Christianity's bishops, priests, and caretakers: "Overnight, it seemed, he created 'a Christianity whose bishops and clergy had had their social horizons blown wide open by finding the openhanded Constantine in their midst.'"[25] Oh, and one more privilege: the church was exempted from having to pay any tax.

It was most surprising for the leader of the Roman Empire to change course so dramatically in such a short period of time. Formerly the Christians in that vast empire met in secret; they were persecuted, mainly poor, and socially marginalized. But after Constantine's rise, they were admired, and their movement quickly gained status, even to the point of being spoiled. Christians were grateful. Understandably, they elevated Constantine—who had a rather checkered rise to power—to heroic status. In the Orthodox churches, he is still known as "an equal to the apostles (*isapostolos*)."

Constantine is one of history's great patrons of Christian architecture. He commissioned numerous church buildings, preferring the basilica format for his projects. This was the architecture he knew. It was the architecture of Rome. And it became the architecture of church buildings for the next thousand years.

From Basilicas to Cathedrals: The Illustrious Heyday of Church Buildings

The day after Constantine's Milvian Bridge victory in AD 312, he marched triumphantly into Rome, but this time he did not emulate previous Roman victors when they strutted into the city. What was notably absent was the standard visit to the capitol building to make sacrificial offerings to the Roman gods. Rather, Jesus Christ—in his view—was the source of his victory.[26]

To avoid offending his pagan citizens, Constantine refused to demolish the other temples to make room for his personal project. Rather, he chose a less conspicuous location for his new structure that would honor Jesus Christ. His church was to be located near the Caelian Hill, just inside Rome's city walls. Perhaps with a little vindictiveness, this new edifice was to be built on the site of a Roman fort that housed the emperor's cavalry. This was the residence for the elite, mounted soldiers that Constantine had just defeated.

The site Constantine chose is today the famous Papal Archbasilica of St. John in Lateran. This is the cathedral church of Rome, the official episcopal seat of the Pope. It is often considered to be the oldest active church building in the Western world and is venerated as the mother church for the Roman Catholic denomination.

Within months, Constantine's engineers and architects were building a brand new facility for worship. They found the architecture of the Roman temple to be unfit for the needs of Christian worship. Besides, the Roman temple was mainly an area elevated for sacrificing animals. The people gathered outside in the open air of the courtyard and waited for the meat of the sacrificial victims. The only sacrifice that was to take place within the Christian church was the Eucharist, and it was to be taken together, almost like a family meal.

Strangely, Constantine and his advisors chose the basilica as the archetype for the church. This decision would have been odd for Romans, because the basilica was not a building used for religion. The Roman basilica was a large rectangular building used for civic gatherings: business dealings, law courts, buying and selling products, money changing, town meetings, "to see and be seen."[27] It was a multipurpose facility, a wedding of public space with religious piety. Constantine's chosen design for his churches was quite distinct from Rome's pagan temples.

Constantine provided ample room in the construction of this monument to Christ. The building was about two hundred fifty feet long and one hundred eighty feet wide.[28] A central nave ("nave" means "ship") would be flanked by four spacious aisles held up by huge columns. There would be a clerestory at the upper part of the nave for windows, in order to bring light and fresh air into the building. At the end of the nave was an apse—the semicircular half-dome which would later depict Jesus the Victor, or perhaps a large cross or depictions of the holy apostles. Below the apse were benches for clergy, an altar, and a ceremonial seat (*cathedra*) for the presiding bishop, who in Constantine's world would become a high-ranking official in his empire.

Constantine's Lateran basilica was magnificent, held up by marble columns, gilded and ornamented with gold. Over three thousand people could congregate inside its walls. Large baptismal ceremonies could take place within the octagonal baptistery. A bishop's residence was attached, with quarters for staff also. This was a turning point in the history of Western architecture, "a new kind of public building and a symbol of the triumph of Christianity."[29]

This architectural symbol of Christianity's triumph would dominate for hundreds of years. And it naturally lent itself to displaying sacred art—mosaics depicting biblical scenes, pious chapels along the aisles, elegant and elaborate altars, floor décor, and holy artistry inside the apse—which served as a focal point from the moment the congregants entered the nave. Gold was often used by artists, especially in decorating the splendid apse. Christian art flourished in the basilica. And whereas competing temples were ubiquitous—due to so many Greek and Roman gods that were worshiped, the Christian basilica would be a place of unity. Constantine's vision was of a unified people, all gathering in a temple much larger than the minor ones that speckled Roman cities. Christian basilicas would be for the masses. Many, many people could worship under one roof. Christendom had begun.

The Roman basilica was improved and elaborated upon throughout the medieval world in a style of church architecture known today as Romanesque. Shortly after the turn of the millennium, however, in the eleventh and twelfth centuries, a new and more daring style of architecture began to emerge. We know it today as Gothic, although by all accounts that is a very imprecise word for it.[30]

In the history of Christianity, the eleventh century is synonymous with the Great Schism of 1054, when the church split into two halves, East and West. That year stands as a testament to how intensely political humans can become, even at the cost of destroying Christian unity. Pope Leo IX and Patriarch Michael Cerularius inflicted serious, long-lasting damage to the church when they split the Christian world into Roman Catholic and Eastern Orthodox. The damage has yet to be repaired.

Perhaps the single most important development of this era, however, was not theological in nature at all, but was rather the collective accomplishment of Christendom—its wonderful cathedrals. What caused Christians to build spectacular, magnificent, colossal churches all across Christendom? They became the most definitive and lasting feature of the High Middle Ages (roughly 1000 to 1300).

The patient and meticulous work put into these titanic edifices is breathtaking. Countless years were spent erecting these behemoths that transcend the power of one man, or even one generation. The scale of construction offers us several insights: These people were intensely committed to the church, communities worked selflessly together to create a house of worship they could be proud of, and the vast majority of community resources were devoted to the task of constructing these truly impressive cathedrals. It took decades or even more than a century to complete them, so most of the people who worked on them never saw their completion.

In the eleventh and twelfth centuries, church architecture began to make a shift from the Romanesque to this Gothic style, as hundreds of staggering, tastefully designed churches ascended from the earth. It was a creative time as the traditional, thick Romanesque style was being challenged by the lighter, more inspiring Gothic. Initially, the term "Gothic" was meant to be pejorative, implying an association more with paganism (the Goths—who conquered Rome) than with Christendom. But the label stuck.

The ground plan of the old church basilica—dating back to Constantine—was rather simple. It was cruciform (cross-shaped), it contained three naves with huge columns leading to the high (elevated) altar, and it presented an apse ("arch" or "vault"). Generally people would enter the nave located on the west side of the building and face the east as they walked in. Once inside they would be dazzled by the awe-inspiring apse with its intricate depictions of Jesus, Mary, and the holy apostles.

However, in the High Middle Ages, this standard Romanesque style that had survived a millennium began to be challenged by the Gothic, a style very different, yet refreshing to many. While

Romanesque churches were intentionally solemn and meditative, the Gothic style was intentionally bright, beckoning parishioners to look and think outwardly. It was a subtle difference with profound effects. From the inside, Gothic style bathed congregants in light; from the outside, the needle point spires caused them to raise their heads upward and cast their thoughts to the heavens. Whereas Romanesque style is earthy, round, and practical, Gothic style is airy, vertical, and tall. It was the invention of the "flying buttress"—a strong masonry arch that transferred the weight of the roof outward—that allowed this development to take place.[31]

In an age of illiteracy, these towering churches served as the forum for mass religious education through art. Stained-glass windows told the stories of the Bible, the history of the church, and the life to come. All persons in the community would have been intimately connected to their church through the rhythms of life: baptisms, weddings, frequent Masses and holy days, and funerals. It was a place of refuge and could be seen from afar. The church was a source of pride. It took the entire community working in sacrificial service for generations to create one.

A cathedral, the most important church in a diocese, often took more than a century to complete. The amazing Cologne Cathedral in Germany was constructed between 1248 and 1880. But even in modern times these structures require patience. Barcelona's famous basilica, *La Sagrada Familia*, has been under construction since 1882 and will not be completed until 2026, or later.

Throughout the medieval world, church buildings—like the old Roman basilica—were multi-use complexes. They were places for business. Pilgrims rested there during their journeys. Entertainment took place outside on the steps. The church was shelter from the elements or asylum during war. A professional clergy was on call to hear confessions, to offer prayers and blessings, or to listen to the anxiety of a troubled soul and offer healing.

It is impressive that these architectural wonders have been preserved. However, it is sad that in Europe most of these churches are frequented more by tourists catching a glimpse of the past than by worshipers offering up praise to the One who inspired the buildings in the first place.

From Altars to Pulpits: The Protestant Preference

Initially, the Protestant Reformation had little impact on church buildings. In regions that joined the Reformation, Catholic churches were simply turned into Protestant ones. However, the *interior* of these churches could be dramatically impacted.

Early in the history of church architecture, church buildings included a pulpit, known in Latin as an *ambo* (or in Greek as an *ambon*). The word *ambo* means "crest of a hill." Not a bad description of the early pulpit, since it was slightly elevated, usually by a few steps.[32] Jewish synagogues had their version of this which was called a *migdal* ("tower" in Hebrew). Due to the influence of Arabic, however, the word used by Jews today is *bimah* (from *al-minbar*). Presumably, the *migdal* was adopted by Christians for use in the basilica-based church buildings.

Resting on the ambo was usually a rounded, sometimes elaborately carved lectern used for teaching. Often, they were impressive pieces carved out of marble or wood. Priests could place their texts upon it and could be seen by the congregation since the ambo sat upon an elevated platform, known today as a podium. (In English the terminology gets confusing, since the terms lectern, podium, and pulpit are often used interchangeably.) Ambos were of many different shapes: round, square, or polygonal. Later in church history an overhead sounding board was installed just above the speaker for acoustic purposes. Using a small roof over the head of the speaker to amplify the sound is a strategy commonly employed in the Muslim version of the pulpit—the *minbar*.[33]

This elevated lectern was not commonly used for preaching. It was used for reading. In fact, the word *lectern* is from the Latin word *lectus*, meaning "to read." However, the most important preacher of the first millennium—John Chrysostom (AD 349–407)—did, in fact, use it for preaching. This was uncommon, however, largely because ambos were not standard in the church building until the sixth century. But when the ambo became common, it was typical that a reader would ascend it and read the Scripture for the day and then step down.

The ambo could be located in several different places in the basilica, but typically it was placed in the nave near the front. It could be centered at the axis of the building, although often it was built off to one side. What was very clear, however, was that the ambo played a minor role in comparison to the altar—where the Eucharist was celebrated.

In Judaism, the Temple contained a central altar for sacrificing animals as well as offerings such as wine, grain, and incense.[34] In Christianity, however, the sacrifices were bloodless. The blood had been shed once for all, in the passion and crucifixion of Jesus. The altar, however, remained firmly as a vital part of church architecture, largely because of the formative period of the Christian liturgy wherein John Chrysostom—yet again—played a major part. Chrysostom conceived of the Christian worship service as a sacrifice, albeit a bloodless sacrifice, which needed an altar from which to act out the dramatic events and to consecrate the "host," the body (sacramental bread) of Jesus. Thus, the notion of a sacrifice, as we explored in the previous chapter, remained very much alive. The idea of re-enacting the "Last Supper" on a table—where Jesus broke bread with his disciples—was also a rich metaphor. But Latin Christians preferred the term *altare*, which has survived in the Western church traditions and no doubt has helped preserve the Eucharist as a type of sacrifice. This was most explicitly the case in Roman Catholicism.

Protestants placed more focus on the ambo and lectern than on the altar. Indeed, it was common for the churches that joined the Protestant Reformation to rotate the furnishings ninety degrees so that the attention was no longer on the altar but on a pulpit that was located off to one side. Protestant churches very quickly began to shift the attention of their congregants from the "sacrifice of the Mass" to the rigorous explication of the word. In this case, the word was most definitely the Bible, the Word of God.

Experts often claim that Protestantism caused literacy to surge. Why? It was because they had the burden of proof. Catholicism was established, normative, expected. However, Protestants had to *prove* to people that the Catholic way of doing things was fundamentally off. First and foremost, their brazen leader Martin Luther set the tone by preaching endless sermons about why he was right and the Pope was wrong. As a result, Protestant society emphasized the pulpit—the teaching. Preachers gave lengthy sermons, typically an hour or more, to prove that their interpretation of the faith was superior to the faith that had sustained the population for centuries.

Changing the mind of a society was no easy task, but Protestant pastors had several newer technologies at their disposal, such as Gutenberg's printing press, which was invented in the mid-fifteenth century. They also launched innovative approaches for teaching the Bible. Luther pioneered the "slow, labor-intensive work" of catechizing through his *Small Catechism*.[35] He also had to engage in constant debates with Catholic leaders in both written and spoken forms. Eventually Protestants also had to devote equal amounts of time toward explaining why their approach to reform was superior to the approach taken by the Protestant pastor in the neighboring city!

Thus, the pulpit was propelled to a position of great prominence it had never enjoyed before. One historian explains: "The size and grandeur of newly built Protestant pulpits were permanent reminders of the paramountcy of the sermon, and led to the drastic restructuring of Reformed church interiors from Ireland to Lithuania."[36] Hourglasses were put on the pulpit, not to rush the preacher, but to emphasize the point that any good sermon must go on *at least* one hour, with the most gifted rhetoricians expected to prove that they could exhort the public for two![37]

The sermon quickly became the dominant aspect—by far—of the Protestant church service. We will look at this topic in more detail in Chapter Six, but suffice it to say that some churches endured sermons four times a week, and the public was strongly encouraged to attend, even fined or punished if they missed—as in Calvin's Geneva. There was nothing uncommon whatsoever in asking a parish to come to church twice on Sundays. "Everywhere sermons were the great occasions of the week."[38] And when the sermon ended—this was most conspicuously the case in the Church of Scotland—parents were expected to drill their children to ensure that they understood the content of the sermon that day.[39]

Bigger and Better: The Rise of the Stage

The rise in stature of the Protestant stage was in many ways a natural progression. After all, the Latin word *pulpitum* can actually be translated as "stage." So the change in terminology from "pulpit" to "stage" that has taken place in many Protestant circles is perfectly reasonable. However, the rise of colossal Protestant church buildings is unique and is linked to the rise of the New World—of America.

It is difficult to name great Catholic preachers. Catholicism, even in the United States, emphasizes the liturgy, the Eucharist, and the established ritual far more than the ability of the priest to deliver a sermon. Contrast this to Protestantism, where it is quite easy to name prominent preachers. All of this is a natural consequence of the Protestant Reformation. Early reformers faced an uphill battle. They had to say, in effect, "Forget what you've always heard. It is corrupt. You should listen to me." Catholic priests, on the other hand, had the weight of history and tradition on their side. They were duly ordained in the apostolic succession of the church. A priest became authoritative simply by being ordained a priest. He did not have to compete for his authority. Once he finished his training, he was consecrated by a bishop to lead a parish church.

For Protestant pastors it was not so easy. They had to earn respect. They had to earn their pulpits. They had to win their credibility in a way quite different from the Catholic system. For better or for worse, this had the effect of creating something akin to a personality cult in Protestantism. Pastors did not necessarily rely on the strength of a particular brand. They had to cultivate their own. This is what Luther, Calvin, Zwingli, and Menno Simons had to do. They had to build up a body of people through persuasion. They had to offer something new and exciting to their followers, something unique that could capture the allegiance of people.

As Europeans heard the Protestant claims about God, they often became interested enough to want to learn more. For the laity, a lot was on the line: their souls. If the Protestants were right, the Catholic Church had become corrupt. The Protestants boldly encouraged people to read the Bible—*sola scriptura*—in order to determine who was right. What followed was a lively era of Scripture reading, increased literacy, biblical scholarship, and a general increase of book knowledge due to persistent questioning. Protestants were nothing if they weren't bookish. One prominent historian put it this way: "There can be no doubt that the effort of catechizing and the task of listening to a weekly diet of abstract ideas from the pulpit made Protestant Europe a society generally more book-conscious, and perhaps also more literate, than Catholic Europe."[40] The result, although unintentional, was that in the Protestant churches the instrument of God's word became supremely important. If this preacher is correct, a layman reasoned, he has saved my soul from condemnation.

In Protestantism, the pulpit rose to new heights, both figuratively and literally. Indeed, in some cases the altar disappeared from the floorplan of the church. One can scarcely imagine today a Catholic Mass without the Eucharist at the end. Communion-less Protestant services are common. But imagine a Protestant service without a sermon. It is hardly possible.

The cult of personality in Protestantism is by no means cultish in the most negative sense. But it is true in the most literal sense. Early on a culture developed around important leaders of the Lutherans, Calvinists, Mennonites, Wesleyans, and more. In most cases, these Protestant pastors did not like their names being affixed to their interpretation of the gospel, but alas, they could do little to keep this from happening. After all, it was their teaching that caused the movement.

In the New World, Protestant pastors took their cues from their English counterparts such as John Wesley (1703–1791), George Whitefield (1714–1770), and Charles Spurgeon (1834–1892). Wesley really got the ball rolling when he was banned from preaching in Anglican churches and moved to the open air. When his denomination marginalized him, he coined that now-famous phrase, "All the world is my parish." He disregarded denominational lines in his preaching. Although Wesley considered himself an Anglican until his death, he can be considered today as the father of non-denominational Christianity. Perhaps most importantly, he influenced Whitefield, who carried this mentality to America and became the most famous personality in the New World during his seven long visits beginning in 1740.

America never had an "established" denomination, as did virtually all European nations. It was therefore a free-for-all, pristine territory for fast-talking evangelists. This peculiar situation led to the camp revival culture in America, where thousands gathered outdoors on the frontier to hear preachers of all sorts. Makeshift stages were set up. Tree stumps served as pulpits. The loud, clear voice of a preacher could carry for hundreds of yards.

Historians call this the era of the Great Awakening in America. The Cane Ridge Revival of 1801, which took place in frontier Kentucky, was the most important of these events. It drew together thousands of people from various Christian denominations at a time when physical isolation from other human beings was common in the virgin land of manifest destiny. People coming together from all sorts of Christian backgrounds, fellowshipping, celebrating Communion, relying on each other, making connections . . . this was the seedbed for Protestant ecumenism—for Christian unity—in the United States. It is a form of Christianity that continues to the present day.

Today in the United States, people are not so much committed to a denomination as they are to a type of worship, or to a particular pastor's interpretation of the faith. In this context, denominational loyalties fade away. One's experience becomes the key to one's interpretation of Christianity. The truth of the gospel is revealed in experience. Not unlike John Wesley's notion of a "warming of the heart," these camp revivals provided more than academic, erudite explications of biblical texts. In many ways, they were holy ground—a setting where God broke through to the common man and woman.

In addition to bringing about the unique phenomenon of American ecumenism, the open-air revivals were an archetype for the modern Pentecostal movement. Properly sanctioned ministers of the more highbrow establishment churches watched in horror as American audiences jumped and cried out in worship revivals, and wept openly without reserve. Often times the revival preachers were not even formally educated, nor were they properly ordained. These camp revivals held no respect for one's pedigree. The preacher who drew crowds spoke to the heart. Pioneer life was terribly difficult, and persnickety arguments over Greek words were entirely out of place.

Church buildings were unimportant in this context; a covered wagon could be holy enough if the Spirit was there. Gothic spires and awe-inspiring stained glass were part of the old world. The new world was different. In the new world, people went "down to the river to pray." They confessed their sin by moonlight. All the pent-up anxiety—the angst of stillborn children, lack of any kind of health care, ruined harvests, bitter winters, and most importantly that terrible isolation—begged for divine release. The revivals were a place where people could come together and lean on one another and share their painfully heavy burdens. These momentous events touched the American consciousness much more profoundly than did the priestly vestments and ornate basilicas of the old world.

One famous American preacher who made a transformative impact on church architecture was Charles Grandison Finney (1792–1875). Finney was trained as a lawyer, but after a dramatic religious conversion he decided to give himself to Christ. Initially a Presbyterian, he eschewed religious parochialism and pled with his listeners to convert to Jesus Christ as Lord. His message caught on in Rochester, New York, during a revival in 1830 and 1831.

Finney, like Wesley and Whitefield before him, was "bitterly opposed by leaders of the older churches."[41] These evangelists were trailblazers, reformers, and innovators at a time when Christianity was guarded by gatekeepers at every turn. Indeed, Finney became an important Evangelical social activist, opposing alcoholism, slavery, gluttony, and luxury. He became a champion for the mentally ill, for women, for the emancipation of slaves, and for equal access to education—including for slaves.

From 1851 to 1866, Finney served as president of Oberlin College in Ohio. Oberlin was ground zero for social activism during Finney's day. The college accepted women as well as African

Americans, when almost no other institution did so. Finney was a man way ahead of his time. He "encouraged women to speak publicly at his meetings," and became highly active in the Underground Railroad, assisting escaped slaves in their quest to cross the Ohio River into freedom. Through it all, Finney never gave up his central message of repentance and Christian holiness. He believed that only through "a transformation of inner life" could one truly claim to have been converted to the religion of Christ. Finney's preaching and activism opened the pathway for many who had previously been marginalized, especially women and African Americans.[42]

Finney's ministry was patterned on the extraordinarily innovative model of itinerant preaching that George Whitefield had pioneered a generation before him. However, the difference was that Finney managed to see the institutionalization of this enthusiastic form of Evangelical Christianity. Finney's conviction held that the message—far more than the building—took precedence, and church buildings began to account for that critical change. Evangelical Protestant churches were destined to become auditoriums and stages. Altars became tables, not so much for bread and wine, but as a place where people could come forward and express their true repentance. Indeed, Finney's name is coterminous with the American Evangelical phenomenon of the "altar call."

My Pepperdine colleague Bradley Griffin is an expert on Finney, particularly on Finney's impact on church architecture. He points out that Finney's Chatham Street Chapel was first a famous theater—the Chatham Garden Theatre. Finney oversaw major renovations to the chapel, most importantly the moving of the pit floor to stage level,

> . . . ostensibly for the purpose of facilitating audience
> response to the altar call. . . . There were no visual or
> physical boundaries to separate the audience from the
> stage. When Finney invited members of the audience

to come forward during the altar call, he was literally inviting them into the world of the stage. They would leave their seats to join him at the front of the stage, a physical move that paralleled the feeling of being swept up into the world of the romantic drama or into the immense landscape of a panorama.[43]

Finney foresaw—or perhaps we could say he pioneered—the blending of sacred and profane, of clergy and laity, of the dramatic with the holy.

The critical point here is that Finney's preaching demanded a response. He was responsible for what became known as the "anxious bench" or the "mourner's bench" where penitent churchgoers would go for prayer and support at the front of the building. This practice continues in many Evangelical denominations, including my own. Finney wanted to see an open, honest, and authentic conversion, so he gave people the tools to express their genuine faith and remorse for sin. People were given a way out of their desperation; the altar call gave them a platform for saying to the Christians around them: "Here am I. In need of God's grace. A sinner in need of a Savior." It was a brilliant strategy that encouraged a response. It took religion out of the hands of the authorities and put it back into the hands of the individual. And while many critiqued the anxious bench and other "gimmicks" like it, it worked for people. They responded. By the tens of thousands. Even millions. And millions still respond in this way.

Many preachers who came after Finney adopted his ingenious methods with even greater effect than he enjoyed. Dwight Moody (1837–1899) in Chicago, Aimee Semple McPherson (1890–1944) in Los Angeles, and, of course, Billy Graham (1918–present), who became the most successful Evangelical preacher in all of Christian history. Common to all of these famous preachers is that they were center stage. The Eucharist, baptism, altars, sacred tables, art, architecture—all of this was secondary. At center stage was a preacher. The man with a message. And the message, today, remains at the center of virtually all Evangelical Protestant church services. Evangelical church buildings account for this shift in focus. Thus, for better or for worse, these churches are virtually indistinguishable from an auditorium. The pulpit has become the stage and the preacher has become a performer. Evangelical Christians have become the audience.

Finney's methods went global alongside the Evangelical movement's advance. By the end of the twentieth century, these same methods could be found all over the world. One of the most obvious examples is in the Yoido Full Gospel Church in Seoul, South Korea. Pastored by the dynamic Pentecostal minister David Yonggi Cho (1936–present), this congregation is today the largest in the world. It includes an impressive auditorium with a stage for the preacher, who is nearly surrounded by onlookers. Much like in a standard theater, there is a chamber below for the orchestra. Little difference can be detected between this church building and a massive movie theater. The one crucial distinction is that rather than a movie or a play, the top billing is the sermon. Today, the sermon is the "message" from Almighty God.

Another important example of this shifting church architecture is Joel Osteen's (1963–present) Lakewood Church, in Houston, Texas. The church building is actually the former arena for the Houston Rockets professional basketball team. Seventeen thousand people can sit comfortably in this religious arena, absorbing the polished presentations by Pastor Osteen. Clearly in the trajectory of the revivalist frontier preachers, Osteen had virtually no training. His father was the pastor of the church when it was relatively small and humble. But his charisma, his wide smile, and his optimistic messages of confidence, self-reliance, and prosperity have helped to shift the center of gravity of Christianity away from mainline Protestantism and toward a generic, non-denominational approach to faith. While Joel Osteen is technically from the Pentecostal expression of Christianity, his message is non-sectarian. And due to his amazing ability to reach through the airwaves and via satellites to the whole planet, his message of hope, of change, and of self-improvement has taken center stage in global Christianity today. And his message seems to work. In contemporary Christianity, he is widely regarded as "the most popular preacher on the planet."[44]

The United States' most famous example of the stage-like church building, however, is undoubtedly the Crystal Cathedral, built up by the ministry of the powerful televangelist Robert Schuller (1926–2015). Located in Garden Grove, California, this massive glass behemoth inspires all who enter it. Inside this grand worship center, the audience is bathed in light, and their attention is drawn outside in a way that no other building has ever done. Ever since its completion in 1981, this glass cathedral has captivated specialists who study architecture. One historian wrote:

> The "Crystal Cathedral" in Los Angeles, by Philip Johnson, is a church conceived for the age of mass evangelism. It is star-shaped and made entirely of glass on a steel frame. All the resources of modern technology are brought to bear. . . . Facing [the preacher] are television cameras, while microphones relay the service to another congregation in the car-park who can see inside when vast glass doors are swung open.[45]

Charles Finney would have been very proud of this . . . up to a point. He would have loved Schuller's focus on mass evangelism, on showmanship, on the supreme prominence of the stage, and on the vital role that entertainment should play in church. However, he would have been shocked and disturbed by the Crystal Cathedral's inglorious turn of events in 2010. After a bitter quarrel in the Schuller family over who would succeed the patriarch as chief pastor, a split in the church eviscerated the membership. Offerings plummeted and the church filed for bankruptcy. They sold the building to the Roman Catholic Diocese of Orange in 2012. The newly renovated Christ Cathedral will open up for worshipers in the year 2017 with what promises to be an overhauled interior, splendidly suitable for a Roman Catholic Mass.

The Curious Case of Pews

Before we close this chapter, we should mention something virtually all Catholic and Protestant (but not Orthodox) Christians will be familiar with: pews. For the first millennium, Christians typically stood during the public worship assembly. Indeed, most of the world's two hundred fifty million Eastern Orthodox Christians *still* stand during worship. Around the thirteenth century, however, backless stone benches begin to emerge in churches, possibly first in England.[46] By the fifteenth century, wooden benches began to emerge, with backs for reclining during the Mass. However, even then, pews were more the exception than the rule.

It was the Protestant Reformation—with its long and rigorous sermons—that would make the pew become standard furniture inside the church building. Parishioners were expected to sit quietly and listen for long periods. In the Catholic and Orthodox liturgies, people were free to move in and out of the nave. According to liturgical practice, they could take a knee and rise again, breaking the monotony. They could also move over to side chapels inside the church building for lighting candles or paying homage to the Virgin. Even today, it can be a bit disconcerting for a Protestant to attend an Orthodox Divine Liturgy. Often, the people do not show up until well into the liturgy's performance. And the masses of people suddenly appear when it is time for the Eucharist. What might seem offensive to Protestants is quite natural for Orthodox Christians—whose services can last over two hours.

The concept of the "box pew" arose in Protestant Europe, again, probably in England. It was an attempt to allow a greater measure of comfort for the parishioners as they listened to sophisticated, academic treatises on biblical themes. Box pews—still found in old Protestant churches in Europe and in the northeastern United States—would actually belong to a family. The family could decorate the box with windows and even curtains for a bit of privacy. As the sermons became longer, the concern for comfort increased. Cushions might be utilized, and even locks were installed on the door to pew boxes. A series of controversies arose in Protestant churches about whether pew boxes could be willed to the next generation, a practice which effectively prohibited rising social classes from moving forward in their seating. Regardless of their newly acquired wealth, these once-poor families still were marginalized in the social stratification of the pews.

During the first few centuries of Protestantism, pew rentals were a common scheme for raising money for a new church building. And when a church building was constructed, donors had rights on particular pews. Typically, the best seats in the house were closer to the front while the cheap seats were in the back. "But after 1840, there was a fervent High Church reaction against pew-renting, and indeed against pews themselves."[47] The reasoning for this was both scriptural and social. Scripturally, there is no foundation for a pew. Socially, it was ostracizing to the poor, who obviously had little wherewithal to purchase themselves seats other than in the lowliest positions in the church, perhaps even segregated from the greater congregation.

During the 1840s the Anglo-Catholic movement launched a broadside attack against pew rents, social stratification in churches, and segregation based on class inside sacred walls. This movement was enamored with Catholicism and often drew upon Catholicism in order to critique Protestant improprieties. One thing this "Oxford Movement" (as it was often called due to its origins in Oxford University) praised was the Roman Catholic tendency to consider all attendees of a church service as being equals. A nineteenth-century lawyer wrote:

> There is no doubt, however, that before the Reformation, parish-churches were not pewed, that is to say, the floor of the nave or body of the building was never covered, as at present, with close boxes. On the contrary, no exclusive seats, with very few exceptions, were allowed. . . . Persons who have visited Roman Catholic countries, can easily imagine that . . . for whatever may be the errors and the corruptions of that Church, respect of persons within the walls of her sacred buildings, and indulgence of personal ease and accommodation there, are certainly not to be laid to her charge. . . . Nor was the practice of preaching lengthy sermons, or rather of reading long essays, so much in vogue as it was afterwards under the reign of the Puritans, who carried it to a ludicrous extent, or as it is at present in a more moderate degree amongst ourselves.[48]

Protestants today will certainly understand the propensity to critique long sermons, but I suspect that the "indulgence of personal ease and accommodation" is a critique that might still be well-justified.

Nevertheless, the pew has become standard in most churches, and, surprisingly, is even catching on in the Orthodox churches of the Western world. Indeed, a church without pews is today about as common as a church without a pulpit.

Returning Home: The House-Church Antithesis

It is ironic that the earliest Christian church buildings were houses. Under Constantine they suddenly took the shape of large public basilicas, in the late medieval era they reached for the stars with Gothic spires, and then the columns and walls were blown out for the large stages so prominent in the North American Protestant mega-churches. Indeed, there is a striking similarity between the ancient Greek theaters and the modern mega-church auditoriums today.[49] Those who argue that Christianity's church buildings actually come down to us from pagan roots, well, they are correct. But seriously, does the Lord care what type of building people use in order to facilitate their worship of him? I suppose arguments can be made in all directions.

Today, what fascinates me is the present "house-church movement" that is making waves in Evangelical Protestant circles. Out from under the albatross of a crippling church mortgage, these Christians put their money into other things, such as service, mission, and benevolence. It is an exciting movement, but for some reason—maybe it is the church historian in me—the house-church movement does not seem built to last. Homes are bought and sold. But solid brick-and-mortar church buildings stand a better chance of lasting. Well, that is, at least outside of Europe, where church buildings are now being turned into apartments, warehouses, pubs, shops, and even discos. Indeed, in the United States and in Europe, many of the once-great churches have now been turned into mosques, due largely to secularization trends as well as immigration from the Middle East.[50]

As church buildings continue to get larger, the movement to get back to what matters—the people—makes good sense. Private homes certainly provide an intimacy and warmth unavailable in the arenas packed by followers of Joel Osteen or Benny Hinn. It is only fair to point out, however, that mega-churches are often quite adept at providing the house-church experience *in addition to* the concert aura of Sunday mornings. They, too, have discovered the magic of house fellowship. For example, Pastor Yonggi Cho, of the half-million-member Yoido Full Gospel Church in South Korea, gives credit to women-led cell groups for being the great source of growth in his humongous congregation. It is common for mega-churches to have thriving cell-group ministries in order to capture that early-church experience, which may signal a deep human need for more intimate worship settings.

But, we can only suppose, the amazing rock band performances with fog machines and awesome lights and hip videos won't be leaving Sunday morning worship anytime soon.

Notes

[1]Quotation from Justin Bieber taken from Olivia Waxman, "See the Strangest Quotes from Justin Bieber's Latest Interview," *Time*, 28 September 2015, located at: http://time.com/4052800/justin-bieber-complex-magazine-interview-taco-bell-church/.

[2]This phrase was made popular in the 1990s by the Church of Christ singing group AVB (Acapella Vocal Band). The song "U Can't Go 2 Church" was included on the 1991 album *What's Your Tag Say?*

[3]See the online version of the dictionary: http://www.oed.com/view/Entry/32760?rskey=RRPysT&result=1#eid.

[4]There is an extensive body of research on the etymology of *ekklesia*, although less has been done on the term *Kyriakos*, from which we get the word "church." See Roy Bowen Ward, "*Ekklesia: A Word Study*," in *Restoration Quarterly* 2:4 (1958). Ward writes that the word "church" "passed into the Gothic languages through the barbaric invasions, probably as *kirika*. From this comes the English *church*, the Scottish *Kirk*, the German *Kirche*, and other modern language derivations, including Slavonic forms."

[5]My friend and former colleague Rev. Michael Jones was pastor at the church (Trinity United) during the closure. In the aftermath of the events, he wrote a helpful book: *Empty Houses: A Pastoral Approach to Congregational Closures* (Charleston, SC: Booksurge, 2004).

[6]Mollie Ziegler Hemingway, "Twenty-First Century Excommunication," *The Wall Street Journal*, 7 October 2011, located at http://online.wsj.com/news/articles/SB10001424052970203476804576614932308302042?mg=reno64-sj&url=http%3A%2F%2Fonline.wsj.com%2Farticle%2FSB10001424052970203476804576614932308302042.html.

[7]Valerie Bauerlein, "Church Fight Heads to Court," *The Wall Street Journal*, 16 April 2013, located at http://online.wsj.com/news/articles/SB10001424127887324010704578418983895885100.

[8]See Everett Ferguson, *Backgrounds of Early Christianity*, 3rd Edition (Grand Rapids: Eerdmans, 2003), 244–245.

[9]See *The Instructor* 3:11 ("Going to Church"), located at http://www.newadvent.org/fathers/02093.htm. Translated by William Wilson; revised and edited for New Advent by Kevin Knight.

[10]See Deborah Amos and Alison Meuse, "Via Satellite, Tracking the Plunder of Middle East Cultural History," 11 March 2015, located at http://www.npr.org/sections/parallels/2015/03/10/392077801/via-satellite-tracking-the-plunder-of-middle-east-cultural-history. See also Andrew Curry, "Here Are the Ancient Sites ISIS Has Damaged and Destroyed," 1 September 2015, located at http://news.nationalgeographic.com/2015/09/150901-isis-destruction-looting-ancient-sites-iraq-syria-archaeology/.

[11]L. Michael White, "Dura-Europos," in *Encyclopedia of Early Christianity*, 2nd Edition, ed. Everett Ferguson (New York: Routledge, 1999), 353.

[12] Diarmaid MacCulloch, *Christianity: The First Three Thousand Years* (New York: Penguin, 2009), 179.

[13] See Yale University's online exhibition of Dura-Europos at http://artgallery .yale.edu/online-feature/dura-europos-excavating-antiquity.

[14] Everett Ferguson, *Early Christians Speak*, 3rd Edition (Abilene, TX: Abilene Christian University Press, 1999), 74.

[15] Additionally, another pagan emperor arose after Constantine: the despised Julian (AD 361–363), known to historians as Julian the Apostate. Julian tried to steer the Roman Empire away from its newfound embrace of Christianity and back toward its traditional panoply of gods and belief systems. It was too late, however. Christianity had already taken root.

[16] Paul Maier, *Eusebius: The Church History* (Grand Rapids: Kregel, 2007), 305.

[17] Ibid., 306.

[18] I am using Paul Maier's translation of Eusebius's careful recording of the Edict of Milan. See Maier, 322ff.

[19] Ibid., 323.

[20] Ibid., 327.

[21] Ibid.

[22] Ibid.

[23] Ramsay MacMullen, *Christianizing the Roman Empire: AD 100–400* (New Haven, CT: Yale University Press, 1984), 53.

[24] Ibid., 49.

[25] Ibid.

[26] My history of the Christian basilica comes from Robert Louis Wilken, *The First Thousand Years: A Global History of Christianity* (New Haven, CT: Yale University Press, 2012), 83–84, and 136–138.

[27] Ibid., 137.

[28] Ibid., 84.

[29] Ibid.

[30] A very good history of church architecture—a large book with full-page illustrations—is Edward Norman, *The House of God: Church Architecture, Style and History* (London: Thames and Hudson, 1990).

[31] See Robert Scott, *The Gothic Enterprise: A Guide to Understanding the Medieval Cathedral* (Berkeley: University of California Press, 2003).

[32] See Gregory Armstrong, "Ambo," in *Encyclopedia of Early Christianity*, 2nd Edition, 41.

[33] Diarmaid MacCulloch argues that the overhead sounding board did not arise until the sixteenth century. See his book *The Reformation: A History* (New York: Penguin, 2003), 327.

[34] Daniel Sahas, "Altar," in *Encyclopedia of Early Christianity*, 2nd Edition, 39.

[35] MacCulloch, *The Reformation*, 587.

[36] Ibid., 585.

[37] Ibid., 586.

[38] Ibid.

[39] Ibid., 587.

[40] Ibid., 588.

[41] Mark Noll, *The Old Religion in a New World* (Grand Rapids: Eerdmans, 2002), 98.

[42] Ibid., 97–98.

[43] See Bradley Griffin, "From Filth to Faith: Creating Holy Ground in New York's Five Points," *Ecumenica Journal* 2:1 (2009), 37–51.

[44] See Michael Mooney, "Why Joel Osteen Is the Most Popular Preacher on the Planet," *Success*, 11 January 2016, located at: http://www.success.com/article/why-joel-osteen-is-the-most-popular-preacher-on-the-planet.

[45] Norman, 289.

[46] See, for example, the Church of England's Council for the Care of Churches, "Seating in churches," April 2004, located at http://www.leicester.anglican.org/site-includes/uploads/wygwam/Seating.pdf.

[47] Chris Brooks and Andrew Saint, eds., *The Victorian Church: Architecture and Society* (Manchester, UK: Manchester University Press, 1995), 41.

[48] John Coke Fowler, *Church Pews, Their Origin and Legal Incidents* (London, UK: Francis and John Rivington, 1844), 7. This book is located at: http://anglicanhistory.org/misc/freechurch/fowler_pews1844.html.

[49] See Professor Barbara McManus's webpage for understanding the structure of the Greek theater: https://www2.cnr.edu/home/bmcmanus/tragedy_theater.html.

[50] See, for example, Jesse Coburn, "As German Church Becomes Mosque, Neighbors Start to Shed Unease," *New York Times*, 23 July 2015, located at: http://www.nytimes.com/2015/07/24/world/europe/as-german-church-becomes-mosque-neighbors-start-to-shed-unease.html?_r=0. See also the article by Daniel Greenfield, "Building an Islamic State in America, One Church at a Time," *Frontpage Mag*, 27 August 2015, located at: http://www.frontpagemag.com/fpm/259932/building-islamic-state-america-one-church-time-daniel-greenfield. I cannot endorse the alarmist tone of the article, but several of the examples cited therein are well-known.

Chapter 5

God's Managers
Bishops, Priests, and Pastors

"Why did the priesthood come into a religion that began without it and, indeed, opposed it?"[1]

—Garry Wills

In a scathing critique of the priesthood, Roman Catholic historian Garry Wills comes across as extremely bitter against his church, and, most notably, against the priesthood. According to everyone who knows him, however, Wills is a faithful Catholic. In his book *Why I Am a Catholic*, he writes, "I am a born Catholic. I have never stopped going to Mass, saying the rosary, studying the Gospels. I have never even considered leaving the church. I would lose my faith in God before losing my faith in it."[2] If Wills is so devoted to his Catholic faith, what caused him to write the 2013 book *Why Priests? A Failed Tradition*? This opened up a huge can of worms and spawned within the Roman Catholic Church some uncomfortable conversations that continue to the present.

Gary Wills is not some obscure, disgruntled yahoo. He holds a PhD from Yale in the Classics, he won a Pulitzer Prize in 1993 for his work on President Lincoln, and he has authored about forty substantive books and countless articles. Respected Catholic journalist John Allen Jr., describes him in the highest of terms:

> ... perhaps the most distinguished Catholic intellectual
> in America over the last 50 years ... one of the most fas-
> cinating personalities American Catholicism has ever
> produced ... one of America's most distinguished non-
> fiction writers, period. .... Wills is regarded as America's
> premier presidential historian, with acclaimed studies
> of Washington, Jefferson, Madison, Lincoln, Kennedy,
> and Nixon. .... Wills is also an accomplished expert on
> antiquity. .... Yet this consummate intellectual is also
> one of the country's most acclaimed reporters, with
> a keen eye for detail and a knack for being where the
> action is.[3]

He's a true renaissance man, a dying breed in an age of academic specialization.

For all of his popular appeal, Wills remains a committed Catholic, praying the rosary and attending Mass with dogged commitment. However, there is no blind sentimentality within him. His eyes are wide open, and he has been among his church's fiercest critics. His willingness to critique what many perceive to be a corrupt institution has made him highly popular among secularists. It is said that this precocious Catholic boy from Atlanta "took the secular world by storm."[4] Yet he remained religious, making him something of a paradox.

A Catholic Broadside

Wills's critiques are relentless and unabashed. He clearly loves the many priests with whom he has worked and worshiped throughout his life. So why question their legitimacy? His answer is this: "It is not a personal issue but a historical one." When his critics argue that apostolic succession and the real presence of Christ in the Eucharist would not be legitimate without the priest, he scoffs, pointing out that both of these teachings are unbiblical and completely unnecessary. He does not want priests in the Catholic Church:

> Some think that the dwindling number of priests can be remedied by the addition of women priests, or married priests, or openly gay priests. In fact, the real solution is: no priests. It should not be difficult to imagine a Christianity without priests. Read carefully through the entire New Testament and you will not find an individual human priest mentioned in the Christian communities. Only one book of the New Testament, the Letter to Hebrews, mentions an individual priest, and he is unique—Jesus. He has no followers in that office, according to the Letter.[5]

Wills spills the beans on the anti-Protestant bias that exists—albeit usually pretty quiet—within the Catholic Church. He was taught that Protestants simply want their "ears tickled" instead of focusing on the mystery of the real presence of Christ in the Eucharist. The Catholic bias is not just against Protestants, however. It is against non-Catholic priests in general, including Eastern Orthodox ones.

Not only does Wills lambast the institution of the priesthood; he goes to the very heart of the Catholic faith with his critique of the papacy—that most sacred Catholic institution. Wills launches scathing criticism against the whole notion of Peter being the first Pope:

> There is no historical evidence for Peter being bishop anywhere—least of all at Rome, where the office of bishop did not exist in the first century CE . . . the linear "apostolic succession" is a chain of historical fabrications. . . . Even if we grant the Roman myths, and say

> that the Catholic priesthood is valid, how is it Christian
> to make that priesthood a means for excluding all
> Christians but Roman Catholics?[6]

According to Wills, Jesus was a "biting critic of the priests of his day," and if people studied the historical record, they would see that the vast institution of the priesthood is really a house built of cards.[7]

Sounding like anything but a devout Catholic, Wills is most strident against the notion of the supposed priestly "ability to change bread and wine into the body and blood of Jesus Christ."[8] Catholic teaching holds that priests are able to perform this miracle with regularity. A priest must be present for the miracle of transubstantiation to occur. A congregation of committed disciples cannot do it; the priest is the only one with this power. As Thomas Aquinas—the Catholic Church's chief theological architect—reasoned, "A priest is established as the mediator between God and the people. A person who stands in need of a mediator with God cannot approach him on his own."[9] According to Wills, this is profoundly unChristian. The Bible, rather, tells us: "There is one God and one mediator between God and mankind, the man Christ Jesus, who gave himself as a ransom for all people" (1 Tim. 2:5). Similarly, in Hebrews 9:15, "For this reason Christ is the mediator of a new covenant, that those who are called may receive the promised eternal inheritance."

In some parts of his book, Wills comes across as a man extremely angry at the institution of the priesthood. In one chapter, he provides several examples of bad priests. He states that since priests have no family of their own, they often befriend members of the church, and some of them abuse the relationship. One priest he knew often came to his house to watch television and would tell the children to be silent so as not to disturb him. This same priest would critique Wills's wife for not cooking beef. After a while, she withdrew the offer to cook for him and, instead, they would take him out for pizza. Later, after they had cut ties with this priest, Wills and his wife considered themselves lucky that he did not extend his hedonism to their children. "As we know from many victims' stories, some priests who molested children got access to them by befriending and visiting their parents on a regular basis, using a surrogate family as a stalking horse for designs on its children."[10] Unfortunately, far too many people were betrayed by that relationship that was supposed to be one of a holy mediator between God and people.

Wills also recounts priests routinely getting out of parking and speeding tickets. Priests are able to cut in line, especially at the golf course. They are happy to receive extravagant gifts from wealthy members of the church, such as luxury cars and in many cases over-the-top residences. Throughout his years, Wills has become more appreciative of Jesus's warnings that his followers should not strive for pre-eminence: "Anyone who wants to be first must be the very last, and the servant of all" (Mark 9:35). Jesus also warned his disciples that they should take no gold or silver with them during their travels, not even an extra pair of sandals or an extra tunic (Matt. 10:9–10). Rather, they were to avoid luxury, and they were most certainly expected to avoid wealth, since "it is hard for a rich man to enter the kingdom of heaven"; indeed, it is "easier for a camel to go through the eye of a needle" (Matt. 19:23–24). Wills then cuts to the chase: "Saint Peter's Basilica and the Vatican Palace cannot claim true descent from that pair of sandals and that single tunic."[11]

Protestant Protests

Catholics do not have the market cornered when it comes to critiquing their leadership. I was raised a Protestant, and I've always known that "having the preacher for lunch" did not necessarily mean he was coming over to eat. Protestants can be every bit as acerbic when it comes to picking apart the pastor, and especially his sermon, during the Sunday lunch hour. However, truth be told, there is nothing shocking about Protestants criticizing their pastors. Catholics are not prone to do this. For Protestants, however, it's in our DNA. We protest. That's why they named us "Protestants." We have always protested, from Luther until now, and we always will.

George Barna, founder of the Christian think-tank The Barna Group, is but one Protestant who has deep misgivings with the way Protestantism has elevated the role of the pastor. Touted by *Christianity Today* as being Evangelicalism's "most-quoted statistician," Barna's opinions matter to a large proportion of the United States' Protestants.[12] And, like Wills, he is disturbed by what the office of the Christian pastor has evolved into. In his co-authored book *Pagan Christianity?* he unleashes a critique similar to that of Wills.[13]

Pagan Christianity? is caustic in its criticism. Almost nothing escapes the notice of Barna and his co-author, Frank Viola. In their view, we Christians have got it all wrong. We don't follow the Bible at all; rather, we have substituted the practices of the early Christians with worldly things geared to entertain and to bring us comfort and self-satisfaction. Their plea is that we start doing Christianity "by the book" rather than by the pagan practices that have crept in over two millennia.

Frankly, I found the book to be scorching and overly bitter in places, no holds barred, often unfair. In the view of the authors, our Sunday morning sermons are oratory performances borrowed more from Greek culture than from the New Testament. They claim our penchant for dressing up on Sundays is absolutely at odds with clear New Testament teaching, aimed more at impressing each other than pleasing God. Our endless positions—from Chief Executive Pastors to Music Ministers to Youth Coordinators to Sound Technicians—are all unbiblical. We borrow our models of leadership from the business world, even to the point of using labels like CFO and Senior Associate in the titles we use to describe our ministers. Whereas the Bible exalted the humble, often declaring the ministers as being *diakonos*, or "deacons," a term that literally means "servants," we have turned the leadership of our churches into a corporate ladder with embarrassingly large salaries and lucrative benefits. We've professionalized the ministry— end-of-year bonuses, financial incentives, retirement portfolios, unbridled authority, staff performance reviews—to the point that it is beyond recognition. The New Testament leaders gave freely of themselves without counting the cost. No sabbaticals or furloughs. No salaries. Ministry was sacrificial. Other-worldly. More fasting than feasting. We've got this all backwards now.

Brutal. Embarrassing. Don't let the non-Christian world read this stuff. Definitely painful reading . . . especially for those of us who have spent our lives in the church and know that at least some of the criticism is spot on. While Protestants might hate to admit it, at least some of these critiques actually resonate with most of us.

In the chapter on pastors—the longest in the book—Barna and Viola refer to the church minister as an "obstacle." He gets in the way. Rather than encouraging an egalitarian model where every member functions as a minister, the pastor has hijacked the system by claiming to be "the" minister. Our pastors have somehow undermined the notion of the priesthood of all believers, which is so fundamental to the New Testament model. Sometimes the Barna-Viola critique hits below the belt:

> [Ephesians 4:11] is the only verse in the entire New
> Testament where the word *pastor* is used. One solitary
> verse is a mighty scanty piece of evidence on which to
> hang the Protestant faith! In this regard, there seems to
> be more biblical authority for snake handling than there
> is for the present-day pastor. Roman Catholics have
> made the same error with the word *priest*. You can find

the word *priest* used in the New Testament three times. In every case, it refers to all Christians.[14]

They conclude that we have turned this solitary mention of a pastor—basically a shepherd—into the Chief Executive Officer of the local assembly of believers. And we pay a punishing price for this costly mistake.

In the view of Barna and Viola, the leadership within Christianity became politicized early on. Eventually two classes of people developed: clergy and laity. The "office" of the bishop was fixed by the mid-third century.[15] Constantine came along in the fourth century and elevated the role of the bishop and showered bishops with ample salaries in order to maintain control over his unruly empire. In order to safeguard this holy club, the elites developed a system of legitimization called "apostolic succession."

In other words, someone could not become a priest or pastor without members of "the system" allowing them to. It was cronyism at its best. "Ordination" became a highly nepotistic enterprise. The leadership of the church favored certain families in order to keep the reins tightly in their own hands. In some cases, even Popes—supposedly celibate—had their own sons succeed them in the papal palaces. Around the year 1000, celibacy became mandatory for priests so that church property could not be passed on within families. Rather, it stayed in the possession of the church. And the church benefited tremendously from this arrangement. The wives of those priests who were suddenly forced to become "celibate" became divorcees, illegitimates with tremendous shame to bear.[16]

The Protestants offered few improvements. Luther and Calvin argued for the priesthood of all believers, but clearly they ruled the roost, even to the point of authorizing the ejection and even the death of those who challenged their leadership or teachings.

In our modern era, the world of Christian psychology has turned the pastor into not only a minister who preaches and teaches, but a counselor who provides care and healing to an entire congregation.[17] All of these things are now part of the pastor's job description, in addition to running his church, as an entrepreneur would run a local business.

In all fairness, Barna and Viola do not lay blame exclusively at the feet of the gatekeepers and pastors. The people are largely to blame, too, for perpetuating an unbiblical system. And pastors are as damaged as everyone else due to this impossible job description. Barna provides statistics showing just how burned out pastors routinely become. Nearly 100 percent of pastors feel pressure to have a perfect family. Around 70 percent of them claim to have no close friends. About 80 percent of them are depressed or discouraged in their job. The pastorate has become a revolving door, as the average tenure in a particular congregation is only four years long.[18]

Their final indictment is that we in the church, those of us who have perpetuated this system, have got what we asked for, because

> Jesus Christ never intended any person to sport all
> the hats a present-day pastor is expected to wear. He
> never intended any one person to bear such a load. The
> demands of the pastorate are crushing; they will drain
> any mortal dry. . . . The pastoral profession dictates . . .
> how pastors are to dress, speak, and act. This is one of
> the major reasons why many pastors live very artificial
> lives. In this regard, the pastoral role fosters dishonesty.[19]

After reading this section of the book, one has to ask why anyone would go into professional ministry at all. Indeed, according to Barna and Viola, it is hazardous to one's health.

A Personal Digression

Before delving into the history of the priest and pastor, I should pause for a moment to show my cards. For twenty-two years I was a pastor, preacher, minister—call it what you will. I served congregations in Texas, Alberta, and California. I experienced all of the highs and lows that come with the territory. From driving a vanload of kids to play "capture the flag," to preparing three or four Bible lessons per week, to holding the hand of a church member who was soon to depart this earth, I wore all of the hats that come with the position.

And it was an honor. Performing weddings. Baptizing a couple's child. Being asked to lead funeral ceremonies. Counseling a marriage that was on the rocks. Visiting a family with a new baby in the hospital. Pastors are given a tremendous amount of trust by their church members. Whether one agrees with the existence of such a position or not, it is an honor to serve people in this regard. In very few other professions does a person receive such a fair hearing as he or she does in the ministry. When the pastor speaks, the people truly listen.

I would not say that all pastors hold tremendous *power*. I think power is the wrong word. Perhaps it would be more appropriate to say *confidence*. At the root of the word, confidence is two Latin words: *con fide*, or, "with faith." People almost automatically trust their pastor. They allow him into their lives and homes. They listen to what the pastor has to say. And they listen to him often. Our faith is shaped profoundly by our pastors. The Christian faith is in many ways passed down through the pastors. They are the keepers of the keys, the ones who stoke the fires throughout the ages, the ones who preserve the treasury of faith that has been built up from centuries before.

I have no axe to grind against pastors. None whatsoever. I side with them. I see myself as one among their ranks. I spent years in universities preparing to be a pastor. I took the tests, put in the time, wrote the papers, fulfilled the internships, pored over the Scriptures, learned the foreign languages, and faithfully drove to the church and took my place in the assembly, day after day, year after year.

And while I do have misgivings about the origins of the pastor and how this role came to be what it is, I cannot say with any certainty that it is an institution that should go away. Like any American Christian, I have been deeply saddened by the sex-abuse scandals both in the Catholic and Protestant churches. Trust has been betrayed on a level most of us will never fully comprehend. I have watched the occasional pastor who has virtual control over his flock, treating it as if it were his own little tribe and he is the chief. Like most others, I wince when I turn the channel to pompous television ministers who seem so divorced from reality, begging for money, living extravagantly, parading on television as if they were celebrities. These are the stories that grab our attention. "If it bleeds, it leads," they say in the world of newspaper publishing. The shocking and hyperbolic stories about pastors—and their sins—are the only ones we hear about. The mansions. The affairs. The private jets. The fiascos. We hear about these leaders and wonder whether they are from God or the devil. Who could harm a child so callously? Who could fleece a group of people in such a way? Who else could get away with that kind of behavior for so long? On national television!

But I am convinced those stories are relatively rare. I know many pastors, and they are good men and women. They were pulled into ministry not because of egos that needed to be stroked each Sunday. They went into ministry because they felt it was a place where they could make a difference. Ministers are among the most self-sacrificial people I have ever known. People call on them constantly, and they don't complain. They get criticized but are not allowed to criticize in return. (That would be un-Christlike.) They went into this business first and foremost because they love God. They had a spiritual encounter at some point in their lives and found it to be immensely helpful in turning their own lives around. And so they go into ministry wanting to offer the same help and care that they probably received from other good and kind pastors along the way.

For all the talk about pastors' shortcomings, what about the encouragement notes they wrote, or the sacks of food they delivered, or the late-night phone conversations they had, or the endless hospital visits? Unfortunately none of that stuff makes the headlines. We *expect* that from pastors. The reason the juicy stories grab our attention is because we never expected those things to occur for a man or woman "of the cloth." They are above that. And it's interesting to see them fail once in a while, to fall short of their calling.

I went into ministry because my life fell apart, and it was the church and its servants who helped me up. My grandfather, a preacher for nearly seven decades, was always there for me, always believing in me. When my life sank to very low depths, it was my preacher—in that little church in eastern New Mexico—who met with me and encouraged me to keep moving forward. It was my preacher—his name was Larry Foster—who realized that I might thrive at a Christian university. It was that small-town preacher with a huge heart who believed enough in me to write me encouraging letters while I was studying at college.

I shudder to think what might have happened to me had my grandfather and Larry Foster not taken the time to get me back on my feet again. I must admit I was not the easiest person to mentor at that time in my life. At times I was a brat. But they overlooked those issues. They realized the ignorance of my youth and helped me to envision a future for my life at a time when I had little hope. Their investment in me was inexplicable. I had nothing to offer in return. I was in receiving mode. They gave to me freely in spite of the fact that I was in no position to give back. I stand forever in their debt.

I have a lot invested in the contents of this chapter. I *understand* the role of a church pastor, from both sides. And while I do have some concerns about the role of pastor and what it has evolved into, I will forever respect the position. I certainly have empathy for the people who have been burned by pastors. I have visited with people who have been subjected to abuse. I have utmost respect for people who were hurt deeply by pastors, yet still manage to keep their Christian faith.

I can even sympathize with those people who were so affected that they left the Christian religion altogether. I was once at a conference when a man found out that I taught church history, and he proceeded to tell me about the abuse he suffered at the hands of a Catholic priest. We were standing in the buffet line filling our plates with food. It occurred to me that this man was wounded and simply could not keep this pain to himself.

Garry Wills and George Barna envision a priestless, pastorless Christianity. My gut instinct is that priests and pastors will always be a central part of the church. We can quibble about Greek words and what they mean, but every group of people needs a leader, a gifted person who is respected by the people. No gathering can function with any semblance of order without a person willing to stand and lead. It makes little sense to have an assembly without someone who will stick his or her neck out and take charge. No business can run that way, no family, no non-profit organization, no court, and no nation. We need leaders, and as the Bible states, those "who direct the affairs of the church well are worthy of double honor, especially those whose work is preaching and teaching" (1 Tim. 5:17). Thus, while I am deeply aware of the bad and the ugly that goes on in ministry, I still have great hope that they are outweighed by those who are righteous and by the many good deeds that come from their godly lives.

The Biblical Era of Church Leadership

The term "clergy" actually comes from the Greek word *kleros*. Historically, that word meant "lot"—either a parcel of land, or a token used in order to "cast lots." It is unclear how the Greek term crossed over into meaning "clergy," that class of people who hold leading positions in the church. What we do know is that many of the church fathers such as Clement of Alexandria (AD 150–215) used the term with regularity, and it has been in the Christian vocabulary ever since.[20] Some historians have argued that the term "clergy" later evolved to mean "the elected ones" or had the connotation of being chosen.[21] This later understanding makes sense, based on that ancient practice of "casting lots"—meaning that someone was chosen by divine or supernatural means.

A distinction between clergy and laity is rooted in the Bible. There is no need to go into the distinction between the priests (Levites) and the non-priests in the Old Testament, but that is not completely irrelevant to the topic, since a priestly caste developed early on in church history. Nevertheless, it is clear from the New Testament that during the ministry of Paul certain categories began to emerge—whether we call them clergy, ordained individuals, or church officials. They were leaders who were sanctioned by apostolic authority to have specific roles in the church. Everybody else was part of the "laity," which comes from the Greek word *laos*, which simply means "people."

We can take a quick survey here of some of the most formative passages that shed light on the so-called "offices" of the New Testament church. In some cases, I have provided the Greek term used, although using the English alphabet. I have done this because in some cases the Greek term is still used in churches, for example in the case of "overseers," which is a simple and straightforward translation of the Greek words *epi* (over) and *scopos* (to see). Some churches, however, choose to use the actual Greek word. Take, for example, the Episcopal Church. Translated literally, that would be

"The Overseer Church." This is not uncommon in church parlance. For example, baptism, Eucharist, apostles, and amen are among the many words that have been brought over from the Greek (even Hebrew) text into English without much change.

In Acts 14:23, we are told that "Paul and Barnabas appointed elders [*presbuterous*] for them in each church and, with prayer and fasting, committed them to the Lord, in whom they had put their trust."

In Acts 20:28, Paul gives the following directives to the leaders of the church in Ephesus: "Keep watch over yourselves and all the flock of which the Holy Spirit has made you overseers [*episcopous*]. Be shepherds [*poimainein*] of the church of God, which he bought with his own blood." It is important to point out that whereas in Acts 14 *Paul and Barnabas* did the appointing, here in Acts 20 Paul says it was *the Holy Spirit* who gave these individuals their authority.

Ephesians 4:11 reads: "So Christ himself gave the apostles [*apostolous*], the prophets [*prophetas*], the evangelists [*euangelistas*], the pastors [*poimenas*] and teachers [*didaskalous*], to equip his people for works of service." Notice that in this case we are told that *Christ himself* provided these positions for the church.

In Philippians 1:1, Paul addresses his letter, "To all God's holy people in Christ Jesus at Philippi, together with the overseers [*episcopois*] and deacons [*diakonois*]." This passage seems to suggest a clerical class as opposed to a lay class. Otherwise, why wouldn't Paul simply address the letter to the Christians at Philippi?

In 1 Timothy 3—a crucial chapter in the New Testament for understanding church leadership—Paul lays out the qualities that should be exemplified in the lives of overseers [*episcopeis*] and deacons [*diakonous*, or "servants"]. Again, it is clear that Paul is advocating a certain class of people: overseers and deacons to lead the church. In both cases, Paul emphasizes that the candidate for either overseer or deacon should be well-known for his integrity and effectiveness as a family man. In both cases, Paul explicitly mentions that the person should "manage his own family well and see that his children obey him," and he must be "faithful to his wife." Paul also mentions, explicitly, that neither overseers nor deacons should "indulge in much wine," indicating that drunkenness may have been a problem in the church. Paul emphasizes that these men are to be well-respected Christians, not recent converts. They should be "trustworthy in everything." They should be "gentle" men, not quarrelsome. And they should not be "lovers of money."

In 1 Timothy 4:14, Paul lays down the foundation for what has become known as the rite of "ordination" in the history of Christianity. He writes, "Do not neglect your gift, which was given you through prophecy when the body of elders [*presbuteriou*] laid their hands on you." Incidentally, the word "presbytery"—as in the Presbyterian Church—comes from this word, and it is usually translated into English as "elder."

However, Catholics and Eastern Orthodox Christians understand the term *presbyteros* to mean "priest." The word "priest" has its origins in the Greek word *presbyteros*, but it came down to English through other, much older languages such as Old Icelandic, Old Swedish, Old English, Old Dutch, and Old High German. Different variations on the word were "priast," "preost," "priester," and the Latin words *prester* and *prevost*. In most Christian traditions, the notion of "laying on of hands" is still closely linked to the legitimization of a candidate for formal ministry. A person is duly "ordained" whenever others in higher authority put their hands on an individual in a sacred and consecrated setting.

In 2 Timothy 4:5, Paul wrote to Timothy, "Keep your head in all situations, endure hardship, do the work of an evangelist, discharge all the duties of your ministry." This passage, as in Ephesians 4:11, seems to indicate that Timothy would have understood what Paul meant by the "duties" of an evangelist. Some churches continue to use "evangelist" as the preferred term for their minister.

One question that comes up in church history is whether the evangelist had authority over the eldership (presbytery) or whether the eldership had authority over the evangelist. There is no clear consensus, but either interpretation can be supported in the New Testament. In some cases, we see Paul and Barnabas serving as evangelists while establishing elderships. This also seems to be true in the case of Timothy; one gets the sense that Paul is instructing Timothy in how to select elders and deacons. There seems to be a certain authority that Paul has invested into Timothy, for example, when he tells him: "Command and teach these things. Don't let anyone look down on you because you are young. . . . The body of elders laid their hands on you" (1 Tim. 4:11–14). On the other hand, the elders seem to be the decision-makers in the churches. It is possible that the biblical evangelists had a unique and apostolic authority invested into them by the apostles, and that this authority petered out as the first and second generations of evangelists passed away.

In Titus 1:5–9, another letter from Paul to a younger evangelist, Paul directs Titus to "appoint elders in every town." Again, we have an example of an evangelist having authority over the eldership, at least in the sense that he is able to appoint—and presumably dismiss—elders. Another interesting aspect of this passage is that Paul employs both words—*presbyterous* as well as *episcopon*—in the same context, clearly using them interchangeably. In this sense, an elder is the same person as an overseer.

We should here introduce that English word "bishop." The word comes from the Greek word *episcopos*, which is literally translated "over-seer." In Old English, the word became "piscop" or "bisceop." Thus, the English word *bishop* is clearly rooted in the pronunciation of the word *e-piscop-os*. Older churches such as the Roman Catholic and Orthodox families prefer to use the English word *bishop* to refer to this position, whereas low-church traditions and non-hierarchical groups tend to prefer the term "elders" or in some cases "overseers."

Before moving on to the next section, we should draw attention to that interesting passage in Romans 16:1 which reads, "I commend to you our sister Phoebe, a deacon of the church in Cenchreae." This has given rise to debates in Christian history about whether the role of deacon could be fulfilled by a woman. Deacons were commissioned to do many different tasks in the New Testament church. Everett Ferguson defines them as "the assistants of spiritual leaders in the church, performing various services on behalf of the people." In later church history, the position evolved and had many more responsibilities, such as distributing the Eucharist, assisting during the liturgy, acting as ushers, administering the benevolence on behalf of the church, ministering to those in prison, and burying the dead, among many other duties. The deacons were the "eyes and ears of the bishop," and they were often called upon to serve in the role of bishop once they had been tested and approved. In fact, Ferguson writes, "Bishops were more often chosen from the ranks of the diaconate than from the presbyterate."[22]

However, could a woman serve in this role? They certainly did, at many times in church history, including very early on. Around the year AD 112, a Roman governor named Pliny the Younger wrote a letter to the Emperor Trajan asking about how he should deal with Christians. In that famous letter—probably the earliest surviving document about Christians that we have from a non-Christian perspective—Pliny refers to two female deaconesses with the following words: "Accordingly, I judged it all the more necessary to find out what the truth was by torturing two female slaves who were called deaconesses. But I discovered nothing else but depraved, excessive superstition."[23] Extensive information about deaconesses comes in the third century, and we learn that while they did not perform baptisms, they did assist in baptisms, particularly in the case of females, since they removed all their clothing for the sacrament and received the oil of anointing.

Deaconesses did not normally teach men, but they did provide post-baptismal instruction to other women. In some places, the deaconess was required to be a virgin or a widow. The Council of Chalcedon (AD 451) set the minimum age of a deaconess at forty, and they were forbidden to marry after the appointment. As believer's baptism declined in Christianity, the role of the deaconess likewise declined, since this primary duty of the deaconess was no longer necessary. Deaconesses persisted longer in the East, but as the position of deacon morphed into a preparation ground for the priesthood, the need for the office of the deaconess was diminished.[24]

The Evolution of Church Leadership in the Church Fathers

As we have highlighted in previous chapters, a key document for our understanding here is the *Didache*, also known as "The Teaching of the Lord Given to the Gentiles by the Twelve Apostles."[25] The *Didache* is such a vital text because it provides us with a noncanonical window into the church in the period just after the apostolic era, perhaps as early as AD 70. It is a document that "presents a church still in close proximity to Judaism and still developing its distinctive institutions." It was "highly valued in the early church."[26]

Describing leadership in the churches, the *Didache* presents four positions: apostles, prophets, overseers (*episcopous*), and deacons. We must be quick to point out here, however, that these are not fixed offices; they often bleed into one another. The *Didache* uses them interchangeably. Those who imagine a static hierarchy in the early church will have to look elsewhere, at later texts.

The most detailed discussion in the *Didache* pertains to the prophet, which was a position that we might label as itinerant preacher. He was a man who traveled around, preaching and teaching in the churches. Sometimes he remained in a place for a fairly substantial amount of time, but sometimes he might move on after a short stay.

The *Didache* privileges these prophets and apostles who participate in the ministry of teaching. However, these individuals were not minor dictators, since the church members themselves were to watch and listen carefully in order to make a judgment on them. If a teacher's conduct and teaching matched that of the apostles, then he was to be respected, and all were to "welcome him as [they] would the Lord." If he "wandered from the right path" in either teaching or lifestyle, then he was to be ignored.[27] In the *Didache*, an unmistakable egalitarianism can be seen in the church leadership, a relational quality that petered out in the first few centuries of the Christian faith in favor of hierarchy.

But teachers were worthy of great respect indeed, if they were deemed to be worthy. The *Didache* commands, "Every apostle who arrives among you is to be welcomed as if he were the Lord."[28] By the word "apostle," the authors of the *Didache* obviously had in mind people other than the Twelve. In its most literal sense, the term simply meant "someone who is sent." However, in this case it was obviously someone who was sent with authority. He was representing the authority of the apostles themselves.

In the first and second centuries, an apostle was often understood as being a missionary, sent out to spread the gospel. Irenaeus, an important second-century church father, refers to the seventy disciples [Luke 10; some manuscripts specify seventy-two] sent out by Jesus as being apostles.[29] Some of the church fathers referred to the associates of the Twelve and of Paul as being "apostolic," an obvious attempt to elevate their authority above that of the ordinary church member. While the term was applied with relative liberality, it was clear by the beginning of the second century that "apostles were often spoken of as belonging to the past."[30]

If we understand the *Didache* to mean "missionaries" when it uses the words "apostles" and "prophets," then the text makes good sense. In one place, the text records the following:

> Every apostle who arrives among you is to be welcomed as if he were the Lord. But normally he must not stay with you for more than one day, but he may stay a second day if this is necessary. However, if he stays a third day, then he is a false prophet! When he leaves you, an apostle must receive nothing except enough food to sustain him until the next night's lodgings. However, if he asks for money, then he is a false prophet![31]

The text comes down pretty hard on these traveling preachers, or missionaries. They were carefully scrutinized. The world portrayed is not the one of "apostolic succession" that developed later, one where priests and bishops are esteemed by the nature of their office. Rather, in the *Didache* we see something closer to a house-church movement where people are more or less equal, and teachers are worthy of special treatment only if they are judged to be authentic.

The *Didache* urges the congregations to watch these traveling "apostles" or "prophets" to make sure that "they follow the Way of the Lord." They are not to indulge in banquet food. If the itinerant minister does so, then "he is a false prophet." If this traveling apostle says, "Give me money—or anything like that," then "you should not listen to that man."[32] Ouch. Many of the televangelists of our day would not pass that test.

Again, the egalitarian ethos in the church should be pointed out here. The *Didache* gives tremendous latitude to the congregation in judging the credibility of a traveling minister: "Now anyone coming in the Lord's name should be made welcome; then you can test him, using your own insight to see if he is genuine or a fraud."[33] If the man is simply passing through, then he should be shown hospitality, but only for two or three days. If he decides to settle down in the community, then he must be able to work and provide for himself because "he is not to live in idleness."[34] One cannot help but to think of Paul's command that "the one who is unwilling to work shall not eat" (2 Thes. 3:10). The *Didache* has a strong word for the itinerant minister who breaks any of these rules: "He is a Christ-monger [or, Christ-peddler]. Be on the watch for such people."[35] Clearly, there was still a sense of "people power" at this stage of development in what we now call the "clergy."

If, however, a "true prophet" settled in a community, then he was to be given special honor. Indeed, he was to be given the "first fruits" since he was "worthy of his food."[36] Thus, teachers and preachers of the gospel were not to be overly scrutinized once they proved their genuine faith. They were to be respected. However, they were not to be left alone to lead the church as an autocrat would do. The church was clearly a team, and the teacher played a critical role. The sacerdotalism that began to develop in the second century eroded this sense of equal fellowship, creating a professional clerical class that dominated right up until modern times. One could say that the egalitarian house-church movement of recent years is an attempt to re-capture that profound sense of fellowship and equality on display in the *Didache*.

The other two offices mentioned in the *Didache* are elders (literally: *episcopous*, a term interpreted in Roman Catholic and Orthodox traditions as meaning "bishops") and deacons. The descriptions are straightforward, inspired obviously by the Pastoral Epistles:

> Select for yourselves bishops [*episcopous*, or, literally,
> "overseers"] and deacons: men who are worthy of the
> Lord, humble, not greedy for money, honest, and well
> tested, because these too carry out for you the service
> of the prophets and teachers. Therefore, you should not

despise them but treat them as your honored men like
the prophets and teachers.[37]

Again, what we see here is not a dictatorial class. Rather, this is a
leadership that has been tested and approved by the people.

It is notable that the *Didache* seems to blend the roles of prophets, teachers, overseers (or, bishops), deacons, and apostles. The
distinct offices that came to define the medieval church were still
developing. The terms for ministerial leadership are almost inter-
changeable in the *Didache*. It appears that a leader was not defined
by a specific office; rather, he was defined by the ministry that he
carried out. In other words, a man who was rooted in a congregation and had earned the trust of the people quite naturally came
to be understood as an overseer. A man who conducted himself
as a servant of Christ was simply known as a "servant"—or, literally, a deacon.

So who was in charge in the first-century church? Obviously
the original apostles conducted themselves with authority, and the
community followed their lead. And somehow James—the brother
of Jesus—and Paul were allowed to that high altar of leadership.
But after them it becomes less clear. The *Didache* uses several leadership terms interchangeably, and within a couple of centuries we
see the rise of very powerful and authoritative bishops—a group of
leaders who essentially governed the churches. In time, the bishops of the largest and most important cities became known as the
patriarchs. The bishops of Antioch, Alexandria, and Rome became
especially revered. Soon added to them was Jerusalem—being the
mother church and homeland of Jesus. And later the list included
Constantinople, or, New Rome.

But what happened before all of that? How did the church
maintain a sense of structure and unity in the first two or three centuries? These are very difficult questions to answer, and scholars

have devoted unbelievable amounts of work to the task of answering them.

What can be said is this: it was not a simple picture. Clearly, the world of the first and second century was not extremely well-connected, as we understand it today. One of the marvelous aspects of Paul's ministry was that he was able to travel so far and wide without losing his life. Indeed, we are told by him that he nearly died numerous times. Christians can only assume that God had a plan in keeping him alive through all of the shipwrecks, illnesses, beatings, and injuries (2 Cor. 11:23ff).

Paul did whatever he could to try to be a unifying force through his visits, his letters, and his ordaining of like-minded people (like Timothy and Titus) to carry on the work in local contexts. However, as the church grew, this became an impossible task. Different kinds of Christian traditions developed. It was not unlike what we have today: charismatics, ascetics, rich and poor churches, Gnostics, Jewish-Christian communities, and some rather academic Christians. Some of the churches were surprisingly immature, while others were praised for their faithfulness.

As Christianity spread—and it did spread rapidly—it diversified. Soon there was no possible way to keep all the churches on the same page. This is the primary reason Constantine called the Council of Nicaea in AD 325. He wanted to bring the Christian leaders together to sort out what Christianity is. What are the core beliefs? How are Christians to conduct their public worship? Who is to be admitted into the ranks of the clergy? Who is to be excommunicated from the faith? Who should touch the Eucharist first— the deacons or the elders? (Yes, this question was hotly debated, and the conclusion was that deacons must "remain within their own bounds, knowing that they are the ministers of the bishop and the inferiors of the presbyters.")[38]

The point here is that the Christians of the first few centuries did not conduct their affairs in a systematic way. They were scattered about, living under different governments. Their beliefs and practices varied widely from place to place. In the fifth century, at the councils of Ephesus (AD 431) and Chalcedon (AD 451), the church began to split formally. "Nestorians" and others—such as the illustrious Armenian Church—were no longer considered in fellowship with the larger body of churches.

The Orthodox and Catholic notions of a "priesthood" and of "apostolic succession" developed fairly early in Christian history, for obvious reasons. How should the authority and integrity of church teaching be maintained in a ragtag situation where Christian doctrine was still in an embryonic state? Several church fathers came to the rescue here and tried to systematize Christianity in a way that bequeathed a system of checks and balances to the churches.

Clement of Rome—a church father in the late first century—makes parallels between Christian ministry and the Old Testament priestly services. However, the connection is only analogical and not a pattern by any means. By the third century, however, the Old Testament priesthood was regularly invoked as an archetype for Christian leadership. Cyprian (AD 200–258) was one of the important church fathers who made this connection between the Levitical priesthood and the Christian church. By that time, the understanding of a clergy maintaining charge over Christianity was fixed, and this pattern remained well into the modern era. Indeed, it is still prominent.

With great effectiveness, Catholics, Orthodox, and most Protestant denominations still use an ordained, officially licensed clergy to run the affairs of the church. The egalitarianism of the earliest decades is gone—if it ever was strong in the first place. This longstanding question—whether there was ever an egalitarian, consensus-based approach to church leadership—is vigorously debated. There are those who believe a system of ordination and succession is necessary, and there are those few (globally very few) who prefer a local, community-based leadership model that they believe pervades the New Testament era.

What happened between Clement of Rome at the end of the first century and Cyprian at the beginning of the third? The short version is that the church felt it needed to safeguard its teachings; therefore it needed to carefully monitor the legitimacy of the clergy. Already in the New Testament—seen clearly in the epistles—pretenders with evil motives were invading the churches and taking charge. John's epistles are particularly hard on these guys. He calls them "antichrists." He accuses them of being "counterfeits." They deny the incarnation of Christ. They are "false prophets." John even names one of these men in his third epistle: "Diotrephes, who loves to be first. . . . I will call attention to what he is doing, spreading malicious nonsense about us. . . . He even refuses to welcome other believers. He also stops those who want to do so and puts them out of the church."

Thus, by the time Clement of Rome—considered to be the first "father of the church"—came along, the church needed a systematized and authoritative order so that charlatans like Diotrephes would not be able to sneak into the churches and take over. Clement of Rome (to distinguish him from other church fathers named Clement) is considered the lynchpin in the Orthodox-Roman Catholic notion of "apostolic succession." He is considered one of the first Roman Popes. We only have one of his extant writings, his *Letter to the Corinthians*, dated to around the year AD 80 (although some historians place it in the 90s). Clement's letter shows a clear sense of the development of a priesthood and a fairly organized clerical class. He writes:

> The Apostles received the gospel for us from the Lord
> Jesus Christ; and Jesus Christ was sent from God. . . .
> Christ, therefore, is from God, and the Apostles are
> from Christ. . . . The Apostles went forth in the complete

assurance of the Holy Spirit. . . . They preached and they appointed their earliest converts, testing them by the spirit, to be the bishops and deacons of future believers. Nor was this a novelty: for bishops and deacons had been written about a long time earlier. Indeed, Scripture somewhere says: "I will set up their bishops in righteousness and their deacons in faith."[39]

Few passages in the history of Christianity have made a more lasting impression than this one. It signaled the beginning of what became known as *apostolic succession*: God sent Jesus Christ. Jesus appointed apostles. Apostles selected overseers and deacons. And on and on the succession goes—down to the present . . . down to the local parish today.

At the end of Clement's passage above, one notices a little defensiveness. He argues that "this is not a novelty." In other words, he needed to allay fears and concerns that he was dreaming up some system out of thin air. His quote of Isaiah 60:17 is a very loose translation, and it comes from the Septuagint (Hebrew Bible in Greek), and it is not recognizable at all in English.[40] But somehow Clement tries to take that passage and argue that the old Hebrew Scriptures foretold how the structure of the early church should work.

Later in Clement's letter he argues that bishops should serve until death and be succeeded by "other approved men." Here again is another precedent that is still with us. In all fairness, Clement is clear that these men should be truly worthy. They should be men who were "appointed by other illustrious men with the consent of the whole Church." They will be men who have "ministered to the flock of Christ without blame, humbly, peaceably and with dignity." They will be men who have "for many years received the commendations of all." Therefore, it should be considered "unjust that they be removed from the ministry."

In other words, the office of bishop is a lifelong position. This is one reason why the resignation of a Pope is cause for alarm. When Benedict XVI stepped down from the papacy in 2013—being replaced by Pope Francis—it was considered scandalous. It had not happened since the year 1415. And the last time before that was 1294.

Conclusion

It would take us beyond the scope of this book to discuss in any detail the evolution of the Christian clergy from the third century to the present day, but in certain ways it has changed surprisingly little. The pattern was set by the second or third century, and still today the vast majority of Christians live their religious lives under the authority of a priest or pastor who is accountable to a bishop. This model pertains to the Roman Catholic Church— which amounts to half of the worldwide Christian membership, the Orthodox Churches, and many of the Protestants, such as Anglicans, Methodists, and Lutherans. Even many of the very recent Pentecostal denominations are organized under a powerful bishopric, as in the case of the Church of God in Christ, the United States' largest Pentecostal denomination.

Some Christian fellowships are much less hierarchical. But even then, the authority of the church usually rests in the hands of a board of bishops or elders. In my fellowship, the Churches of Christ, our churches are almost always governed by an eldership. We have "priests," although we call them "ministers," who work under the authority of elders, or, overseers.

The main complaint that some high-church traditions have with fellowships such as the Churches of Christ is this—that they are not valid since the system of "episcopal succession" was broken off at some point in history. In this critique, they are correct. Churches of Christ, and low-church traditions like them, do not try to prove a two thousand-year unbroken connection to the apostles. Low-church traditions generally argue that authority comes directly from God, not through a magical "line of succession." The worthy elder or bishop or overseer in such a group will be a person who is respected in the congregation. The Holy Spirit works through the consensus of the faithful, rather than through an unbroken chain of authority passed down through the clerical ranks.

Whether one is high church (apostolic succession-based) or low church (locally elected leaders) is not the primary issue today. Church officials will debate such things until kingdom come. And, in my view, these disputes are actually coming along quite well as Christianity, worldwide, is becoming more ecumenical. We have learned how to maintain our civility, even when we disagree profoundly. In my classes, I like to write on the whiteboard: "I may not always agree with you, but I will always respect you." And I believe Christianity as a whole is slowly adopting this mantra, or something like it.

It is a great time to be a Christian. Members of the faith are realizing that our own narrow interpretations of Christianity are useful, but not *absolute*. I teach young people—often known as millennials. And these people have virtually no concern about whether someone is Anglican, Lutheran, or Catholic. They switch churches often. They have almost no denominational loyalty. What is more important is that they are, simply, Christians.

In closing, I think that we should look back on the history of Christianity's clergy as being, overall, a good thing. Although all of these leaders have been imperfect individuals, these brave men and women kept the faith alive for two millennia. It was passed down. And here we are, with a precious faith that was bequeathed to us by thousands of monks, priests, overseers, nuns, catechists, and deacons. They have all played a part in keeping the flame aglow.

Admirable clergy such as Billy Graham and Rick Warren have done far more good than bad in their role as mega-pastors. I am thankful that they had their input so far, and that a man like Warren is still in his prime. These good souls did their part to improve a faith that will outlive all of us by centuries. Every pastor should aspire to be a responsible steward of the faith that was handed down to him or her. The Christian faith is much bigger than any of us. We do our best with it, with humility. And then others pick up where we left off. And so it goes. For centuries.

As we make our way into the twenty-first century, we are witnessing a profound change in the nature of a Christian priest and pastor. For many centuries, priests and pastors were only males. In the second half of the nineteenth century, however, women began to be ordained in some of the more progressive denominations such as the Unitarians, Universalists, Congregationalists, Salvation Army, Methodists, and Presbyterians. These were always contested moves, but ordination of women is today accepted in many denominations. In 1976, the Catholic Church had a major discussion over the ordination of female priests, although up until now the decision has been that priests must be male. The fact that the issue was even discussed is somewhat surprising. Nevertheless, denomination after denomination continues to change course on this issue, allowing women the role of priest, bishop, and even primate (highest ranking clergy)—as in the case of the Episcopal Church, Christian Church (Disciples of Christ), Evangelical Lutheran Church in America, and more. Numerous Pentecostal fellowships ordain women—and have done so since the beginning days of the movement in the early twentieth century. Since 2006, females have outnumbered males in seminaries and divinity schools across the United States.[41]

Let us return to the Garry Wills question that opened this chapter: Why did the priesthood come into a religion that began without it and, indeed, opposed it? The answer to that question just might be this: the church *needed* it.

Notes

[1] Garry Wills, *Why Priests? A Failed Tradition* (New York: Viking, 2013), 1.

[2] Garry Wills, *Why I am a Catholic* (New York: Houghton Mifflin, 2002), 13.

[3] John Allen Jr., "'Poped out' Wills seeks broader horizons," *National Catholic Reporter*, 21 November 2008, located at: http://ncronline.org/news/people /poped-out-wills-seeks-broader-horizons.

[4] Ibid.

[5] Wills, *Why Priests?*, 1–2.

[6] Ibid., 2–3.

[7] Ibid., 3.

[8] Ibid., 20.

[9] Ibid.

[10] Ibid., 32.

[11] Ibid.

[12] Tim Stafford, "The Third Coming of George Barna," *Christianity Today*, 5 August 2002, located at: http://www.christianitytoday.com/ct/2002/august5 /third-coming-of-george-barna.html.

[13] Frank Viola and George Barna, *Pagan Christianity?* (Carol Stream, IL: Tyndale, 2012).

[14] Ibid., 106–107. Ephesians 4:11–12 reads, "So Christ himself gave the apostles, the prophets, the evangelists, the pastors and teachers, to equip his people for works of service, so that the body of Christ may be built up."

[15] Ibid., 113.

[16] Incidentally, Garry Wills wrote a very influential book that dealt with the history and the present reality of what he considers to be the errors of priestly celibacy. See *Papal Sin: Structures of Deceit* (New York: Image, 2001).

[17] Viola and Barna, 134.

[18] Ibid., 138–139.

[19] Ibid., 139.

[20] See Joseph Lienhard, "Clergy," in *Encyclopedia of Early Christianity,* 2nd Edition (New York: Routledge, 1999), 265.

[21] See Wim Blockmans and Peter Hoppenbrouwers, *Introduction to Medieval Europe, 300–1500*, 2nd Edition (New York: Routledge, 2014), 57.

[22] See Ferguson, "Deacon," in *Encyclopedia of Early Christianity,* 2nd Edition, 321.

[23] This translation is by James O'Donnell of Georgetown University. See http://faculty.georgetown.edu/jod/texts/pliny.html.

[24] See Ferguson, "Deaconness," in *Encyclopedia of Early Christianity,* 2nd Edition, 322.

[25] The translation that I am using here is: Thomas O'Loughlin, *The Didache* (Grand Rapids: Baker, 2010).

[26] Everett Ferguson, "Didache," in *Encyclopedia of Early Christianity*, 2nd Edition, 328.

[27] See Didache 11:2.

[28] Ibid., 11:4.

[29] See Everett Ferguson, "Apostle," in *Encyclopedia of Early Christianity*, 2nd Edition, 89.

[30] Ibid.

[31] Didache 11:4–6.

[32] Ibid., 11:8–12.

[33] Ibid., 12:1.

[34] Ibid., 12:4.

[35] Ibid., 12:5. The alternative translation for "Christ-peddler" comes from Aaron Milavec, *The Didache* (Collegeville, MN: Liturgical Press, 2003), 31.

[36] Didache 13:1.

[37] Ibid., 15:1–2.

[38] This debate was addressed in Canon 18 of the Council of Nicaea documents. See New Advent (a Roman Catholic translation) here: http://www.newadvent.org/fathers/3801.htm.

[39] I have used the translation of William Jurgens, *The Faith of the Fathers*, Vol. 1 (Collegeville, MN: Liturgical Press, 1970), 10.

[40] Ibid., 13.

[41] See Neela Banerjee, "Clergywomen Find Hard Path to Bigger Pulpit," *New York Times*, 26 August 2006, located at http://www.nytimes.com/2006/08/26/us/26clergy.html?n=Top%2FReference%2FTimes%20Topics%2FSubjects%2FD%2FDiscrimination&_r=0.

Chapter 6

Preaching
How Christians Proclaim the Faith

*"I believe in God, the Father Almighty,
the Maker of heaven and earth.
And in Jesus Christ, His only Son, our Lord."*

—The Apostles' Creed

CHRISTIANS BELIEVE VERY DIFFERENT THINGS about what is at the heart of the faith. What is most crucial? The word *crucial* has at its core the Latin word *cruc*, which means "cross." In other words, what is the "crux" of what we believe as Christians? There is no doubt that some would say that the cross is at the very crux of Christian faith. The Roman Catholic Church emphasizes the cross like no other group. Walk into a Catholic Church on any continent and you will come face to face with the suffering Jesus—on a cross. But is that the *most* central aspect of Christian faith?

I would argue that an emphasis on the passion of Jesus must be balanced with the resurrection, where we get a clearer sense of the hope and glory offered to us as believers in the Christian story. Indeed, the method of Jesus's execution is not nearly as critical to the story as is his resurrection. Placing the cross at the center of Christian faith is to miss the uniqueness of Jesus's contribution to humanity. *Many* people died by crucifixion in the Greco-Roman world. However, resurrection was not so common. It is resurrection that separates Jesus from all who came before him, or since.

The Crux of the Matter

So what *is* at the crux of the Christian faith? Christians from all epochs have concluded very different things. Go to any church and you will receive a slightly peculiar emphasis on what really matters in Christianity. We are able to witness what a community values by looking at the architecture, listening to the teachings, and observing the rituals. Quite obviously, Roman Catholic Churches emphasize the Mass. Eastern Orthodox Churches emphasize the Divine Liturgy. Typically, Protestants emphasize the sermon, although in recent years there has been a strong emphasis on the worship experience.

Mass, Divine Liturgy, sermons. These are all quite different things. Throughout the ages, Christian communities concluded that certain aspects of faith needed to receive more attention than others. Loving one's neighbor received a higher billing than selling everything one has in order to give the proceeds to the poor. Thus, the teachings passed down in song, in public prayer, and in the church's writings will vary according to that particular bent of Christianity. While a Catholic Mass will give ample attention to the Virgin Mary, an Evangelical Protestant service will usually ignore her. Rather, an Evangelical sermon might emphasize the central importance of studying the Bible in order to please God with one's personal conduct.

So how do we determine what is *crucial* in Christianity? Do we look to the Bible or to the Virgin? Do we look at the teachings of Jesus or the teachings of Paul? Perhaps we should focus on the historic creeds, since that is what the most important leaders of Christianity have deemed to be absolutely vital. Maybe the prayers are what matter most, since that is how we communicate with God.

The short answer to all of these questions is Yes. A conscientious disciple of Jesus will look at all of them and try to discern what is *most* critical to a life of following Christ. However, across the spectrum of global Christianity there is no consensus as to which is, absolutely, the most important thing. Christians in all times and places have emphasized different aspects of Christian teaching. They dogmatize and institutionalize certain aspects of the faith. They preserve some teachings. They relinquish others. If Peter or Paul watched a Greek Orthodox liturgy today, would he understand what was happening? If Jesus watched Joel Osteen preach a sermon, would he be proud? If the early Christians witnessed a Catholic Mass, would they say, "Exactly. That's precisely what we were trying to establish"?

In this chapter, we explore the evolution of Christian teaching, both in content and in how it was delivered. Obviously this is a massive topic, but in this chapter we are going to step back and take a broad survey of some of the ways Christians have reinforced and preserved the faith throughout the centuries. This chapter will be broken into small sections so we can avoid the feeling that we are drinking water from a firehose.

First, we will look at the some of the earliest sermons in the Bible. We will try to figure out the New Testament *kerygma*, or, "preaching."[1] What was central in the preaching of Jesus? What did Christianity's earliest sermons actually emphasize?

Second, in order to understand what the church fathers thought to be the most central and most sacred teachings, we will discuss the most important creeds in the history of Christianity. We will begin with the Council of Jerusalem in Acts 15—an oft-neglected text. We will then look at the earliest versions of the sacred creeds in Christianity. We'll pay a brief visit to the earliest Ecumenical Councils to see what they perceived as being most crucial for Christian thought and practice.

Third, we will look at the various methods used by Christians to preserve and inculcate the faith today. We will try to understand the development of the Catholic Mass, the Eastern Orthodoxy Divine Liturgy, and the Protestant sermon. We will also touch on the notion of Christian catechism (teaching), and how churches have used catechesis to train the young and the converts.

At the conclusion of the chapter, we will highlight some of the more recent, cutting edge approaches Christians are using—worldwide—to disseminate and reinforce the teachings of Christ.

We will pause at the end of the chapter to consider the merits (and perhaps a few demerits) of all of these different approaches, commenting briefly on their effectiveness and faithfulness to the traditions of the early church.

Preaching in the New Testament

Jesus was a preacher. In the Gospel of Luke, Jesus launched his public ministry with a sermon (Luke 4:14–32). It was a quintessentially Jewish approach that would have been normal in his context. On the Sabbath, Jesus went into the synagogue, as was customary for him. He took on the role of a teacher or preacher. Luke tells us that this also was customary for Jesus. He was a teacher of the Law, a rabbi. However, on this day, Jesus did something that stirred up the crowds. He stood up to read from the scroll of Isaiah. (A few have tried to argue that Jesus was illiterate. This is nonsense. Even at the launching of his ministry he was respected for his status as a teacher.[2]) He read a famous passage: "The Spirit of the Lord is on me, because he has anointed me to proclaim good news to the poor. He has sent me to proclaim freedom for the prisoners and recovery of sight for the blind, to set the oppressed free, to proclaim the year of the Lord's favor." Clearly, Jesus believed he was anointed by God to preach. After the Scripture reading, he began his sermon with the following words: "Today this scripture is fulfilled in your hearing."

That sermon did not go over well. At first everyone was impressed, but after Jesus delivered a discourse on how "no prophet is accepted in his hometown," the people turned on him and "drove him out of town." Indeed, they tried to kill him, but he escaped, and word began to spread widely about his preaching abilities. Repeatedly in Luke 4, we are told that the people were "amazed" at Jesus, because "his words had authority."

How could someone so gifted in preaching become so divisive to his hearers? What was it that caused some to flock to Jesus and others to despise him?

I am fascinated by how Jesus gets portrayed in film, sermons, pop culture, public conversations, and books. People have radically different interpretations of him. In Christian parlance, for someone to act "Christlike" is to conform to some gentle version of Christ that is, frankly, unbiblical. Sometimes people equate tolerance with Jesus, as if his chief virtue was "live and let live." But one careful reading through any of the four canonical Gospels demonstrates beyond a reasonable doubt that this man preached with conviction—conviction that was often extremely offensive to his hearers. Jesus at times became angry with those who questioned or opposed him. Yes, he could be gentle and kind on occasion, but a sentence or two later he would get fired up about something. He was prone to go from zero to sixty in a single passage! Let me give an example.

In Matthew 18 and 19, we see Jesus interacting with children. Here we get the gentle Jesus. He is loving and caring. He dotes on some of the children, treating them with care and dignity. Bible scholars like to point out that this attitude toward children was not common in the ancient Near East. In a context where children were bought, sold, abandoned, and routinely exploited, Jesus

> ... called a little child to him ... and he said, "Truly
> I tell you, unless you change and become like little

children, you will never enter the kingdom of heaven.
Therefore, whoever takes the lowly position of this child
is the greatest in the kingdom of heaven. And whoever
welcomes one such child in my name welcomes me."
(Matt. 18:2–5)

However—and here's where we get the "other" Jesus—if anyone
exploits or otherwise harms a child . . . watch out! The reader can
certainly understand the fire in Jesus's voice and the distress on
his face when he warns his listeners:

If anyone causes one of these little ones—those who
believe in me—to stumble, it would be better for them
to have a large millstone hung round their neck and to
be drowned in the depths of the sea. Woe to the world
because of the things that cause people to stumble! . . .
Woe to the person through whom they come! If your
hand or your foot causes you to stumble, cut it off! . . . It
is better for you to enter life maimed or crippled than to
. . . be thrown into eternal fire! (Matt. 18:6–8)

Some people have tried to explain this flaring of Jesus's temper by
appealing to his use of hyperbole, perhaps as a form of humorous
exaggeration. I disagree. It seems to me that he is condemning the
mistreatment of children, and in very strong terms. While Jesus
does not explicitly condemn violators with a death sentence, he
certainly doesn't rule it out. He also seems to say that if a person
is tempted—perhaps tempted to abuse a child—they should take
drastic measures to remove themselves from the temptation.

Jesus spoke with great authority, and he was not afraid to
offend his hearers. In the famous Sermon on the Mount (Matt. 5–7),
Jesus gave what is probably the best known speech in Western civilization. It was essentially a condensed version of what he thought
to be the righteous life. It is his longest sermon recorded in the

Gospels. People who like sermons that are focused, that deal with only one text or topic, will be disappointed here, because Jesus covers a lot of ground in this sermon:

- He blesses the have-nots in this world.
- He condemns the religious teachers of his day.
- He reinterprets several of the Ten Commandments by, apparently, making them stricter—for example, instead of avoiding murder, we should not even get angry with people.
- He condemns vengeance in the strongest of terms, upending the Old Testament's command of "eye for eye and tooth for tooth."
- He condemns people who do good just to receive praise from others.
- He teaches his disciples to pray short prayers, and to pray in such a way as to not draw attention to themselves.
- He condemns demonstrative fasting, saying that it should be done secretly.
- He condemns storing up money and possessions.
- He commands his hearers to avoid worrying.
- He condemns judging others.
- He urges people to ask God for "good gifts."
- He provides the Golden Rule: "Do to others what you would have them do to you."
- He condemns false prophets and false disciples.

That, in a nutshell, is the *kerygma*, the central preaching, of Jesus, at least as recorded in the Sermon on the Mount.

Jesus said much more than this, of course. And he did much more. He raised dead people, healed people of various diseases and disabilities, mentored a group of men we call apostles, and confronted demons and teachers with whom he disagreed. Indeed, the Gospel of John closes with the following words: "Jesus did many other things as well. If every one of them were written down, I suppose that even the whole world would not have room for the books that would be written" (21:25).

So how did Christianity get passed down to us as a religion based on the death, burial, and resurrection of Jesus? The answer to that question is difficult, because our written records are incomplete, but we gain helpful insight from the writings of Paul. Paul's writings are perhaps the oldest Christian writings we have in hand. And while that is an important fact, it is equally important to realize that Paul's writings occurred *after* the events described in the Gospels. Some scholars argue that the Sermon on the Mount actually comes after Paul, since Paul's writings are the earliest writings we have. That is incorrect, however. The Sermon on the Mount— obviously—occurred before Paul's writings. Yet, in the textual tradition, it appears that the Gospels were written down *after* Paul's earliest epistles. It would be utterly erroneous, however, to think that Paul actually wrote before the events of the Gospels *ever occurred*!

Paul's *kerygma*, his central proclamation, was not exactly the same as Jesus's message. Yes, Paul did echo much of what Jesus said, but his central thesis is found in his *magnum opus*, the book of Romans. That book has been analyzed and reanalyzed by scholars over the centuries. I can add little here. Nevertheless, some unmistakable themes appear in Romans, and we can point to a few of them:

- Paul has been chosen by Christ to be an apostle and to preach the gospel to Gentiles. This is his "priestly duty" (1:1–5; see also 15:14–22).
- God is not concerned only about "his" people, the Jews. God reaches out to Gentiles as well (2–3).
- Humans stand in condemnation before God because of their sins (2–3).

- God's plan was to send Jesus to be a sacrifice of atonement (3:25).
- Those who put their faith in Jesus will be saved from condemnation (5).
- Obedience to Christ results in "eternal life" rather than in death (6).
- Even those who are saved by trusting in Jesus Christ still struggle with sin (7:7–25).
- Those who trust in Christ are adopted by God, and God becomes their Father (8:15–17).
- Critical to Christian faith and practice is the notion of selfless love: love for God, love for others, love for self. "Love is the fulfilment of [God's] law" (13:10).
- Disciples of Jesus Christ should "stop passing judgment on one another" (14:13).
- Christians should accept one another, as Christ accepted them in spite of their weaknesses (15:7).
- Christ is working through Paul's life and preaching, accompanied by signs and wonders (15:15–19).

We can see that the teachings of Jesus and of Paul are not exactly the same thing. Much is shared in their teachings, but we get crucial additions from Paul, particularly the idea that by trusting in Christ one can achieve salvation from sin. It could be argued that Jesus spoke of this while in the flesh, but Paul's discussion of the resurrection is sophisticated. To many, it is the lynchpin of the gospel. It certainly seems to be Paul's *kerygma*. Jesus did it. Paul explained it.

So why do Christians place so much emphasis on the authority of Paul when, in fact, he was not one of the twelve apostles? The answer is because the apostles recognized and confirmed Paul's authority (Acts 15:22). They accepted him as a card-carrying member of the apostolate. In their view, he was not marginal at all. Indeed, we can see in the Bible that they revered Paul, considered his writings to be "Scripture" (2 Pet. 3:15–16), and even allowed him to correct their interpretations on occasion (Gal. 2). Further, in Galatians 1 and 2, we see Paul's version of how he and his message came to be seen as being crucial to Christian proclamation.

First, Paul tells us that he was commissioned not by men but by Jesus, indeed by God himself (Gal. 1:1). Paul did not receive his teaching "from any man." Rather, the gospel he preached was received directly "by revelation from Jesus Christ" (Gal. 1:12).

Second, Paul provides a chronology to establish his pedigree. He tells us that he used to persecute the followers of Jesus. But God called him to preach to *Gentiles* because, presumably, the task of the Twelve was to preach to Jews. Paul then tells us that he immediately went to Arabia, but then later returned to Damascus (where Paul was first converted to Christ). Then, "after three years," Paul "went up to Jerusalem to get acquainted with Cephas [Peter] and stayed with him fifteen days." Paul also came to know James, the brother of Jesus, during that time. Paul interrupts the story to tell us, "I assure you before God that what I am writing to you is no lie" (Gal. 1:18–20).

Paul then traveled to other places to start his preaching ministry. Christians were surprised to see that this was the person who formerly persecuted them. Nevertheless, Paul traveled and preached "for fourteen years," presumably earning the full acceptance of the leading figures of Christianity. After this fourteen-year period of preaching, Paul returned to Jerusalem to speak privately with the most "esteemed" Christian leaders. In his words, "I wanted to be sure I was not running . . . my race in vain." Thus, he presented his gospel to those "esteemed as leaders" in the Christian community, as a comparison, and "they added nothing to my message" (Gal. 2:1–6). Paul's presentation to the apostles went splendidly. He wrote of that eventful meeting: "They recognized that

I had been entrusted with the task of preaching the gospel to the uncircumcised just as Peter had been to the circumcised" (Gal. 2:7).

The results of that decisive meeting were this: God was using Peter to preach to Jews, and he was using Paul to preach to Gentiles. Peter and Paul. The great pillars of Christianity, even to the present day. However, Paul tells us right away, in virtually the next verse, that he "opposed Peter to his face, for he stood condemned." Paul was angry at Peter for withdrawing from Gentiles. Peter was caving in to Jews who insisted on keeping the long-held Jewish teaching that there must be a wall of separation between Jews and Gentiles. Paul wanted to demolish that wall. In Paul's view, Peter was out of line. Indeed, if Peter were to win this conflict, then "Christ died for nothing" (Gal. 2:21). Thus, Paul rebuked Peter publicly, "in front of them all," and presumably won the battle (Gal. 2:14). Otherwise, the Christian faith might have been restricted to Jews. By Paul's dogged persistence, however, it morphed into a faith for all, even those despised, uncircumcised Gentiles!

Clearly, Paul's understanding is what we proclaim in the churches today. It has profoundly shaped the Christian *kerygma*— the most fundamental teaching of Christian faith. Otherwise we followers of Jesus would be Jewish. Paul changed that. Christian "preaching" forevermore would include the notion that Gentiles are full participants in God's plans for humanity. And the Christian "gospel" would be indelibly linked to Paul's most cherished ideals.[3]

We Believe: A History of the Creed

If you ask an Evangelical Protestant which of the Christian creeds he happens to recite, he might mention John 3:16, "For God so loved the world that he gave his only begotten Son, that whosoever believes in him will not perish but will have everlasting life." Or if he watches Joel Osteen's popular telecasts, he might recite the creed that "the smiling preacher" proclaims every time he stands to preach:

This is my Bible. I am what it says I am. I have what it says
    I have.[4]
I can do what it says I can do.
Today, I will be taught the Word of God. I boldly confess:
My mind is alert, my heart is receptive. I will never be
    the same.
I am about to receive the incorruptible, indestructible,
    ever-living seed
Of the Word of God.
I will never be the same. Never, never, never. I will never
    be the same.
In Jesus' name.
Amen.[5]

This creed is recited not only by Pastor Osteen's church each Sunday morning, but it is recited in unison by tens of thousands of people who watch him on television, as well as by those who attend his huge "Night of Hope" speaking engagements that take place in arenas and stadiums all across the United States, and beyond. It is ironic that a creed that has only been around a few decades has come to such prominence, especially when we consider the nature of creeds. They are intended to be concise confessions of faith that summarize the most precious ideas within a particular faith community.

The word "creed" comes from the Latin word *credo*, which means "I believe."[6] I must confess that I came to understand the entire notion of a creed much later than most. In my religious community—the Churches of Christ—we actually take pride in the fact that we have "No creed but the Bible." This cherished slogan presents a fair bit of irony, however. It is like having a statement of faith that we have no statement of faith. In many ways, I love it, however. It is rather brilliant in the sense that we refuse to "boil it down" in favor of an idea or set of ideas that may marginalize other important and scriptural ideas. We remain people of the good Book rather than people who tend to focus on a particular set of teachings from the good Book. Fortunately for us, we don't have to recite our creed—the entire Bible—by memory.

My religious community has tried throughout its two hundred years of history to construct a core set of ideas that might unite our fellowship. Walter Scott, one of our early evangelists, tried to summarize Christian teaching into his famous "five-finger exercise": hear, believe, repent, confess, and be baptized. The long version went like this: "Hear the gospel, believe the gospel, repent of one's sins, confess the name of Jesus, and be baptized for the forgiveness of sins." Scott boldly claimed that "he had restored not only the true *method* of proclaiming the gospel but the true, ancient gospel itself." The founder of the movement—Alexander Campbell—approved heartily, referring to Walter Scott as "the first successful proclaimer of this ancient gospel."[7]

Thus, while we in the Churches of Christ claim to have no creed, there is almost an innate obligation to construct *something* that might stand as our *kerygma*—our most sacred convictions. Our movement came up with a few of these sayings, some of which have survived to the present. However, as far as constructing an official creed that arises out of a collective voice from our churches—we have resisted that process. The chief reason our movement never pounded out a formal creed is because of our heavy emphasis on congregational autonomy. We take pride in the fact that our congregations—led by local elders—have no dominion over any other congregations in our fellowship. Each congregation comes to its own consensus. How our movement has managed to remain "a" movement is a minor miracle: no creeds, no hierarchy, no central headquarters, and no guidebook such as the Book of Common Prayer, Book of Concord, or anything of that nature. In the early 1800s, this approach to church organization was rather novel. However, in the twentieth century, as the so-called "non-denominational" movement spread terrifically, it gradually became commonplace.

Through the years, when colleagues or other acquaintances learned of the peculiar "congregational" structure of my church, their question was inevitably: How do you keep your fellowship together without any formal structure? This is a good question that even those of us in the Churches of Christ struggle to answer. Often we mention our Bible colleges, our newspapers (and the powerful editors who choose who gets to contribute to them), or our various lectureships that occur annually. However, the bottom line is that we have held together fairly well for two hundred years. We have experienced divisions. In fact, our movement—known these days as the "Stone Campbell Movement" or the "Restoration Movement"—has split into several fairly distinct fellowships during its history. We have the Christian Church (Disciples of Christ), the Christian Churches, the Churches of Christ, and the International Churches of Christ. Many smaller sub-fellowships have separated within these larger groups.

The bigger question, however, is this: How does *any* church manage to keep itself together? And the answer to that question is twofold: people and beliefs. How does a church establish cohesion and continuity with its people and its beliefs? The most effective way of accomplishing that kind of unity and stability is through some sense of control. A clergy must be controlled by a rather tight system of ordination: a leader must be approved by an already-approved governing body. A candidate for ordination must study the beliefs and practices of that particular fellowship. Once a candidate satisfies the governing authorities in that church, then he or she is ordained.

Beliefs, however, are controlled through creeds—carefully and thoughtfully constructed confessions of faith. Of course, every confession of faith requires other layers of control. In other words, each creed needs authoritative interpreters. The layers of authority and control will vary over time. For example, the American Constitution had its original framers, but every generation of officially licensed (call it ordained) judges must revisit the layers of authority and perhaps subtly reinterpret the meaning of that original document. Some creeds last a long time—such as the Nicene Creed. Others, however, are fleeting. They stick around for a few generations, suffer neglect, and then fall out of use.

What is Christianity's *kerygma*—its central proclamation, its core convictions, its preaching? This is our central question of this chapter. As we saw in the previous section on Jesus and Paul, the earliest Christian *kerygma* was summarized by Jesus in his famous Sermon on the Mount and then a little later by Paul in his most important epistle, Romans. But what about the other apostles? Did they just stick to these core convictions of Jesus and Paul? Or did they come up with some sort of consensus about what should be preached in their tiny movement that was destined to become the largest religion on the planet?

Some of the earliest Christians held an important meeting; it is recounted in Acts 15. This text does not receive the attention it deserves. Indeed, this Acts 15 conference served as an archetype for the extremely important church councils that would follow in its wake a few centuries later. That gathering is known as the Council of Jerusalem. Traditionally it is dated in AD 50.

The context of the council is this: the early Christians could not agree about whether converts to Christ had to be circumcised. The larger questions—which Paul addresses in detail in Romans and in other epistles—was to what extent converts to Christianity had to "become" Jewish. Paul's analogy was that they were to be "grafted in" to Judaism, thereby becoming part of the "chosen people" of Israel (Rom. 11). However, if these Gentiles were to somehow become adopted Jews, then must they follow the Laws of Moses?

The Council of Jerusalem met to consider all of these issues regarding the extent to which Gentile converts to Christianity had to adopt Judaism. It was terribly complicated because Jews had many, many customs and laws—as a quick glance through Leviticus makes clear. So the key players in this conference—Peter, James, Paul, and Barnabas—each had their say. Peter began by arguing essentially that God had accepted Gentiles to become part of "his" people. Next, Barnabas and Paul discussed their ministry to the Gentiles, which they claimed had been extremely successful because it had been blessed by God. Finally, James spoke up and pronounced a judgment: the Gentiles who responded to the preaching of the apostles were to observe the following rules listed in Acts 15:29:

- Abstain from food sacrificed to idols.
- Abstain from blood.
- Abstain from the meat of strangled animals.
- Abstain from sexual immorality (in other words, observe Jewish sexual norms and not Gentile ones).

While this list was not a creed per se, a pattern of authoritative decisions was established that would become crucial in the following centuries, especially in the fourth century, at a time when Christian beliefs were wildly diverse.

The Nicene Creed

The first major council was at Nicaea in AD 325. It is still the most important council that the Christian religion has ever convened. This council set the standard for Christian orthodoxy. The context of the council is an interesting one.[8] The powerful emperor, Constantine—the man who made Christianity legal in the Roman Empire and who himself became a champion of the faith—invited the widely scattered bishops of Christendom to a place near his palace, located today in the town of Iznik in northwest Turkey.

Of the eighteen hundred or so bishops who were invited, about three hundred showed up. The Pope of Rome was elderly and had to send representatives. However, Santa Claus was there! His actual name was Nicholas of Myra. He deserves mention because he was probably the only bishop present at the council that virtually any Christian would recognize today.

Constantine gave the opening lecture. In it, he made it clear that Christianity's fortunes had changed. Not only was it legal, but it was preferred. It was to be endowed with riches, with liberal clerical salaries, with sumptuous buildings, and with great imperial favor (incidentally, many Christians believe this was a catastrophic turn for the faith). Constantine presided over the council, participated in some of the discussions (although he did not vote), and in many ways was the person who brought unity and cohesion to the bishops by suggesting the word *homo-ousios*. This word needs to be explained further, due to its huge significance in the annals of Christian history.

Constantine offered the term *homo-ousios* to the bishops at Nicaea as a word that could concisely explain the unity of God the Father and God the Son, and how both of them could be divine at the same time. At first the bishops were leery of his suggestion, since this precise word is not biblical. Eventually, however, they warmed up to it, and it is today a lynchpin of Christian orthodoxy.

Homo-ousios is a helpful term that manages to uphold unity in the Godhead's diversity. The Latin equivalent to this word is *consubstantialis*. In English, we don't typically use the term *homo-ousios*. However, we do use the Latin term, although we have Anglicized it to "consubstantial." In other words, God and Jesus are of the same substance. They are con-substantial. As a result, Jesus can be properly considered part of God's very nature. Constantine's suggestion was brilliant, and it is a core reason why the Eastern Orthodox Churches bequeath to him an extremely honorable title: Saint Constantine the Great, Equal to the Apostles.[9]

The Council of Nicaea accomplished a lot of things. It settled a standard date for Easter, solved a couple of local church schisms in Egypt and Syria, and decided how to deal with the "lapsed" Christians who had forsaken Christ during intense persecution (and wanted back into the church once it became legal). The council also recognized the great bishoprics of Alexandria, Antioch, Rome, and Jerusalem as supreme in all of Christendom. (Constantinople was the fifth and final "patriarchate" to be added, in AD 381, at the First Council of Constantinople. It was declared to be the "New Rome," since Constantine moved the imperial capital there in AD 330.) The council also established much more order in the church by tightening up some administrative matters. The council ruled, for example, that a bishop could not ordain a priest from another diocese. The most important and perhaps most lasting accomplishment of the Council of Nicaea was that it took steps to establish a formal creed.

The famous Nicene Creed was actually an expansion of earlier versions of a standard Christian profession of faith that virtually all Christians everywhere could proclaim. It would, ideally, be sort of a universal *kerygma* for the Christian church. The history of the Nicene Creed is extremely complicated and is an academic discipline in itself. Where did it begin? Perhaps the earliest version of it, a very rough archetype for it, is found in Scripture.

It could be argued that an archetypal creed is found in the Old Testament, a passage that all Jews hold in the highest regard, the *Shema*: "Hear, O Israel: the LORD our God, the LORD is one" (Deut. 6:4). That passage has been understood to be the most fundamental expression of faith for Jews for well over two millennia. It is an extremely succinct profession of faith that all Jews recite heartily as the core of their belief system.

An early New Testament profession of faith—intended to distill what a Christian believes at the core—is found in 1 Corinthians 15:3–7: "What I received I passed on to you as of first importance: that Christ died for our sins according to the Scriptures, that he was buried, that he was raised on the third day according to the

Scriptures, and that he appeared to Cephas, and then to the Twelve." It is short and sweet. It expresses the most fundamental truth, what Paul considered to be "of first importance." Christ died for our sins, was buried, and resurrected.

When Jesus gave the "Great Commission" to his apostles shortly before his ascension, he ordered them to go out and make disciples of all nations, ". . . baptizing them in the name of the Father and of the Son and of the Holy Spirit, and teaching them to obey everything I have commanded" (Matt. 28:19–20). But what exactly did Jesus want them to teach their converts? Everything? Obviously they would not remember everything. So early on in Christianity the disciples were put in a situation where they had to make judgments about what was absolutely crucial, particularly at the point of baptism.

In the second century, the Apostles' Creed emerged as a concise formulation of Christian faith. It has been dated to around AD 140 and is often called "the oldest creed of the church."[10] It is of critical importance here because virtually all Christian creeds have their origins in the Apostles' Creed:

> I believe in God, the Father Almighty, the Maker of
>   heaven and earth.
> And in Jesus Christ, His only Son, our Lord:
> Who was conceived by the Holy Ghost, born of the
>   virgin Mary,
> Suffered under Pontius Pilate, was crucified, died, and
>   buried;
> He descended into hell.
> The third day He arose again from the dead;
> He ascended into heaven,
> And [sits] on the right hand of God the Father Almighty;
> From thence he shall come to judge the quick and
>   the dead.

> I believe in the Holy Ghost; the holy catholic [or,
>   universal] church;
> The communion of saints; the forgiveness of sins;
> The resurrection of the body; and the life everlasting.
> Amen.

Every Christian would do well to memorize this powerful statement of faith. I would argue that it is the best one we have, since it avoids the theological quarrels that developed later.

During the Council of Nicaea a huge theological controversy dominated Nicaea's proceedings. It had to do with a clergyman/theologian from North Africa named Arius (AD 250–336). A participant in the Council of Nicaea, Arius was extremely articulate and persuasive. The reason he became the embodiment of heresy was his claim that "there was a time when the Son did not exist." What did he mean by that? He believed that Jesus was a created being. Jesus was superior to humans, but inferior to God, Arius contended. After all, Jesus seemed to place himself in a position lower than God when he said things like: "Why do you call me good? No one is good—except God alone" (Luke 18:19).

Arius was extremely influential. A good percentage of Christians who came after him believed he had got it right. In fact, his "heresy" persisted for several centuries after his death. At Nicaea, however, the bishops roundly condemned him, and as a result Constantine exiled him. It is interesting that when the council penned their creed, they attached the following words, clearly aimed at Arius:

> And those that say "There was [a time] when he was not,"
> and "Before he was begotten he was not," and that "He
> came into being from what-is-not," or those that allege,
> that the Son of God is "Of another substance or essence,"
> or "created," or "changeable," or "alterable," these the

Catholic and Apostolic Church anathematizes [that is, condemns].[11]

And that pretty much covered it. Arius's ideas on the nature of Jesus were thenceforth considered heretical, blasphemous, and even dangerous to one's soul.

The Nicene Creed, as we know it, was not actually completed at the Council of Nicaea in 325. Rather, what we know today as the Nicene Creed dates to the First Council of Constantinople in 381. In the centuries of church history, several different versions of the Nicene Creed show up. The one that most of us have inherited goes like this:

I believe in one God, the Father Almighty,
Maker of heaven and earth, and of all things visible
    and invisible.

And in one Lord Jesus Christ, the only-begotten Son
    of God,
Begotten of the Father before all worlds;
God of God, Light of Light, very God of very God;
Begotten, not made, being of one substance with
    the Father,
By whom all things were made.
Who, for us men and for our salvation, came down
    from heaven,
And was incarnate by the Holy Spirit of the virgin Mary,
    and was made man;
And was crucified for us under Pontius Pilate;
He suffered and was buried; and the third day He
    rose again,
According to the Scriptures; and ascended into heaven,
And sits on the right hand of the Father;

And He shall come again, with glory, to judge the quick
and the dead;
Whose kingdom shall have no end.

And I believe in the Holy Ghost, the Lord and Giver
of Life;
Who proceeds from the Father [and the Son];
Who with the Father and the Son together is worshipped
and glorified;
Who spoke by the prophets;
And I believe in one holy catholic and apostolic Church.
I acknowledge one baptism for the remission of sins;
And I look for the resurrection of the dead, and the life of
the world to come.
Amen.[12]

It is obvious that the architects of the creed wanted to send a message: Arius was wrong. Jesus was "begotten," not "made," as Arius had argued. Jesus was "of one substance" with the Father. Jesus was not subordinate to God; rather, he was "very God of very God." These were all attempts to preserve the mystery of worshiping Jesus, but they were also intended to eradicate Arianism.[13]

As a side note, three words in the Nicene Creed have wreaked havoc on Christianity for centuries. It is that little phrase in the section pertaining to the Holy Spirit that reads: "and the Son." The original version of the creed did not have those words, but the Western churches began using it in the creed in the sixth century.[14] In Latin the word that translates "and the son" is *filioque*. The ancient Eastern Orthodox Churches, however, never added the *filioque* clause. As a result of this addition, Christianity divided between the East (Orthodox) and the West (Roman Catholic), in the year 1054. That division remains today.

Earlier in the chapter, we looked at some of the key teachings from Jesus and Paul and explored how they came to be interpreted and later enshrined by the church fathers in the form of creeds. Still today, seventeen centuries later, their painstaking work is understood by Christians to be *the* standard for defining what Christians believe. Roman Catholics, Eastern Orthodox Christians, and the vast majority of Protestants readily agree that the Apostles' Creed and the Nicene Creed sufficiently define their faith.[15] It is our *kerygma*. It is our most central and sacred teaching. This is what we preach.

Liturgy, Mass, and Sermon

Christians have proclaimed and safeguarded Christian teaching in numerous ways across the centuries: by creating a biblical canon, by writing creeds, by mission work, and by training the younger generations through catechism. However, three of the most common techniques still with us are the Eastern Orthodox Divine Liturgy, the Roman Catholic Mass, and the Protestant sermon. While there is certainly crossover between the three approaches, in this section we will attempt to make it clear what we mean when we talk about each of them.

Early in Christianity, baptismal and Eucharistic services were developed, and we have discussed them in previous chapters. Out of these important sacramental services arose a splendid array of services known as liturgies. The heyday of liturgies was from the fourth to the seventh centuries. It was an incredibly rich time for the development of Christian worship services that are still with us today in the Eastern Orthodox and Roman Catholic Churches.

Protestants sometimes scratch their heads and wonder why these ancient liturgies are still so prevalent after a millennium and a half. Times have changed. Culture has moved on. Relevance must remain at the center of everything we do as Christians, right? Wrong, according to Orthodox and Catholic Christians. Each liturgy is a rich repository of faith. It is a method of preserving our faith. We do well to memorize these liturgies and recite them during our days on earth. This would anchor us to the church fathers. Instead of allowing culture to lead our Christian teaching into many and various and uncontrolled directions, the liturgical traditions of the church keep us grounded in faith. The liturgies are where we encounter our most sacred beliefs and practices.

Liturgies arose for a variety of reasons. Chiefly, they were created to bring order to public worship services. As the apostle Paul argued explicitly, worship should be orderly (1 Cor. 14). Liturgies were a way for the clergy to stay on the same page and to bring a sense of stability at a time when Christianity was growing prolifically—both in numbers and in territory. It was becoming impossible to keep the Christian faith together as it spread into Africa, central Asia, northern Europe, India, and even all the way into China. Liturgies traveled with priests and missionaries. Wherever Christianity was planted, the liturgies were there, maintaining a relatively coherent picture of what constituted the Christian religion.

There were other key reasons motivating the creation of liturgies:

1. They preserved "best practices" for church services. They were archetypes of how to worship well.
2. Many early clergymen were illiterate or insufficiently trained. Liturgies gave them support so that even they could lead a public worship service.
3. Liturgies preserved the *kerygma*. The most sacred ideas and beliefs were preserved in liturgy, to be recited day after day, year after year, century after century.
4. Arius and other "heretics" of the first few centuries had made Christian leaders extremely alarmed at what could happen to Christian doctrine without proper supervision. People's souls were at stake. Liturgies preserved truth. This is why the changing of liturgies continues to be cause for alarm, inevitably causing controversy.[16]

The esteemed Orthodox theologian Bishop Timothy Ware has written beautifully about how the liturgy encapsulates the core of Christian doctrine:

> The Orthodox approach to religion is fundamentally a liturgical approach, which understands doctrine in the context of divine worship. It is no coincidence that the word "Orthodoxy" should signify alike right belief and right worship, for the two things are inseparable. . . . Dogma is not only an intellectual system apprehended by the clergy and expounded to the laity, but a field of vision wherein all things on earth are seen in their relation to things in heaven, first and foremost through liturgical celebration.[17]

Ware goes on to explain that, for Orthodox Christians, "Christianity is a liturgical religion." He argues that "worship comes first, doctrine and discipline second." If people are interested in Orthodoxy, they should not first read books. Rather, they should attend the Divine Liturgy, for that is where one can find the soul of the Orthodox Church. Attending the liturgy is the way people get to know Christian belief in a context of history and in sublime beauty. Orthodox Christians do not evangelize by bringing people to Bible studies. Rather, as Jesus invited Andrew, they invite people to "Come and see" (John 1:39).

As Timothy Ware rightly points out, "The basic pattern of services is the same in the Orthodox as in the Roman Catholic Church."[18] What follows is his itemization of the services shared by both fellowships, Orthodox and Roman Catholic:

1. Divine Liturgy: known by Catholics as "Mass." This is the Eucharist. It is celebrated daily in most Roman Catholic settings. In most Orthodox parishes, it is celebrated only on Sundays and feast days.

2. Divine Office. This is also known as the Liturgy of the Hours.[19] These are the regularly scheduled prayers that go back to the earliest days of the church, largely in imitation of the ancient Jewish times for prayer. They were rigorously practiced by many of the monastic orders in the following order:

   a. Matins: often prayed at midnight, known as the "Night Office"

   b. Lauds: the "Dawn Prayer," often prayed at 3:00 A.M.

   c. Prime: prayed around 6:00 A.M.

   d. Terce: prayed around 9:00 A.M.

   e. Sext: prayed around 12:00 noon

   f. None: prayed around 3:00 P.M.

   g. Vespers: evening prayer, often celebrated at 6:00 P.M.

   h. Compline: night prayer, generally around 9:00 P.M.

The two most important of these times for prayer are Matins and Vespers, and they are still celebrated widely in Roman Catholic, Orthodox, and even many Anglican churches.

3. Occasional Offices. These are the services that are held for special occasions such as baptism, marriage, monastic commitment, royal coronations, consecration of a church, and the burial of the dead.[20]

When Protestants attend Orthodox services and more traditional Roman Catholic services, they typically feel like the service is rote, and perhaps even out of date. While some Catholic churches have become more progressive, the Orthodox churches are extremely conservative. Their services are sung or chanted. They believe the early church services functioned that way, similar to Jewish chanting.[21] Incense is common. The Orthodox Church services will be in an ancient language, for example, New Testament Greek (in

Greek Orthodox churches) or in Old Church Slavonic (in Russian Orthodox churches).

The Roman Catholic Churches held services in Latin until the 1960s, when they modernized their liturgy. This was a massive change for the church. But the transition occurred quite rapidly, and now Roman Catholics only occasionally see a Latin Mass either on television in a traditional Mass in Rome, or in one of the few Latin Rite liturgies that can be found. Like the Protestants half a millennium before, the Roman Catholic Church has decided to move in the direction of progressivism and cultural relevance. They have adopted many Protestant practices in their quest to connect to modern society.

The ancient Orthodox Christians do not share this concern with cultural relevance. They are proud of the fact that they have maintained continuity with the fathers of the church who settled the liturgy hundreds of years before. There is an element of staunchly defending the church's traditions, rather than allowing society to mold and shape what Christians should believe. Orthodox Christians believe that to assimilate too much to contemporary culture is to surrender one's convictions, resulting in a faith that is no longer prophetic but is rather a mirror of the society around it.

The liturgies of the Roman Catholic and Orthodox Churches are rich, sophisticated, and pregnant with meaning. They are full of early church practices, Bible readings, many different forms of prayer, and beautifully sung songs that go back centuries. Scripture readings are based on a lectionary—a three-year cycle in the Roman Catholic Church (and many mainline Protestant fellowships) and a one-year cycle in the Orthodox churches. The Gospels are the most prominent texts in both of these churches, although there is an attempt to read widely from the entire canon throughout the lectionary cycle. An observer will witness the *Kyrie eleison* ("Lord, have mercy"), a time for the kiss of peace, an offering from the people, the *Sanctus* ("Holy, Holy, Holy"), the Words of Institution from Jesus ("This is my body . . . take and eat"), intercessory prayer for the living as well as the dead, and the Lord's Prayer ("Our Father"). While mainline Protestants have kept some of these practices, many of them have fallen into disuse. Some Protestant churches have even dropped the frequency of the Eucharist to just a few times per year. Such a thing would be anathema in both Roman Catholic and Orthodox churches.

What about the concept of delivering a sermon? Did the early church preach anything like the sermons we are used to today? Do Roman Catholics and Orthodox Churches have sermons?

In Orthodox and Roman Catholic spheres, the sermon is typically known as the homily. The word "homily" was originally a Greek term that meant "conversation," "instruction," or "lecture." Early on in church history, it was an informal word, as opposed to the more formal word *logos*, which can be translated as "sermon." The homily was distinct from the concepts of evangelizing or even instructing new converts in a catechetical (formal teaching) setting. It had a fairly precise meaning.[22]

The earliest collection of Christian homilies comes from a church father named Origen (AD 185–254). His homilies focused on biblical texts. He tried to extract meaning from biblical books, preferring an allegorical approach, though some of his interpretations were literal. For example, it is claimed that Origen may have castrated himself due to his literal reading of Matthew 19:12.[23]

During the fourth century, when Christianity suddenly became legal and highly favored by Constantine, the preaching of the homily became almost exclusively the responsibility of the bishops, and they preached from their official chair, or throne. This is where we get the expression *ex cathedra* which means "from the chair." Bishops made their most authoritative statements from the bishop's chair.

The fourth century saw the golden age of preaching. Highly skilled rhetoricians in the empire delivered sermons that are still considered to be the greatest in the history of Christianity. Three of the brightest lights during that era are known as the Cappadocian Fathers: Basil the Great (330–379), Gregory of Nazianzus (329–390), and Gregory of Nyssa (335–395). These were Greek-speaking men with great training in rhetoric, and they were praised highly for their extraordinary oratorical prowess and theological sophistication. These three are deeply revered in the Orthodox families of Christianity.

The greatest preacher in all of Christian history, however, is John Chrysostom (349–407). His name means "Golden Mouth." Chrysostom was the Archbishop of Constantinople from AD 398 to 404. All through his career he preached at least once each day, and often more. On feast days his sermons could last for two hours.

The most celebrated preacher in the Latin sphere of influence was Augustine (354–430). Hundreds of his sermons survive. For many years Augustine was a professor of rhetoric, and he mastered the discipline on all levels. His sermons were lively, ". . . filled with plays on sounds and words, stylistic flourishes, and aphorisms."[24] Augustine's sermons were much shorter than his Greek counterparts, often only around ten minutes (which helps to explain why Roman Catholic sermons still hover around ten minutes). Augustine "stylized" the Latin homily due to his powerful influence. After him, it was common for authors to put his sermons into collections for use by the priests. For hundreds of years these sermons were then read by priests to congregations in the Latin-speaking West.

No other person has impacted the culture of preaching in the Western world as Augustine did. He was a master of the art of persuasion, and it was to Augustine that the Reformers turned both for theology as well as for how to teach that theology. Outside of

Scripture, no one and nothing else had more influence on the mind of Martin Luther than Augustine's sermons and writings.

It is generally thought that after this early golden age of preaching—the fourth century—the quality of sermons and homilies declined.[25] The great Cappadocian Fathers, Chrysostom, and Augustine remained the archetypes; to deviate from them in style and content was to miss the mark. This was a far cry from the first century, where "it seems that any member of a congregation or visiting Christian could be asked to speak. Soon, however, preaching became a task restricted to the clergy."[26] In the second century, preaching was further restricted, mainly to the office of the bishop. Priests and deacons could then read the sermons that had been duly authorized by the bishops of the church. This general tendency persisted for many centuries.

After the fourth and fifth centuries, virtually all Christians who went through catechetical training used the Cappadocian Fathers, Chrysostom, and Augustine as their guides.[27] It was as if their systemization of Christianity was the standard for all time. In many ways, their approach to catechesis (teaching) is still with us.

When Luther's Reformation broke out in 1517, the central idea was that of *sola scriptura*—Scripture alone. Initially, Luther thought that any reasonable person could read the Bible and reach the same conclusions as he did. It was a disaster. Just a few years into the Reformation, the German Peasants' War arose, taking with it around one hundred thousand lives. It was clear to Luther and his fellow Reformation leaders that the Bible had to be *taught*. Simply putting it into the hands of the people would not do. People needed to become educated in Lutheran interpretations before gaining access to the hallowed—even dangerous—Scriptures. Historian Diarmaid MacCulloch writes:

> The long-term task for Protestants was to show people
> how to use the Bible in a disciplined way and still love

it: to build on the officially provided resources so that
everyone could make Reformation their own, rather
than merely passively accepting what their betters
[Luther and company] decided for them. Central to this
task was preaching: disciplined presentation of the word
by a duly authorized minister.[28]

In Scotland, newly ordained ministers were given a Bible and "a
key to unlock the pulpit."[29] No, this was not theological egalitarianism. The Protestants became every bit as protective as the Catholics
when it came to safeguarding the preaching of the gospel.

In Protestantism, however, there was an unmistakable development that became obvious inside the church buildings. As we
noted earlier, the pulpits became huge, ornate, and often central.
Preaching became the most important feature of the congregational assembly. The altar—the communion table—got down-
played in favor of an often gargantuan pulpit. Previously, pulpits
were quite modest, but they became grand and opulent during the
Reformation. And in many cases that legacy of the Reformation is
still seen in the pulpits across the Protestant world.

In an odd return to the days of Augustine, the pastor of a
Protestant congregation came to be respected as a rhetorician.
Preaching a sermon became a theatrical performance. And, most
importantly, the frequency of sermons increased exponentially. "In
Shakespeare's London there were a hundred sermons each week."
In Transylvania's Reformed churches, it was common for each
parish to feature four sermons per week.

The drama surrounding the sermon was palpable: there was a
prolonged ringing of the church bells and long readings of Scripture
beforehand, the doors of the church were closed and even locked,
parishioners (especially in Scotland) would shout out "Amen"
after an important point was made in the sermon.[30] The sermon
did not end after church services, either, as members—especially

children—could be called upon to explain the meaning of what they had just heard.

All of this lends credence to the theory that Protestantism tended to promote education better than its Catholic or Orthodox counterparts. MacCulloch writes, "There can be no doubt that the effort of catechizing and the task of listening to a weekly diet of abstract ideas from the pulpit made Protestant Europe a society generally more book-conscious, and perhaps also more literate, than Catholic Europe."[31] And the Protestant catechism could be exacting. Indeed, the Protestant approach to catechism—with numerous printed materials—became "a massive enterprise on a European-wide scale, a very competitive commercial market. Lutheran Germany produced around thirty or forty different new editions of printed catechisms every decade after 1550, and more than a thousand different catechisms produced in England between 1530 and 1740.[32] It got to the point where "Protestant clergy were so busy preaching and catechizing that they had little time for quiet and reflection."[33] Indeed. Perhaps that tendency is still with us.

The Protestant proclivity for education manifested itself again in the late eighteenth century with the work of Robert Raikes (1736–1811). Christians have Raikes to thank for the concept of Sunday School, which he created in 1780, in Gloucester, England. Times were miserable for England. It was the beginning of the industrial revolution, and cities became crowded. Poor children and orphans were routinely put to work in the factories and mills rather than in school, as education was for the upper classes. Sundays were supposed to be a day of rest, but the kids who had been crammed into an enclosed space for six days needed to blow steam. In their time off, many of them became big troublemakers. And that's where Robert Raikes came onto the scene.

Raikes was a newspaper publisher, and he publicized his belief that the working children needed to receive basic education, and the only time to do it was on Sunday. Raikes considered it a win-win situation: the neighborhoods would benefit by not having delinquents running loose, and children would benefit by receiving secular and Christian education.

In 1780, Raikes and his friend Rev. Thomas Stock (1749–1803) established their first Sunday School program in Sooty Alley, Gloucester, just opposite the city prison. Many unsung heroes stepped up by contributing, teaching, writing curriculum, and holding Sunday School gatherings in their homes and yards. As a printer, Raikes was strategically positioned to publicize the charitable work, and the progressive Evangelical community rallied around him immediately. Notably, the popular writer and activist Hannah More (1745–1833) got on board, as did William Wilberforce (1759–1833), Britain's famous opponent of slavery. John Wesley's (1703–1791) endorsement opened the floodgates. With the support of figures such as these, the movement's future was secure. Even adults started attending Sunday School to receive basic training in reading and writing. Offshoot programs expanded at breakneck speed.

The Sunday Schools began by ministering to boys aged five to fifteen. Programs quickly expanded to girls. Classes usually ran from 8 to 10 A.M. and paused for church and lunch. Afternoon classes went from 2 P.M. to as late as 6 P.M. Most programs were incentive-based. Children received prizes for learning, such as shoes, clothes, books, and candy.

In Britain alone, the legacy of the Sunday School Movement is massive. Until Britain's Elementary Education Act of 1870, it was the only source of formal education for most children. One institution—the Stockport Sunday School in London—accommodated five thousand students. Estimates are that by the 1830s around a fourth of Britain's kids, or 1.2 million, were attending each week. Sunday Schools became a key part of British missions, exporting the concept to churches worldwide. Today, millions of children all over the world attend Sunday School. It has become a necessary, almost assumed, ministry of the church.

Conclusion

The "crux" of Christian teaching shifts with the times. My grandparents spoke to me often about the "hellfire and brimstone" sermons they had heard all their lives. I did not hear such sermons. I was raised with Max Lucado's emphasis on God's unmerited grace. There were times when I wanted some good old-fashioned judgment: you need to follow Jesus or bear the consequences! However, in 2011 when Rob Bell released his book *Love Wins,* it became clear to me that many millennials were basically moving in the direction of universalism. God's grace is big enough to have room for all. Every. Single. One.

And while I have serious misgivings about this exuberant emphasis on unlimited grace, I predict a correction may be just around the corner. The central teaching of Christianity—its *kerygma*—has ebbed and flowed for two thousand years, and it will continue to shift as new generations come to know Christ. One generation focuses on one thing while another generation rises up with different concerns. The Lord knows that the concerns of the 1950s were entirely different than the concerns of the 1960s and 1970s. The cultural *zeitgeist* can change in a flash.

What interests me immensely is how global Christianity seems to be placing a spotlight on the poor at this time in history. While I have little admiration for the blasé universalism so common in American Christianity today, I am touched and motivated by the renewed attention given to the world's poor and marginalized. This is undeniably a part of the *kerygma* of Jesus himself. One look at the Beatitudes makes it evident that Jesus had a deep passion for the poor and neglected. He wanted better for them. He devoted much of his ministry to their causes. He seemed drawn more to lepers, the crippled, and the sinners than he was to the in-crowd or the uber-righteous.

And just as the content of Christianity's *kerygma* gets interpreted and reinterpreted all through history, so does its medium.

It is said that Billy Graham preached to more souls than anyone in the history of Christianity due to his tapping in to electronic media, chiefly television and radio. Today, many of us hear the gospel proclaimed on the Internet. For all the talk of secularization, a thing or two can also be said about how we are on the threshold of a whole new era when it comes to sharing the gospel. People can easily create a Youtube channel and preach to anyone who cares to click. Gospel preaching is more available today than ever before due to the advent of electronic media, especially the Internet.

Just this morning my pastor sent out a Lenten meditation by email. I read from the Scriptures at Biblegateway.com. On television I watched as presidential candidates declared their allegiance to the Christian faith. These new methods of proclaiming the gospel are all around us, at our fingertips. It is a wonderful time to follow Jesus Christ.

However, as opportunities for Christian teaching expand, we hear much talk of a recession of Christianity in the Western world. My hope and prayer is that a new round of preachers and teachers will emerge, equipped not only in the truth of Christian faith but in the skills and relevance necessary to win themselves a hearing. A modern Chrysostom. An American Augustine. A twenty-first century Billy Graham.

And while theological emphases vary, and approaches to preaching evolve, it is my prayer that a new generation will rise up, preaching the message that has been proclaimed for twenty centuries now. I pray they will emphasize those things which are "of first importance":

> That Christ died for our sins according to the Scriptures,
> that he was buried, that he was raised on the third day
> according to the Scriptures, and that he appeared to
> Cephas, and then to the Twelve. (1 Cor. 15:3–7)

Notes

[1] The term *kerygma* can be translated "proclamation" or "preaching." In its verb form, it means "to herald" or "to proclaim." In its verb form, it is found over sixty times in the New Testament. Because of its frequency in the New Testament, it has been the subject of much scholarly discourse. Three things can be said with a large measure of confidence regarding *kerygma*. First, it is a word used to capture the Christian message as a whole. It is a word that was intended to *summarize* the Christian message. Second, it precedes the written New Testament, since the gospel message was proclaimed before it was written. Third, the term "blurs the lines of development from the message *of* Jesus himself to more diverse messages *about* Jesus." Historian Rudolf Bultmann believed the *kerygma* entailed "the conviction that Christ's death and resurrection constituted God's decisive eschatological event." As Bultmann famously put it, "The proclaimer became the proclaimed." However, historians are quick to point out, once someone hears the proclamation *about* Jesus, they immediately must know the proclamation *of* Jesus. See Tucker Ferda, "Kerygma," in *Encyclopedia of the Bible and Its Reception*, Vol. 13 (Berlin: De Gruyter, 2016).

[2] Reza Aslan has argued repeatedly that Jesus was illiterate. See, for example, Belinda Luscombe, "Is Reza Aslan Anti-Christian?" in *Time*, 30 July 2013, located at http://ideas.time.com/2013/07/30/is-reza-aslan-anti-christian/. New Testament scholars tend to disagree with Aslan's claim. See for example Ben Witherington's three-part discussion, "Reading and Writing in Herodian Israel—Was Jesus an Illiterate Peasant?," at *Patheos*, 2 November 2011, located at http://www.patheos.com/blogs/bibleandculture/2011/11/02/reading-and -writing-in-herodian-israel-was-jesus-an-illiterate-peasant-part-one/.

[3] It is important not to overstate the case that Paul was the missionary to Gentiles. As Acts 10 and other passages point out, Peter played a crucial role in the decision to reach out to Gentiles. It seems Peter may have balked at a later stage, but initially he was committed to reaching out to Gentiles.

[4] This particular phrase [I have what it says I have] is always said by Joel, but it is not listed on his website as part of his creed. This creed does not seem to have originated with Joel, since one can find it on the Internet being quoted by various individuals. It is likely that the creed was invented by Osteen's father, Pastor John Osteen (1921–1999), the founder of Lakewood Church in Houston. See John Osteen quoting the creed before preaching: https://www.youtube.com /watch?v=-Ptp4wsKXfA.

[5] See https://www.joelosteen.com/downloadables/pages/downloads /thisismybible_jom.pdf. It is common for media outlets to refer to Joel Osteen as "the smiling preacher." See Phillip Luke Sinitiere, "The rise of the smiling preacher Joel Osteen," in *Christian Century*, 22 July 2015, located at: http:// www.christiancentury.org/blogs/archive/2015-07/rise-smiling-preacher.

[6] For this paragraph I am drawing from Justin Holcomb, *Know the Creeds and Councils* (Grand Rapids: Zondervan, 2014), 11ff.

[7] See Richard Hughes, *Reviving the Ancient Faith: The Story of the Churches of Christ in America* (Abilene, TX: Abilene Christian University Press, 1996), 52–53. Italics are his.

[8] For my description of the Council of Nicaea, I am using Joseph Kelly, *The Ecumenical Councils of the Catholic Church: A History*, 21–25.

[9] Ibid., 22–23.

[10] See Holcomb, 25–27. I use his version of the Apostles' Creed.

[11] Henry Bettenson, *Documents of the Christian Church*, 2nd Edition (Oxford: Oxford University Press, 1963), 25. Bettenson points out that there were several versions of the Nicene Creed early on. However, the official one was actually adopted at the Council of Chalcedon in the year AD 451. When it was adopted, it was acknowledged as being the Creed that was first authored at Nicaea (325) and then amended at Constantinople (381). For this reason, the Nicene Creed is typically known in the scholarly world as the "Nicene-Constantinopolitan Creed."

[12] I have used Holcomb's version, 35–36.

[13] Arianism was not the only heresy that was countered by Nicaea's participants. They also argued against Gnosticism (that the world was created by a lesser deity known as the demiurge) and Sabellianism (that the Trinity was three different modes of the divine).

[14] There is much discussion about when the *filioque* was introduced, and who first proposed integrating it into the creed. Scholars generally agree that the first formal usage of it was at the Third Council of Toledo in AD 589, but it may have been used informally much earlier than that.

[15] The vast majority of Protestants adhere to the Nicene Creed. For example, the World Council of Churches (WCC) uses the Creed as the standard for Orthodoxy. The WCC represents the world's Anglicans, Baptists, Lutherans, Methodists, Reformed, and many United and Independent churches. Over five hundred million Christians—Protestants and Orthodox—are associated with the WCC. In one important WCC document, it is written: "The creed (the Apostles' Creed, the Nicene Creed or both) functions as a summary of the rules that govern Christian use of the word 'God.' That is, the creed functions both as *the guide* to Scripture and Christian living and as *the criterion* of sound teaching." Italics are mine. See "Doctrinal, social and ethical issues (Anna Marie Aagaard), Documents from Sub-committee III," 1 August 2000, located at: https://www.oikoumene.org/en/resources/documents/wcc-programmes /ecumenical-movement-in-the-21st-century/member-churches/special -commission-on-participation-of-orthodox-churches/sub-committee-iii -theological-convergences-and-differences/doctrinal-social-and-ethical-issues -anna-marie-aagaard.

[16] For this short list I have used Everett Ferguson, *Church History*, Vol. 1 (Grand Rapids: Zondervan, 2013), 322.

[17] Timothy Ware, *The Orthodox Church* (London: Penguin, 1997), 266.

[18] Ibid., 267.

[19] For a very helpful explanation of the historic hours for prayer, see the website EWTN, which is Global Catholic Television Network: https://www.ewtn.com/expert/answers/breviary.htm.

[20] See Ware, 267.

[21] Ibid., 268.

[22] Joseph Lienhard, S.J., "Homily," in *Encyclopedia of Early Christianity*, 539. I have relied on this article to develop the early history of homilies.

[23] The early church historian Eusebius reported that Origen took Jesus's teaching "in too literal and absurd a sense, and he was eager to fulfill the Savior's words. . . . So he quickly carried out the Savior's words, trying to do so unnoticed by most of his students. But however much he wished it, he could not possibly hide such a deed." See Eusebius, *The Church History*, book 6, section 8.

[24] Lienhard, 540.

[25] See William Howden, "Preaching," in the *Encyclopedia of Early Christianity*, 940.

[26] Ibid., 942.

[27] See, for example, Everett Ferguson, "Catechesis, Catechumenate," in *Encyclopedia of Early Christianity*, 223.

[28] Diarmaid MacCulloch, *The Reformation: A History* (New York: Penguin, 2003), 585.

[29] Ibid.

[30] Ibid., 586.

[31] Ibid., 588.

[32] Ibid., 587.

[33] Ibid.

Chapter 7

Church Music
From Jerusalem to Chris Tomlin

*"I would rather have written that hymn of Wesley's,
'Jesus, Lover of My Soul,' than to have the fame
of all the kings that ever sat on the earth."*

—Henry Ward Beecher

By now, readers will know that I grew up in the Churches of Christ, a tradition that is often associated with its rather staunch approach to church music. For many decades we have worshiped in the acapella tradition. While things are changing, for much of our recent history we have been known as a Protestant group that did not use instruments.

Church Music: A Personal Testimony

Acapella music was, for many years, a sacred cow doctrine in the Churches of Christ. It was a line in the sand; it still is for many. Many of our members considered the teaching to be non-negotiable; for over a century it was a central part of the Church of Christ identity. If you flirted with instrumental music in the church, you were well on your way to leaving the Church of Christ orbit. Why?

Simply put, because the New Testament does not authorize instrumental music . . . or such was the argument.

Virtually every Church of Christ member will take a stand on this issue. Forget the nature of the Trinity. We are content to leave that doctrine a mystery. Each individual must make his or her own decision of how the hypostatic union brings together the three substances of the persons of God: Father, Son, and Holy Spirit. But acapella music? No room for compromise. Either you used instruments or you did not. This was the litmus test *par excellence*.

Most readers will find all of this off-putting, judgmental, or terribly insular. For those of us growing up in the Churches of Christ, however, it was simply a reality. My generation—which grew up in the 1970s, 80s, and 90s, found it to be a curious doctrine. We knew our particular brand of Protestantism was different from the mainstream denominations, but we considered it a choice that our forefathers had made. And on a good Sunday we realized the beauty that stems from unaccompanied music. Pure voices. No screaming guitars, no organs to vibrate the walls, no drums to drive out the elderly. We knew we had something beautiful in our churches that should be preserved.

Most certainly we understood the seriousness of the issue. For some, salvation was at stake. But those of us from the moderate wing of the movement, especially the younger folks, thought that the intensity surrounding this highly charged issue was strange. We grew up listening to Amy Grant, Michael W. Smith, Steven Curtis Chapman, and D.C. Talk. These were Christian artists who were trying to give young Christians an alternative to secular music. We respected the decisions of our most conservative elders, but at a fundamental level we failed to comprehend the intensity of this issue. Most of us younger folk had the sense that acapella music was from a bygone era. Nevertheless, we respected our elders. They were good men, highly committed to the church. So we refused to create a fuss.

As a result of this reluctance to allow our music to evolve with the times, however, the Churches of Christ began to look out of sync with the surrounding society. We brought our friends to worship, and they tended to fixate on that elephant in the auditorium: "Why don't you guys have instruments?"

In addition, our songs tended to be written decades if not centuries before. The 1980s kids as well as the millennials did not resonate with the old hymns, like "Standing on the Promises" and "I Come to the Garden Alone." They just didn't connect anymore. Certainly these are songs that command respect. They sustained the Churches of Christ and a host of other denominations for ages. But culture has a way of moving on. And younger people realized what was at stake.

To disallow one's church from evolving with the times is to isolate its young people and place them in an impossible situation. How can we expect younger church members to listen to Adele, Bieber, Beyonce, and Drake from Monday to Saturday and then spend Sundays singing Isaac Watts and Fanny J. Crosby? It just doesn't fit. After all, Watts and Crosby wrote their songs at a time when that style of music was common. Now we're singing songs in church that are a century or two old, without instruments, and with lyrics that hardly make sense to modern sensibilities.

And the young Church of Christ members *are* moving on. Many of them leave when they go off to college and realize their acapella tradition has put a straitjacket on their desire to worship the Lord. They head to non-denominational churches where the music is much more closely aligned to their preferences. Or perhaps they worship God by strumming guitars in their dorm rooms in order to get that spiritually satisfying experience of God.

It seems to me, a teacher in a Christian university, that most university students who care to attend church services would place music as a top priority in their worship experience. Preachers can be forgiven for long, dry sermons. But a worship service that fails to connect with younger generations is often a good reason for them not to come back.

Speaking personally, the church service I attend worships in the acapella way, at least for now. And I appreciate it. I can get my more contemporary fix by listening to CDs or by tuning in to "Air1," "Shine FM," or "The Fish"—national Christian radio stations. For me, it is not worth it to start a big scandal in the church. Preserving the unity is much more important. It would be wrong for me to make an issue of this since it is just not that important to me. My parents raised me in an acapella congregation, but they never once argued that instruments were somehow less Christian, or more sinful. My mother earned a Master's degree in music and was an accomplished pianist. Like me, she simply chose to respect the wishes of the majority when it came to church music. So she remained silent. For seventy five years . . . and counting.

I have been heartened by those Church of Christ musicians who try to write songs that are more relevant. With great commitment, they attempt to balance musical innovation with loyalty to our movement's roots. With mixed success, they create lyrics and harmonies geared for the twenty-first century.

Many of our churches have incorporated the "worship team" approach where the various parts (soprano, alto, tenor, bass) are led by gifted musicians in front of the congregation, often singing into microphones in order to help people find the proper notes (and to drown out the musically challenged).

I have empathy for those Church of Christ congregations who took the calculated risk and decided to move into the twenty-first century. They knew that they might be cast out if they crossed that line, but some of them did it anyway. They adopted instruments. They usually created a "contemporary" service with instruments, while retaining a "traditional" acapella service for those committed to the old paths. Some of our younger generations have even planted new churches that are fully instrumental. They are brave souls. They realize that they might be fiercely opposed by their parents' peers, and especially by their grandparents' generation. But they made the move anyway . . . often to avoid falling away from Christianity altogether.

It seems to me that Protestant Christianity has undergone a seismic change in the last few decades. For nearly five hundred years, the heart of Protestantism was the sermon. Preachers had a message, and the congregation expected a competent, biblically informed, rigorous explication of a scriptural text. In the last decades of the twentieth century, however, that seems to have changed. The heart of the public Protestant gathering, certainly in Evangelical and charismatic services, seems to have switched to experiencing the music. Sermons are not unimportant, but today younger people expect an experience from their worship gatherings. As a result, the old models for public worship are being challenged as never before. As we analyzed in the last chapter, the Protestant sermon occupies a centrality not found in Catholicism or in Orthodoxy. However, I would argue that music has begun to eclipse the oral proclamation of faith since the 1990s—even earlier—in Evangelical Protestantism.

If I am correct in this analysis, the shift happened alongside the technological revolution. For example, the culture-wide preference for digital texts and iPods over printed media and music CDs. The Internet made music immediately accessible for people, with a click. Since the days of Elvis and even before, young people have shown a deep passion for music. But in the late twentieth century and increasingly into the twenty-first century, music has become something (literally) as attached to younger generations as wallets once were. Think of the ubiquitous ear pods and wires hanging from the ears of millennials. They can't even exercise without being connected to their music. This shift in technology has impacted Evangelical Christianity profoundly in my view, often to the point where music takes center stage in their lives and in their churches. I will not attempt to back up these ideas with statistics or scientific scrutiny, but I will argue that these changes are more or less obvious. Music is more important to Christians—especially to younger Christians—than ever before. And churches that deny this shift will do so at the expense of their youth.

Herein lies a serious problem that my tradition, the Churches of Christ, must face. We have painted ourselves into a corner. We have argued that church music must remain different and distinct. We have urged our young people to accept the old hymns without allowing them much input. And at some point they began to walk away. Music is simply too important to them. And they joined new churches, or started their own.

This chapter shows just how deeply cultural our musical traditions are in the church. From the earliest days of Christianity, music was there. When creative energies were unleashed, music served as a great aid to Christian worship. At its best, church music allowed people to express themselves in a way that nothing else could match. In the worst cases, however, music became an impediment to the worship of God. As theology evolved, new generations of hymn writers were needed. And those churches that suppressed the creative energies of its people did so at great risk—to their own relevance. Such continues to be the case.

Biblical Music

Music comes up rather early in the Bible when we are told that a man named Jubal "was the father of all who play stringed instruments and pipes" (Gen. 4:21). The Hebrew Bible is full of references to music. Military victories were celebrated with instruments. God told Moses to assemble the people by using "trumpets of hammered silver" (Num. 10:2). The lyre—a stringed instrument similar to a harp—is mentioned dozens of times. Cymbals show up repeatedly, most importantly at the Jewish Temple (Ezra 3:10). The most frequently mentioned instrument in the Hebrew Bible is the shofar—the horn from a goat. It is used commonly in Judaism still today. The tambourine turns up several times in the Hebrew Scriptures, often played by women (Ex. 15:20). We see what appears to be a large band of musicians in 1 Chronicles 15. They were accompanied by singing choirs (1 Chron. 15:27) as they transferred the Ark of the Covenant to the city of Jerusalem.

Singing was indispensable to the worship of God in the Jewish Temple.[1] Worship was accompanied by at least twelve male singers between the ages of thirty and fifty. According to the Mishnah, the singers were trained for five years before gaining admission to the Temple choir. The same number of musicians could be expected as well. It is clear from the Psalms that musical praise to God in the Temple was enthusiastic, as displayed in Psalm 150:

> Praise the LORD. . . .
> Praise him with the sounding of the trumpet,
>   praise him with the harp and lyre,
> praise him with tambourine and dancing,
>   praise him with the strings and pipe,
> praise him with the clash of cymbals,
>   praise him with resounding cymbals.
> Let everything that has breath praise the LORD.
> Praise the LORD.

It is curious to notice that while Temple worship was rich in instrumentation, outside of the Temple instruments were frowned upon—certainly in worship.

Rabbi Akiva (AD 50–137)—an extremely influential leader in first and second century Judaism—wrote a splendidly helpful account of worship in the Temple before its destruction in the year AD 70. Basically the approach was responsorial, meaning the leader sang one line and the congregation either repeated it or responded with a chanted "amen" or "hallelujah." Out of the responsorial approach developed antiphonal singing, where one verse (usually of a Psalm) was sung by part of the congregation while the next verse was sung by another part of the congregation.[2]

What did this ancient singing sound like? It was quite different from what we understand as music today. We would describe it today as a chant, consisting of only three or four notes. Rabbi Akiva urged his fellow Jews living in the *diaspora* to chant the Torah daily.[3] It was a pious exercise for the faithful. This chanting became the music of the early church.

It is important to point out that while worship in the Temple was accompanied with instrumentation, the culture within the synagogues developed a musical tradition that was almost exclusively vocal.[4] Further, when the Jewish Temple fell in AD 70, Rabbi Akiva and other leaders prohibited instruments in worship, probably in order to mourn the loss of the Temple. It seemed inappropriate to celebrate with instruments alongside the destruction of something so vital, so central, to Judaism. Some Jewish leaders even wanted to extend a moratorium on instruments in daily life as well.[5]

Christians in the first few centuries of the faith would have been impacted by these facts. The Jewish Temple—where instruments were played—was destroyed. The synagogues—where, initially, Christians met—rarely included instruments, if at all. In addition, Christians were under duress for much of their first three centuries of existence, forcing them to worship in secret or at least very quietly. Noisy instruments might have placed their lives in danger. As a result, early Christianity was a non-instrumental religion. And this practice continued for a long time—for centuries. That is why the term "acapella"—a term meaning "as in the chapel"—came to signify unaccompanied music. Church music was acapella music. To them, instruments did not belong in the chapel. Instruments were associated with Greek religion. Indeed, "Such links with pagan cults reinforced the frequent condemnation of instrumental music by both orthodox Jewish rabbis and early Christians."[6]

The New Testament discusses a few different instruments, including pipes (Matt. 9:23), lyres or harps (Rev. 15:2), trumpets (1 Thes. 4:16), and cymbals (1 Cor. 13:1). Clearly, the church would have been familiar with the instruments of Judaism, as the complete separation of Jews and Christians took many decades, if not a century or more. However, Christians were a people on the move. They did not have the benefit of being settled and organized, so they relied more on the human voice than on instrumentation.

It is clear from several New Testament texts that the early Christians sang with gusto. Jesus and his apostles sang at the Last Supper (Matt. 26:30). Paul and Silas sang while imprisoned (Acts 16:25). Paul mentions singing on several occasions, notably in Ephesians 5:18-20: "Be filled with the Spirit, speaking to one another with psalms, hymns, and songs from the Spirit. Sing and make music from your heart to the Lord, always giving thanks to God the Father for everything, in the name of our Lord Jesus Christ." James, the brother of Jesus who from the city of Jerusalem led the early Christian movement, instructed the early Christians to sing when they were happy (5:13). The book of Revelation features several scenes that include music, instrumentation, and singing.

Church Music in the Patristic Era

Scholars do not sufficiently understand the development of early Christian music.[7] The main reason scholars have trouble studying this era's music is clear: "Neither Jews nor Christians are known to have noted down any of the music they used for worship until at least the sixth or seventh century AD."[8]

We do have some examples of ancient Christian lyrics. For example, Petros Vassiliades tells us, "The earliest known Christian hymn recorded outside of the Bible" is the *Phos Hilaron*, or, "Hail Gladdening Light." This song is still performed in the Eastern Orthodox Vespers service and has been discovered by Protestants in recent years. The song was written "in all probability in Cappadocia, the cradle of the 'early Christian' spirituality."[9] While scholars struggle mightily to reconstruct early church music, some innovative approaches to the research have emerged. One approach is to listen to the music of the most ancient Christian traditions, such as the Ethiopian Orthodox Christians, or the various Middle Eastern forms of Christianity such as Syriac and Assyrian. These groups are ancient, and they have been careful to maintain church tradition. Their habits and practices do not change much over time. These religious communities are often isolated and very conservative. They have been persecuted and marginalized, making them even more entrenched and more proud of who they are. When we analyze these ancient communities, we often catch a glimpse of Christianity's deepest musical roots.

One of the earliest secular references to Christianity is a letter from an imperial official named Pliny the Younger to Roman Emperor Trajan (ruled AD 98–117). The letter was written around 112, and it gives us some insight into the practices of the early church from the perspective of an outsider:

> On an appointed day they had been accustomed to
> meet before daybreak, and to recite a hymn antipho-
> nally [call-and-response style] to Christ, as to a god, and
> to bind themselves by an oath, not for the commission
> of any crime but to abstain from theft, robbery, adul-
> tery and breach of faith, and not to deny a deposit when
> it was claimed. After the conclusion of this ceremony it
> was their custom to depart and meet again to take food;
> but it was ordinary and harmless food.[10]

Pliny found little to worry about, although he did torture two deaconesses in an effort to extract information about this new Jewish movement. The *style* of worship was perfectly consistent with Jewish worship. What was brand new was the *object* of their worship: some Jewish rabbi who seemed to be adored as a god. Pliny dismissed it all as "nothing but a depraved and extravagant superstition." He did note, though, that "many persons of all ages and classes and of both sexes" were converting to Christianity, both in the cities as well as in the countryside.

Liturgical scholar Frank Senn tells us that the early church fathers were virtually united in their condemnation of music, dancing, and showing artistic expression in the context of Christian worship. When it came to music and dancing, his conclusion was clear: the church fathers "disapproved of it most of the time."[11] However, in order to compete with the Greco-Roman religions, as well as with Judaism itself, they needed something more, so they turned to the Scriptures for guidance. What they found there was a style of music that is still practiced tenaciously in most Orthodox Churches.

The apostle Paul seemed to prefer "rational worship" (Romans 12:1) over the flutes, tambourines, and cymbals that were common in the Greek temples.[12] And Paul's view is the one that carried the day, for many centuries. Church music was almost always acapella. Indeed, in the Eastern Orthodox Churches, the music is still unaccompanied. Timothy Ware writes, "In the Orthodox Church today, as in the early Church, all services are sung or chanted. . . . Singing is unaccompanied and instrumental music is not found, except among certain Orthodox in the United States—particularly the Greeks—who are now showing a penchant for the organ or harmonium."[13] Indeed, in an Orthodox service, one gets the sense that the music is from another time, another place. It is rarely replicated outside of church walls.

One might wonder, "How did the worship of God in the Jewish Temple, resplendent with all manner of musical instrumentation, get reduced to the point of singing only?" Here's where the history stands on firmer ground. The reason for the church's dogmatic insistence on acapella music can be placed squarely on the shoulders of the powerful Archbishop of Constantinople John Chrysostom (347–407), who, with Basil the Great and Gregory Nazianzus, formed a theological backdrop for virtually all Orthodox theology and liturgy. Chrysostom is considered the father of the Eastern Orthodox liturgy, and he was no friend of using musical instruments in worship.

Chrysostom's preaching could be harsh and punishing at times. For instance, he asked his listeners the following: "What is it that you are rushing to see in the synagogue of the Jews who fight against God? Tell me, is it to hear trumpeters?" Apparently, by Chrysostom's time, many Jews had reversed course again and had adopted instruments in the worship of God. They had come to terms with the fact that the Temple was not to be rebuilt anytime soon. So their synagogues—once devoid of instruments—had become well-known for having a robust culture of musical accompaniment.

Chrysostom gave his explanation as to why the Jewish Temple fell, and it just may have had something to do with their using instruments in worship:

> Do you wish to see that God hates the worship paid
> with kettledrums, with the lyre, with harps, and other
> instruments? God said, "Take away from me the sound
> of your songs and I will not hear the canticle of your
> harps." . . . Do you run to listen to their trumpets? Do
> you wish to learn that, together with the sacrifices and
> musical instruments and the festivals and the incense,
> God also rejects the temple because of those who enter
> it? He showed this . . . when he gave it over to barbarian
> lands, and later when he utterly destroyed it.[14]

Anyone who ran afoul of Chrysostom's eloquence (remember: his name means "golden-mouthed") could pay for it dearly, as in the case of the instrument-loving Jews. He was notoriously harsh on Jews in his speeches. In recent years, he has been hammered for fomenting anti-Semitism amongst Christians. We have to remember, however, that Chrysostom was active at a time when Christian leaders had to compete in the religious market against Jews as well as pagans. Senn writes, "Thus, the condemnation of the use of musical instruments by the church fathers was not an aesthetic criticism, but a matter of staking out Christian identity and morality."[15]

Christian music was performed in the style of "unaccompanied monophonic chant" for hundreds of years.[16] However, two exceptions are the Ethiopians and the Copts, two closely related church traditions. Ethiopians used such basic instrumentation as the prayer staff and systrum, and the Coptic Christians of Egypt used triangles and cymbals.

For centuries, the chanting of the psalms remained standard practice in Christian worship, mirroring what took place in the synagogues. Indeed, "Christian chant is fundamentally Jewish in origin."[17] Chanting is still quite common in the more ancient Orthodox Christian traditions. The religion of Islam has also maintained this focus on the human voice, as it freely adopted aspects of Christian faith in the seventh century and beyond. The Nestorians and Syriac traditions—still heavily steeped in chanting—were common in Arabia during the years of Muhammad and the compilation of the Quran. Chanting methods evolved over time to become highly complex, even to the point of requiring a high level of expertise. This gave rise to professionally trained choirs. Timothy Ware writes, "Until very recent times all singing in Orthodox churches was usually done by the choir; today, a small but increasing number of parishes . . . are beginning to revive congregational singing."[18]

Armenians and Ethiopians have their "own systems of notation."[19] These systems are nuanced and complex, and there is no way an outsider could understand the music of these ancient tra-ditions without having been trained in them. "Byzantine notation and chant developed through the middle ages, becoming increas-ingly complex, until by the fall of the city [1453] only experts could master them."[20] These liturgies are still a very specialized field of knowledge; entering into this field would be extraordinarily diffi-cult for the religious outsider who does not have decades of infor-mal learning from his or her youth, growing up around it.[21] In addition to learning a foreign language, one would have to learn a unique system of music.

In Western Christendom, church music was dominated by the monophonic style well into the medieval period. Polyphony (multiple parts) began to surface in the liturgies of the eleventh and twelfth centuries, for example in a descant sung above the plainchant melody.[22] Liturgical music in the Western world came to be known as "Gregorian chant" in memory of Pope Gregory the Great (reigned 590–604), although in reality this style of music has "minimal if any association with him."[23] In the thirteenth century, we can witness a rather rapid rise of the use of the organ in the Roman Catholic Mass: "There is clear evidence of the organ being used regularly; it replaced the singing of some liturgical texts in the late fourteenth century."[24]

Protestant Preferences in Music

Not only did Martin Luther launch the Reformation in 1517, but he was chiefly responsible for transforming music in the churches that followed him. A well-known music aficionado, Luther claimed that "next to the Word of God, music deserves the highest praise."[25] Luther was well known for his musical compositions, including his enduring paraphrase of Psalm 46, "A Mighty Fortress Is Our God," which is still sung today. In 1620, a frustrated Jesuit priest made the claim that "Martin Luther destroyed more souls with his hymns than with all his writing and preaching."[26]

Luther wanted the entire congregation to be involved with the music of the church, and his "own hymn-writing set the highest of standards." Luther did not reject medieval church music; rather he "encouraged his followers to preserve it."[27] After all, he was a monk and would have been very familiar with the chanting arrangements practiced in his Augustinian order. However, he baptized church music with Protestant convictions, using new methods such as vernacular language and congregational participation, as well as expressing the deep conviction that music should be *enjoyed*. Not all Protestants were willing to take music into such ambitious and creative directions as Luther did. For example, the more austere Calvinist churches generally opposed music as being frivolous, other than plainly singing the psalms in rigid, metrical form.[28]

Johann Sebastian Bach (1685–1750) is considered by many to be the climax of sacred music, period. This pious Lutheran composed choral masterpieces that are considered by many to be unsurpassable. The brilliant, former Archbishop of Canterbury Rowan Williams once observed that Bach "somehow does a great deal more theology in a few bars of music than most do in many words."[29] Bach's theology and music were "rooted in Luther's theology." Bach was an avid reader of Luther's works, and much of his music is centered on Lutheran motifs such as justification by faith alone.[30]

Hearkening back to Chrysostom, some of the other Protestants, particularly those in the Reformed churches, remained convinced that music should remain outside the walls of the church. In Zurich, Ulrich Zwingli wanted to purify the churches; therefore he "closed all the organs" in 1524, arguing that "music distracted from worship." He even banned the ancient practice of chanting the psalms. John Calvin similarly prohibited instrumental music in the churches.[31] He allowed chanting of the psalms since they were biblical, but writing fresh hymns with creative lyrics was out of the question since the Bible did not authorize this practice.

Indeed, the most radical voices of the Reformation felt that the Bible disallowed singing altogether. At some points their biblical hermeneutic became downright bizarre, as when Conrad Grebel—one of the founders of Anabaptism—wrote the following to fellow-reformer Thomas Muntzer:

> We understand . . . that you have introduced new German hymns. That cannot be for the good, since we find nothing taught in the New Testament about singing, no example of it. . . . Paul very clearly forbids singing in Eph. 5:19 and Col. 3:16 since he says and teaches that they are to *speak* to one another and *teach* one another with psalms and spiritual songs, and if anyone would sing, he should sing and give thanks *in his heart*. Whatever we are not taught by clear passages or examples must be regarded as forbidden, just as if it were written: "This do not; sing not."[32]

It is interesting that, in general, Luther believed that when the Scriptures are silent on a particular matter, the interpreter has the freedom to innovate. However, the more radical reformers interpreted silence as being prohibitive, as in the case of Grebel's interpretations above. It is peculiar and intriguing to read this interpretation from the vantage point of the twenty-first century, well after the turbulent context of first-generation Protestantism.

For Calvin and Zwingli, hymn writing was inherently pompous because it implied that the Word of God was somehow inadequate for the Christian assembly. It is ironic that at a time when Catholic and Lutheran church music was reaching new heights, the Reformed churches were stuck in the "plainchant of medieval monasteries," if they allowed music at all.[33] Sometimes they did paraphrase many of the psalms in order to make them work metrically, but they scarcely went beyond that. And while accuracy was not exactly adhered to in their conversion of the psalms, the practice of memorizing Scripture was amply justified because that's what these more radical Protestants really cared about. First and foremost, they wanted people to know their Bibles.

English Protestantism achieved its zenith in the work of Isaac Watts (1674–1748), the father of English hymnody. Watts was a Nonconformist (Congregationalist) pastor, and he was able to innovate musically without compromising the Bible. He had to tread carefully, however, because his Puritan colleagues were deeply suspicious when it came to music and the arts. His strategy was risky, but ended up being ingenious. Here was his central argument: if the psalms are the sole source for church music, then New Testament teaching gets short-changed. Therefore, it is of utmost importance that Christians sing *the gospel* rather than exclusively the psalms, as was the practice in most of the English churches. Brilliant! How could a Bible-loving Protestant find anything to critique in that?

In spite of the clear sensibility of his argument, Watts did not have a huge impact on the English and Scottish churches early on. They were simply too conservative at that time. Alister McGrath writes: "Watt's breakthrough was generally ignored by Anglicans and Presbyterians."[34] Watts did, however, have a huge impact on John and Charles Wesley and their explosive Methodist movement during in the eighteenth century. And the Wesleys, particularly Charles, shaped Christian hymnody in ways that survive to the present, especially that "warming of the heart" phenomenon so closely associated with the early Methodist movement and subsequent holiness churches. Wesley's song "Jesus, Lover of My Soul" is a prime example of the intimacy between humans and God that he wanted to emphasize in his hymn writing. Many of Charles Wesley's songs today are classics in the Protestant hymnal: "Christ the Lord Is Risen Today," "Hark, the Herald Angels Sing," "O For a Thousand Tongues to Sing," and "Soldiers of Christ, Arise."

Many Protestants remained ambivalent about music for some time. But as pipe organs were integrated into church services, those who held onto plainchant became marginalized and were increasingly viewed as backward and irrelevant. In general, Americans lagged behind the Europeans in the acceptance of instruments and innovation, but it may have had more to do with economics than anything else.

Whatever the case, when the Americans finally caught up, they really made church music their own, forging new paths and innovating on a scale that would make even Martin Luther blush. Prominent American preacher Dwight Moody (1837–1899) toured with a musical sidekick named Ira Sankey. Sankey's melodious performances attracted large audiences, and then Moody would preach to them. They wrote many hymns together that were intended to instruct their Christian hearers in the essentials of theology and discipleship. There is no doubt that Moody's use of Sankey was the template for Billy Graham's use of George Beverly Shea in his massive crusades.

Probably the most prolific hymn writer of the era was Fanny J. Crosby (1820–1915), a blind Methodist woman who had unparalleled success in finding her way into the songbooks of America. She authored thousands of hymns, many of which are still with us, such as: "Blessed Assurance," "Jesus Is Tenderly Calling You Home," and "To God Be the Glory." Crosby and Sankey were close friends, and their style came to be known as the "gospel song," casting a long-lasting spell over American Protestantism. There is little doubt that without Crosby, there would be no Gaither Vocal Band or the Stamps-Baxter Music phenomenon of the twentieth century. Ultimately, however, this style of music found its heartiest proponents in the African American churches at a time when they were experiencing the exuberance of emancipation.

African American Church Music

African Americans have had a significant influence on American music ever since they began claiming church music as their own. With highly participatory styles, call-and-response patterns, exuberant choirs, and a constant stream of remarkably gifted soloists, black gospel music has become a vital part of the landscape of American Christianity. Many of the great African American singers perfected their musical craft in church, singers such as Mahalia Jackson, Marvin Gaye, and Whitney Houston. Indeed, in the African American Protestant church scene, the music is as indispensable as the sermon. One scholar put it this way: "It is impossible to 'have church' without good music. In the African American community, music is to worship as breathing is to life. . . . A good sermon ain't nothing but a song."[35] One visit to an African American church will make this point crystal clear.

Rooted in the slave experience, black gospel is a vivid reminder that America was not "the beautiful" for many of its people. While European-Americans enjoyed the Promised Land in the Americas, this land was a living hell for many African Americans, a nightmare without end and a horrific tragedy. Over time, however, the black church became a refuge, a means to escape the evils of this world. Behind the scenes, unknown to whites, these churches were becoming an "invisible institution" that fostered black leadership, a unique liturgy, and a form of Christianity that, even still, non-blacks know little to nothing about.[36] This is the black-church experience, and it is one reason why black churches can feel foreign to outsiders. They simply do not share the history that has been passed down over the generations of oppression. Unless one is black, it is almost impossible to become an insider to this type of collective memory and inherited pain.

A distinct feature that separates black church music from others is the blurring of the lines between sacred and profane. Religion scholar Christopher Partridge has described this phenomenon as being one of "liminality," with a "mild transgressive appeal."[37] There is a porousness between church and society that is rarely found elsewhere. For example, Whitney Houston sang her party anthem "Queen of the Night" followed by her truly sacred rendition of "Jesus Loves Me" as back-to-back songs on the *Bodyguard* film soundtrack. Smokey Robinson moved smoothly into gospel music after a brilliant career with Motown. Andrae Crouch—often called the father of modern gospel music—worked with Michael Jackson in the studio on weekdays and returned to the pulpit on weekends to pastor the Christ Memorial Church of God in Christ in Pacoima, California.

R&B, hip-hop, and jazz have their roots in the collective experience of the black church. There is no border separating them. Puff Daddy's smash hit "I'll Be Missing You"—a tribute to rapper Notorious B.I.G.—is brilliantly blended in with the melody and chorus of the gospel classic "I'll Fly Away." Considered one of the greatest crossover singles of all time, it brilliantly blends gospel music with the 1980s Police hit "Every Breath You Take." Its haunting lyrics evince a deep faith, a firm belief in life after death, a commitment to prayer, and a conviction that the singer and his beloved friend will see each other's faces again one day. One scholar writes, "It was, and still is, typical for a black composer to take a song written by a white composer, reshape it and improvise it in a folk-like manner, or 'blackenize' it, giving it new life. This is the genius of worship in the African American experience."[38] "I'll Be Missing You" is the quintessential example of a hybridizing process fusing pop music with African American Christianity.

The black-church experience came through clearly in one of Whitney Houston's final songs before her death in 2012. Her hit "I Look to You" was designed as a prayer to God. The song was prescient, sung from the deepest places inside a person who somehow senses that the end is near. In the song, Houston tragically describes how her life has been so difficult, and how her strength has left her, but she looks upward to God—the One to whom she can still turn for strength and ultimately for release.

These are themes that run deep into black gospel's roots. The past continues in the music of the present. The slave ships, the plantations, the loss of personhood . . . these sources of pain live on in the collective memory of a community only beginning to rise from centuries of trauma. Yet faith is the ever-present.

Even a rapper as troubled as Tupac Shakur was bathed in the spirituality of his youth. His biographer wrote, "Tupac was obsessed with God. His lyrics drip with a sense of the divine."[39] His song "So Many Tears" encapsulates the hopes, fears, and profound despair of a young black man struggling with his complicated existence. He feels cursed. He sees no escape from his often self-inflicted problems. Death is welcome because it will end the painful hopelessness of life in the here and now. Hell awaits his soul, but at least it provides escape from the intense sorrow and the inevitable prison sentence. No longer will he have to watch his friends drop, one by one, to violence on the street. No longer will he have to mourn them and fear for his own life. For better or for worse, his "many tears" will finally come to an end.

Tragically, Tupac's lyrics were prophetic. He was killed in a drive-by shooting in 1996, in his prime, at the age of twenty-five. He is a giant in the world of rap and hip-hop today. His music, at once profoundly religious and painfully worldly, has an authenticity that has yet to be equaled. Tupac's music was the work of a prodigy, effortlessly blending the sacred and the profane into one.

In recent years, we have witnessed the rise of such artists as Lecrae and Trip Lee, rappers who share the black experience but with a decidedly Christian outlook on life. They and their peers are the best hope that Christianity has to evangelize a hip-hop culture often associated with misogyny, drugs, and violence. As the influence of American hip-hop expands globally, Lecrae and his cohorts are at the cutting edge of Christian evangelization among the youth. The Christian world needs these bright lights, although it will be an uphill battle. In spite of terrific odds, Lecrae has already managed to reach unprecedented heights in his career, becoming the first artist to top the Billboard and Gospel charts simultaneously.[40]

Church Music Today

Today, in the twenty-first century, we are living in what is arguably the richest period of Christian music composition in history. All around the world, music is indigenizing. As colonial influence recedes in the former colonies, a renewal is taking place. Africans, Asians, and Latin Americans are finding within themselves the courage to create their own music with their own sounds and lyrics. They are tapping into their indigenous musical traditions, although not always without resistance. When many of the missionaries worked in these places, they often associated indigenous music, dancing, and instruments with evil. And many of their early converts became convinced that the only way to worship God was the Western, European way.

What eventually gained traction in the colonial context was something deeply disturbing: the absurd idea that Western music was somehow more righteous than indigenous music. Thus, for example, in Africa there often pops up a vestigial notion that somehow African instruments are inappropriate for Christian worship, especially drums. One Zambian leader put it this way:

> It would be fair to say that most early missionaries to
> Africa did not encourage the use of traditional musical
> instruments in worship. How could their use be allowed
> if they had been used in animistic religion? They had
> been contaminated and would resurrect memories of
> pagan festivities. . . . These missionaries might have

meant well at the time, but in banning the use of these instruments in church, they actually robbed the nationals of part of their valued culture. The damage done in this respect can still be evidenced among some of the older generation of Christians in Zambia who believe that the use of traditional instruments in worship is unchristian and worldly.[41]

However, as that initial generation of colonial converts passed away, the younger generations began rediscovering their roots, their music, their instruments, and their dancing. African Christianity is today bursting with creativity now that it seems to have won the battle over whether it can integrate its own heritage into contemporary church practices.

In China, an amazing thing is happening with a Christian songwriter named Xiao Min, from Henan province.[42] This amazing woman was featured in the documentary *The Cross: Jesus in China*—perhaps the most authentic film perspective into Chinese Christianity yet. Xiao Min is the author of fifteen hundred songs. These songs are known to China's underground Christians as the Canaan Hymns. Xiao Min has no musical training. In fact, she dropped out of school in junior high. She is simply a common field worker who decided to follow Jesus. She has suffered persecution and has even been imprisoned for her Christian convictions. And like many Christians who suffer for Christ, her trials put her in situations where she was able to evangelize. Indeed, she claims to have brought many prisoners to Christ. For thirteen years her husband scoffed at her, but after witnessing her utter transformation, her deep commitment to Christianity, and her nearly miraculous musical abilities, he too decided to follow Jesus. Xiao Min has become something like a celebrity in the Chinese underground church because of her songs. They are sung all across the nation in underground and registered churches alike.

The Protestant movement in Latin America has unleashed creative energies within the churches as well. In recent decades, Pentecostal churches in particular have challenged the Roman Catholic monopoly on church music. However, in my observation, the influence of the United States—particularly when it comes to music—looms large. Many of the old, American classical hymns are sung, simply with Spanish lyrics.

I saw this same phenomenon in South Korea at the massive Yoido Full Gospel Church. Their songs were almost exclusively old American hymns, simply with Korean words. However, these trends will not last forever. As Latinos and Asians make Christianity their own, they will surely capitalize on the richness of their own cultural heritage and musical traditions.

The main problem with indigenization in the Latin American churches is this: the native cultures were so thoroughly obliterated by the Spanish and Portuguese that it is taking time for much of the civilization to rediscover what being an indigenous person even means. Records were so utterly destroyed, the people so vanquished, the traditions and cultures so thoroughly erased, that it is not easy to tap into what indigenous worship might even look like, or sound like. After all, Roman Catholic and Latin culture has had five centuries to enmesh itself, and getting back behind the arrival of Columbus is extremely difficult for professional historians and probably even more so for the masses. Nevertheless, an unmistakable indigenizing process is taking place within Christianity—particularly the less tradition-bound forms of Pentecostal and Evangelical Christianity—and it will only continue to impact the region's church music.

In North America, the twentieth century witnessed the rise of Contemporary Christian Music (CCM). It has roots in the 1960s with the marriage of Jesus to pop culture. Examples here are many: Bob Dylan's conversion to Christ, hits like "Jesus Is Just Alright" made famous by the Doobie Brothers, and the extremely influential

Jesus Movement which spawned several hip churches and denominations on the West Coast. The music of that era began to move east, and eventually—through the remarkable ministry of the Belmont Avenue Church of Christ—landed at Nashville, Tennessee. When that happened, the CCM genre quickly began to take shape.

One of the early CCM figures to rise out of Nashville was Amy Grant, an extremely gifted singer who burst onto the contemporary Christian music scene in 1978 at the tender age of seventeen. "Within a decade, Amy Grant changed the course of sacred music— and in the process, altered the way Christians worship God."[43] Not only did she sell more than thirty million albums, but she crossed over into secular radio in a way no one else did before, or has done since.[44] Grant's ability to reach secular radio listeners did not come without a price, however. She was fiercely criticized for her efforts to go mainstream. Some appreciated her and considered her a hero, like a modern missionary. Others, however, accused her of selling out, especially when her marriage to Gary Chapman broke down and she married Vince Gill—the darling of country music.

Amy weathered the storm, however, and while her music appeals more to the "adult contemporary" crowd today, I think it is safe to say that she has finally won over her critics on all sides. She is remarkably talented musician who hit it big as a teen and matured while in the public eye. Her many fans witnessed her successes, failures, milestones, as well as her ups and downs. She is still an inspiration for those of us who grew up listening to her. And her concerts—often played barefooted—are so pleasantly authentic, as if she is welcoming people into her living room.

Amy Grant was the first of several influential artists who made Christian music cool. Michael W. Smith and Steven Curtis Chapman rose up in the eighties and dominated Christian charts for well over a decade. Others came along in the CCM world such as Newsboys, Jars of Clay, DC Talk, Twila Paris, Third Day, Casting Crowns, and Mercy Me. For the most part, these artists' supporters remained squarely within the somewhat insular CCM world. It is rare to find a Christian artist who can publicly and frequently proclaim Christ, yet continue to appeal to secular audiences. A few have managed to do it, however. For instance, Cliff Richard is a British pop icon who caused only a mild splash in the U.S. with his 1979 hit "We Don't Talk Anymore." However, in the U.K.—his home country—he is a megastar. In his long career, he has sold over two-hundred-fifty-million records![45] The Irish band U2 also comes to mind here, having enjoyed decades of success evidenced in their one-hundred-seventy-million albums sold.[46]

One artist in particular is extremely relevant to the discussion in this chapter: Chris Tomlin. Perhaps no other musician alive today has transformed how we sing in church as this man has. Chris Tomlin is today's Charles Wesley or Fanny Crosby. Like Amy Grant, he has sold around thirty million albums. But his ability to sell albums and fill concert seats is not what makes him so extraordinary. It is his ability to impact the world of church music that puts him on a very short list of artists. Amy Grant, Michael W. Smith, and Casting Crowns enjoyed frequent radio airplay. However, they did not transform the Sunday morning assembly. Chris Tomlin has done that.

Tomlin is a forty-something Texan who has been labeled the "Most Sung Songwriter in the World."[47] His albums top the secular Billboard 200 chart, but they are not primarily aimed at radio airplay. Chris Tomlin writes his songs for churches to sing. They are worship songs. And whether you realize it or not, your Christian friends are singing his music every Sunday . . . and you probably are too, unless your hymnal was published last century. Some of his biggest hits are: "How Great Is Our God," "Jesus Messiah," "Whom Shall I Fear," "Amazing Grace (My Chains are Gone)," "Our God," "Indescribable," "God of This City," "I Will Rise," "We Fall Down," and so many more. Indeed, CNN reports that 128 of Tomlin's songs are regularly sung around the world.[48]

The breathtaking statistics make sense since Tomlin happens to be the songster for the world's largest religion. With Christianity's two and a half billion members, Tomlin certainly does not lack clients. And the people are responding to him in droves. But the secret of Tomlin's success is not the same secret that made the previous artists successful. Tomlin is different. Branding him "the undisputed king of worship music," CNN had this to say of Tomlin: "The stage, the lights, the band—aren't about him. As lively as his shows are, the point is not to get you inside the doors. The point is to get you singing in church."[49] It is altogether common for Tomlin songs to dominate the most-sung songs in churches, according to the company that tracks such things, Christian Copyright Licensing International. And Tomlin is not just for Caucasians, either. All races, all nations, all continents sing his songs. As a comparison, CNN measured Katy Perry's airplay—at the height of her influence in 2012—with Chris Tomlin's songs being sung in church. According to Billboard, Perry stood at 1.4 million plays as opposed to Tomlin's 3.1 million.

Tomlin is impacting church music in profound ways. Churches everywhere want to sing his songs. His new releases are immediately belted out by thousands the week they are released. One expert on Christian music said, "His songs have probably had the most immediate impact on churches that we have seen in history. Even before you get to street release [of a CD], churches are already networked and engaged with his songs."[50]

Historically, it has been uncommon for Christians to sing Billboard chart-toppers in church services. But we have entered a new age where the radio and the church mirror each other when it comes to music. Churches no longer rest content in singing hymns written during previous decades and centuries. Churches, especially churches led by younger generations, prefer to sing the hot-ticket song on the radio *right now*. Why sing Watts, Wesley, and Crosby when you can sing a song that is topping the charts, that is fresh and vogue. Clearly, we have entered a new era in church music.

And what does this mean for Christianity? There are several implications and consequences that are arising out of this new turn of events in church music.

First, churches are trying to become more relevant when it comes to their music. Tradition is out, relevance is in.

Second, churches are uniting as never before. Catholics, Methodists, Presbyterians, Evangelicals, and Baptists are all singing the same thing. This is rare in Christian history. Tomlin is blowing up the rigid borders of denominationalism that have stood for so long. For all of the efforts of ecumenical institutions over the past decade, who would have thought a Texas worship leader would be the one to bring a greater sense of unity to Christendom?

Third, theology becomes dulled. By this I do not mean "dumbed down." Rather, the distinctive teachings of churches—such as my tradition's preference for acapella music—these things are downplayed. Few people care about whether Augustine or Pelagius got it right when they can lift their hands and praise God—no matter their opinion on the finer points of theology.

Fourth, experiential Christianity is taking center stage as more cerebral approaches become de-emphasized. Young people do not church hop in order to hear whether Paul wants women to cover their heads. They want an experience of God. This fact lies at the root of the popularity of megachurches. It is like a concert where people are united in the experience. In the past, some Christian leaders made the argument that "doctrine divides, service unites." Perhaps a fresh spin on that phrase would be "doctrine divides, worship unites."

Fifth, in an age of extreme isolation—people locked onto a computer or phone much of the time—the corporate worship experience is perhaps as important as it has ever been. People hunger for community, and the public worship experience brings people shoulder to shoulder, sharing prayer, singing songs, and fellowshipping. The only question here is whether they know those individuals standing next to them, or whether the concert-like setting makes them simply *feel* part of a community. This is a real dilemma for Christianity today. How do you help Christians feel connected to each other in a crowd of two thousand? There is a strong likelihood that those people will scarcely know the people sitting beside them. While the music makes them *think* they are all in this together, in reality the connections are superficial.

Conclusion

Legend has it that Charles Wesley claimed he would rather write hymns for the church than theology. Theology is rarely recited or memorized, but hymns are sung with regularity.

And this idea brings home an important point: music touches the heart in profound ways, but Christians must be careful not to throw out theology just to feel the Spirit move. Music can and should teach theology, but it can also get theology very, very wrong. I don't mean to sound like Grebel and the Radical Reformers here, but I think we've all sung songs and later wondered, "What did I just say?"

I used to love the song "Imagine" by John Lennon, until I realized it was a song yearning for the end of religion and ridiculing the hope of everlasting life. It is a song profoundly out of sync with Christian orthodoxy. Yet it has become an anthem to people all over the world, including Americans when they welcome in the New Year with the dropping of the big apple in Times Square.

Some of these songs even pop up in church. I recall a preacher once decrying the song "Have You Seen Jesus My Lord?" When I was a youth minister I used to sing this song with the teens. However, after that sermon, I could no longer lead a song that claimed Jesus was same thing as "the white foam at your feet." It equated Jesus with the sunset. That's pantheism. I wonder how the church fathers would have reacted.

Yes, perhaps church music is entering a new epoch where people can write songs, post them on the Internet, and teach them to hundreds of people at a time. And that is a welcome development. The democratization of Christianity is taking place at breakneck speed as blogs and Youtube stations emerge daily. This is all well and good. But at some point, I have to believe, the pendulum will swing the other way. People will want some theology that has roots. They will want an anchor for their beliefs. They will want more than "that feeling" they get when the lights dim and the fog machines are activated.

Experience is something we each yearn for. We have a deep desire to experience God, community, and spiritual awakening. But without some sort of rootedness, we just might lose touch with answers to the "why" questions. Why are we feeling good when we pray the Lord's Prayer with others in the room? Why do we gather on Sunday? Why are we praising Jesus as Messiah? Why do we long to praise our Creator?

Church music has opened many positive doors for us, leading us forward in our quest for community with others and with God. But in the quest for relevance, let us not allow our church music to shut the door to our Christian past, for we are surrounded by a great cloud of witnesses. And they will still speak to us if we will take the time to listen.

Notes

[1] For an excellent discussion of singing in ancient Judaism, see Tim Dowley, *Christian Music: A Global History* (Minneapolis: Fortress Press, 2011), 21. In my discussion of music in the Old Testament, I have relied on Dowley.

[2] See Everett Ferguson, "Music," in *Encyclopedia of Early Christianity*, 2nd Edition (New York: Routledge, 1999), 788.

[3] Dowley, 25.

[4] See Ferguson, Ibid., 787.

[5] Ibid., 789.

[6] Dowley, 24.

[7] Some of the historical narrative in this chapter was first developed in my book *To Whom Does Christianity Belong? Critical Issues in World Christianity* (Minneapolis: Fortress Press, 2015). See chapter 13 entitled "Music."

[8] Andrew Wilson-Dickson, *The Story of Christian Music: From Gregorian Chant to Black Gospel* (Minneapolis: Fortress Press, 2003), 25.

[9] Petros Vassiliades, "From the Pauline Collection to *Phos Hilaron* of Cappadocia," *St. Vladimir's Theological Quarterly* 56:1 (January 2012), 9 and 5.

[10] Henry Bettenson, *Documents of the Christian Church*, 2nd Edition (Oxford: Oxford University Press, 1963), 3–4.

[11] Frank Senn, *The People's Work: A Social History of the Liturgy* (Minneapolis: Fortress Press, 2006), 114.

[12] "Rational worship" is Senn's translation of Romans 12:1. The NIV translates this phrase "proper worship."

[13] Timothy Ware, *The Orthodox Church* (New York: Penguin, 1997), 268.

[14] Quoted in Senn, 118. The source is Chrysostom's *Discourses against Judaizing Christians*, preached in 386 and 387. The quotation comes from Discourse IV.

[15] Senn, 117–118.

[16] David Melling, "Music," in *Blackwell Dictionary of Eastern Christianity*, ed. by K. Parry, D. Melling, D. Brady, S. Griffith, and J. Healey (Oxford: Blackwell, 2001), 328–331. Quotation is from 329.

[17] Ibid., 329.

[18] Ware, 268.

[19] Melling, 329.

[20] Ibid., 330.

[21] See, for example, the careful research of Nina Glibetic, a specialist in the field.

[22] Everett Ferguson, *Church History*, Vol. 1, *From Christ to the Pre-Reformation* (Grand Rapids: Zondervan, 2013), 463.

[23] Ibid., 321.

[24] Ibid., 464.

[25] Carter Lindberg, *The European Reformations*, 2nd Edition (Oxford: Wiley-Blackwell, 2010), 372.

[26] Ibid.

[27] Diarmaid MacCulloch, *The Reformation: A History* (New York: Penguin, 2003), 589.

[28] Ibid., 590.

[29] Rowan Williams, *Where God Happens* (Boston: New Seeds, 2007), 49.

[30] Lindberg, 372.

[31] Ibid., 372–373.

[32] Conrad Grebel, *Letter to Thomas Muntzer (1524)*, located in Keith Stanglin, ed., *The Reformation to the Modern Church* (Minneapolis: Fortress Press, 2014), 137–138. Italics mine.

[33] Alister McGrath, *Christianity's Dangerous Idea: The Protestant Revolution* (New York: HarperOne, 2007), 297.

[34] Ibid., 300.

[35] Pedrito Maynard-Reid, *Diverse Worship: African-American, Caribbean & Hispanic Perspectives* (Downers Grove, IL: InterVarsity Press, 2000), 69. For my understanding of black church music, I am indebted to the wonderful documentary *Rejoice and Shout: A Jubilant Journey Through Gospel Music History* (Magnolia Pictures, 2011) a *tour de force* that should be seen by anyone interested in the topic.

[36] For "invisible institution," see Maynard-Reid, 54.

[37] Christopher Partridge, *The Lyre of Orpheus: Popular Music, The Sacred, and the Profane* (Oxford: Oxford University Press, 2014), 242.

[38] Maynard-Reid, 71.

[39] Michael Eric Dyson, *Holler If You Hear Me: Searching for Tupac Shakur* (New York: Basic Books, 2001), 202.

[40] See Jason Lipshutz, "Grammys 2015: Meet the Lesser-Known Nominees," *Billboard*, 5 December 2014, located at: http://www.billboard.com/articles/events/grammys-2015/6363721/grammys-2015-meet-the-lesser-known-nominees.

[41] Felix Muchimba, *Liberating the African Soul: Comparing African Western Christian Music and Worship Styles* (Colorado Springs: Authentic Publishing, 2008), 62.

[42] There is not much published on Xiao Min. The second disk in *The Cross: Jesus in China* is the best source available on her life. Liao Yiwu mentions her in his highly popular *God is Red* (New York: HarperOne, 2011), 71. There are several websites that briefly discuss her work. See "Xiao Min on Preparing for the Lord's Return," 21 November 2012, located at http://chinesechurchvoices.com/2012/11/21/xiao-min-on-preparing-for-the-lords-return/ (accessed 4 June 2014); and "The Canaan Hymns," located at http://waysoflife.info/Canaan%20Hymns.html (accessed 4 June 2014).

[43] David Murrow, "How a 17-year-old girl changed the way we worship God," 29 April 2014, located at http://www.patheos.com/blogs/churchformen/2014/04/how-a-17-year-old-girl-changed-how-we-worship-god/.

[44] See William Ruhlmann, "Amy Grant," AllMusic, located at: http://www.allmusic.com/artist/amy-grant-mn0000024944/biography.

[45] Dowley, 237.

[46] "U2: What they're still looking for," CBS News, 24 May 2015, located at: http://www.cbsnews.com/news/u2-what-theyre-still-looking-for/3/.

[47] CBN News, "Chris Tomlin Most Sung Songwriter in the World," 2 July 2013, located at: http://www.cbn.com/cbnnews/us/2013/july/chris-tomlin -most-sung-songwriter-in-the-world/?mobile=false.

[48] Eric Marrapodi and Tom Foreman, "Chris Tomlin, king of the sing-along," CNN, 9 March 2013, located at: http://religion.blogs.cnn.com/2013/03/09/the -most-sung-artist-on-the-planet/.

[49] Ibid. I relied on the data in the CNN article for the statistics in this paragraph.

[50] Ibid. The quotation is from Howard Rachinski, the CEO of Christian Copyright Licensing International.

Epilogue

If this book has helped Christians to understand why they do what they do in church, then it has accomplished something significant. I am afraid that Protestants—in their quest for relevance—too often ignore the past. It is not difficult to do. Since the time of the Reformation, Protestants have focused far more on the here and now than on long-held traditions that may or may not be rooted in the Bible. As a result, Protestants have maintained a posture of suspicion toward church history. They give plenty of attention to the biblical era, but there is a sense that whatever is not found in Scripture must be wrong, or at least misguided.

This book has tried to correct that narrow understanding of our collective past. Yes, the biblical era was important. But we kid ourselves if we think we can leap over two thousand years of history and brazenly assert that our current practices are replicates of the churches in Corinth, Thessalonica, or Ephesus. We are products of our time as well as products of our history. It is ignorant to think that we in the twenty-first century have essentially picked up where Paul left off.

As this book has tried to illustrate, we are part of a long-evolving tradition. We have been impacted by many cultures, individuals, texts, and events. Perhaps an appropriate analogy can be found in language. The English language is a massive concoction of Latin, Greek, French, and Anglo-Saxon, with elements of Arabic, Hebrew, Hindi, and more. Similarly, the Christian faith was molded and shaped by numerous entities before it came to us. And when American missionaries spread the gospel to Africa or Asia, they left distinctly American cultural impressions on this ancient faith.

Europe and North America had its chance with Christianity, and now the baton is being passed to other cultures. And those cultures will deal with the Christian faith in their own way—just as we did. The well-known African philosopher John Mbiti once described Africa's newfound Christian faith as

> . . . an African opportunity to mess up Christianity in our own way. For the past two thousand years, other continents, countries, nations and generations have had their chances to do with Christianity as they wished. And we know that they have not been idle! Now Africa has got its chance at last.[1]

One of the most beautiful qualities of Christianity is that it is a borderless faith. It morphs as it finds its way into new civilizations and new lives. Like an unstoppable river, it always finds a way to keep pressing on to new frontiers.[2]

Which culture had the "purist" form of Christianity? Was it "the early church?" Did they get it right? Or was it the era of the church fathers? Was it during the time of Constantine? Did Augustine articulate the Christian faith most perfectly? Perhaps it was in the medieval era that Christendom finally made Christianity what it was intended to be: an entire culture united on the principles of

Christ. Maybe it was the Puritans who implemented Christianity best, with their radically strict interpretations of Christian discipleship. Or perhaps it was during America's Second Great Awakening when Christians finally discovered how to live the Christian faith as God intended? Surely the 1940s and 1950s—before the drugs, the revolutions, feminism, and all that—was the high point in how to live the Christian life.

I'm skeptical. Christians are always a mixed bag, no matter the century. They probably always will be. They get some things right, and some things wrong. There is no utopian past. Anyone who tries to point to an era when they "got it right" is going to be severely disappointed. We have come so far since the days of the early church. Or since the days of Luther. Or since the 1950s.

What is critical is that we understand our *own* checkered pasts. Why? I believe we confront our past in order to improve ourselves in the present. But I also believe there are occasions when we must uphold the past as representing something better than even our best efforts today. There's some good stuff in the past, much to be admired. There's much to be ashamed of as well. As Christians, we should *at least* learn about the past so that we can better comprehend where our ancestors in the faith went wrong, or right. We are arrogant and crude if we think ourselves immune from the same mistakes they made.

In this book, I have tried to help readers understand some basic history about seven different themes: biblical interpretation, baptism, Eucharist, church buildings, pastors, preaching, and music. Hopefully, we will think with a little more humility—and subtlety—when we realize that our interpretations, our sacraments, and our teaching have a history. We stand on the shoulders of others, for better or for worse. And one day we will be the shoulders, and our posterity will stand.

My hope is that readers of this book have learned something about their roots, and, perhaps, have gained some insight into how to improve their future, especially the future of this precious faith.

William Faulkner once wrote: "The past is never dead. It's not even past."[3] I can think of no better expression to summarize what I hope readers will gain from this book.

Notes

[1] John Mbiti, quoted in Noel Davies and Martin Conway, *World Christianity in the 20th Century* (London: SCM Press, 2008), 118.

[2] See Dyron Daughrity, *The Changing World of Christianity: The Global History of a Borderless Religion* (New York: Peter Lang, 2010).

[3] William Faulkner, *Requiem for a Nun* (New York: Random House, 1950), 92.